Glisterings

LaTeX and Other Oddments

Peter Wilson

TeX Users Group
Portland, Oregon, USA

TeX Users Group, Publishing
P.O. Box 2311
Portland, OR 97208-2311
USA
`tug.org/books`

ISBN-13 978-0-9824626-2-1
ISBN-10 0-9824626-2-X
First printing, 2020

CONTENTS

LIST OF FIGURES

INTRODUCTION

> Not all that tempts your wand'ring eyes
> And heedless hearts, is lawful prize;
> Nor all, that glisters, gold.
>
> *Ode to a Favourite Cat*
> THOMAS GRAY

For many years Jeremy Gibbons edited a very successful column in the TeX Users Group journals *TeX and TUG NEWS* and *TUGboat* called *Hey — It works!* [52]. I learnt much from this but apparently not enough to decline when asked to take over the column. On the other hand I have learnt to my cost that the quickest way to get a correct answer to a question on the `comp.text.tex` (`ctt`) newsgroup is to give an incorrect answer. In order not to sully Jeremy's reputation my first thought was to change the title to *Hey — It might work* but after some consideration the new title is as you see it earlier — *Glisterings* — implying that there might be some dross among the nuggets.

The first column was published in *TUGboat* in 2001. When I got to my sixteenth submission I wanted to stop as conditions had changed, both personally and technically. The `ctt` newsgroup was fading, being replaced by the `https://tex.stackexchange.com` website and the questions were much more oriented towards graphics which I was not interested in. My sixteenth column was much the largest and the powers that be decided that it should be split into several columns but, thankfully, they agreed to do the splitting. The end result was a total of twenty seven columns. Almost all the material relates to LaTeX.

They have now been assembled in the volume you are now reading. Originally each column had its own list of References but here they have all been merged into a single list. Also, an index has been added.

When I came to print the results in a two-column book format there were many short columns; sometimes the first column with an empty second column and at others a short second column. To me it looked like there was too much empty space. I decided that it might be an (awful?) idea to fill those spaces with some kind of graphic. Hence the "spidron" graphics that appear; they are described in Chapter 9.

In assembling all the columns into one volume I discovered that I had used some epigraphs more than once. Here every epigraph is unique and there are some that did not appear in the original columns; their ordering is not necessarily the same.[1]

Acknowledgements: *Glisterings* would not have been possible without the support and input of many others. In particular I thank Jeremy Gibbons for his *Hey — It works!* and Barbara Beeton and Karl Berry for their enthusiasm and editorial improvements to the column and this book. There are many others who also contributed, often unknowingly, by asking questions on the various TeX-related mailing lists and to those who questioned and answered, with my grateful thanks to all of you.

I hope you enjoy the collection.

—Peter Wilson
Kenilworth, United Kingdom
`herries.press@earthlink.net`

---

[1] For American readers I am rather pleased with the serendipitous pairing of the first two epigraphs in Chapter 5. For those who have not heard of Amway, try googling it and you might find questions such as, 'Is Amway a pyramid scheme?'

CHAPTER 1

TUGBOAT 22:4, DECEMBER 2001

All that glisters is not gold.

Early 13th century proverb

Several questions on `ctt` recently have been related to comparing two words or strings. To my chagrin I gave an incorrect answer to one of the questions, so I'll now try and redeem myself.

1.1 Checking for an optional argument

If you can meet with triumph and disaster
And treat those two impostors just the same...

If —
RUDYARD KIPLING

If you are defining a new command that has an optional argument you generally need some way of checking whether or not it is present when the macro is called, especially when it should be ignored if it is not present. One convention is to use the LaTeX kernel's `\@empty` macro as the default for the optional argument.

```
\newcommand{\mine}[2][\@empty]{%
%  if #1 is \@empty do nothing else
%  do something
```

To me the obvious way of performing the check was to use TeX's `\ifx` primitive to compare `\@empty` and the actual value of the argument, as in `\testoptarg` here:

```
\newcommand{\testoptarg}[1][\@empty]{%
  \ifx #1\@empty
    Optional (#1) unused%
  \else
    Optional (#1) present%
\fi}
```

But if you try this you can get some odd results:

`\testoptarg` Optional () unused
`\testoptarg[full]` Optional (full) present
`\testoptarg[oops]` psOptional (oops) unused

It was kindly explained to me[1] that `\ifx` checks the following two tokens and in TeX a token is either a command sequence (e.g., `\@empty`) or a single character, like 'o'. In the oops example, `\ifx` checks 'o' and 'o', concludes that they are the same, and hence the strange result. Flipping the token ordering works better as in:

```
\renewcommand{\testoptarg}[1][\@empty]{%
  \ifx\@empty#1
    Optional (#1) unused%
  \else
    Optional (#1) present%
\fi}
```

Now `\testoptarg` and `\testoptarg[\@empty]` will report 'Optional () unused'.

Any other call, for example `\testoptarg[]`, will report 'Optional () present', and in particular `\testoptarg[oops]` reports 'Optional (oops) present'.

1.2 String comparisons

A more general problem along the same lines is to check if two words, or strings, are the same. We can use `\ifx` for this as well. When `\ifx` compares two tokens that are macro names, the result is true if the macros have been defined in the same way, and if their first level replacement texts are the same. So, we define two macros whose replacement texts are the strings, and compare these.

```
\newif\ifsame
\newcommand{\strcfstr}[2]{%
  \samefalse
  \begingroup
    \def\1{#1}\def\2{#2}%
    \ifx\1\2\endgroup \sametrue
    \else    \endgroup
    \fi}
```

The two arguments to `\strcfstr`[2] are the strings to be tested. `\ifsame` is set true if the two strings match character to character. If the arguments are macro names it checks the characters in the names,

---

[1] By, among others, Donald Arseneau, Michael Downes and Stephan Lemke.

[2] The `cf` used in the names of macros is the abbreviation *cf* (from the Latin *confer* = compare).

not their definitions. If there are any spaces in the arguments, each group is reduced to a single space before the strings are compared. `\strcfstr{}{␣}` sets `\ifsame` false but `\strcfstr{␣}{␣␣}` sets it true.[3]

```
\newcommand{\StrCfStr}[2]{%
  \lowercase{\strcfstr{#1}{#2}}}
```

The `\StrCfStr` macro performs a case insensitive test on two strings. For example, it will set `\ifsame` true for any of the pairs (abc, abc), (abc, Abc), (abc, aBc), and so on. It uses `\lowercase` to convert any uppercase letter to a lowercase letter so all the letters will be lowercase at the time `\strcfstr` does the checking. This will not work if the arguments include differently cased macro names as `\lowercase` does not touch those.

The `\strcfstr` and `\StrCfStr` macros have provided all the string testing that I have needed, but I'll show a couple of extensions. One thing is that `\strcfstr` relies on `\def` which is not expandable so, for example, it cannot be used in an `\edef`. Both Victor Eijkhout [38, section 13.8.7] and David Kastrup [69] have presented solutions for this. The other is that you may want to check if a macro expands to a particular string. David's expandable macro also provides a solution for this and Michael Downes [35] gives a somewhat different method using `\expandafter`.

We can use `\strcfstr` as the basis for the macro to string comparison, by using `\expandafters`.

```
\newcommand{\macrocfstr}[2]{%
  \expandafter\strcfstr\expandafter{#1}{#2}}
```

The first argument to `\macrocfstr` is either a string or a macro that is expected to expand to a string. The second argument is the test string.

We can also do a case insensitive test by using `\MacroCfStr`:

```
\newcommand{\MacroCfStr}[2]{%
  \lowercase{\macrocfstr{#1}{#2}}}
```

The `\charscfchars` expandable macro below is based on Victor's code. It is tricky because it uses recursion to perform pairwise comparisons of the individual characters in its two arguments, and it requires two supporting macros. Here is how it starts:

```
\catcode'\^^?=11    % make a letter
\newcommand{\charscfchars}[2]{%
  \IfAllChars#1^^?\Are#2^^?\theSame}
```

---

[3]The ␣ symbol is a printed representation of a space.

`\charscfchars` adds a character at the end of its arguments to mark the ends of the strings. Victor used $ as the marker which meant that neither argument could include $ among the characters. I chose to use ^^? (TEX's notation for the ASCII DEL control character, which is normally invalid TEX). The `\catcode` changes first make ^^? appear to be a letter and then at the end of the macro definitions it is set back to its normal invalid state.

The next macro, `\IfAllChars`, which is presented with some interspersed commentary, does most of the work.

```
\def\IfAllChars#1#2\Are#3#4\TheSame{%
  \if#1^^?\if#3^^?\sametrue
        \else\samefalse\fi
```

The macro takes two pairs of arguments that are delimited by the tokens `\Are` and `\TheSame`. The first pair of arguments are for the first string under test and the second pair for the other string. More specifically, #1 will be the first character in the first string and #2 contains the remaining characters (including the ^^? marker), and similarly for #3 and #4. If the ends of both strings have been reached, then the strings are the same, but if only the end of the first string has been reached, the strings are different. If we are not at the end of the first string there is more work to be done.

```
  \else\if#1#3\IfRest#2\TheSame#4\else
      \samefalse\fi\fi}
```

If the corresponding characters in the two strings are the same then the rest of the character pairs must be checked, otherwise the characters don't match and we are done.

The last of the macros, `\IfRest`, takes three arguments which are delimited by the tokens `\TheSame`, `\else`, and `\fi\fi`. The first two arguments are strings to be compared, and it throws away the third.

```
\def\IfRest#1\TheSame#2\else#3\fi\fi{%
  \fi\fi \IfAllChars#1\Are#2\TheSame}
\catcode'\^^?=15  % return to invalid
```

`\IfRest` recursively calls `\IfAllChars` to compare the strings.

`\charscfchars` can be used as a basis for case insensitive and macro to string comparisons exactly like `\strcfstr`.

Apart from `\charscfchars` being expandable while `\strcfstr` is not, it also ignores all space characters while `\strcfstr` does not. For example, `\charscfchars{ab}{a␣b}` thinks that the arguments are identical but they will be reported as different if `\strcfstr{ab}{a␣b}` is used.

Calm was the day, and through the trembling air
Sweet-breathing Zephyrus did softly play —
A gentle spirit, that lightly did delay
Hot Titan's beams, which then did glister fair.

Prothalamion, EDMUND SPENSER

One of the less frequently asked questions on `ctt` is whether there is a package for typesetting forms, and the answer is 'no'. Nevertheless forms are still typeset via LaTeX.

2.1 Tick boxes

Little boxes on the hillside, little boxes made of ticky tacky.
Little boxes, little boxes, little boxes all the same.

Little boxes
MALVINA REYNOLDS, 1961
(Popularised by Pete Seeger)

One common component of a form is the tick box, also known as a checkbox.

Can you produce a tick box? Yes ☐ No ☐
Can I produce a tick box? Yes ☒ No ☐

The empty boxes above were produced by the `\tickbox` macro defined below, and the `\xbox` command produced the checked box.

```
\newcommand*{\tickbox}{{\fboxsep 0pt%
  \framebox[\height]{\vphantom{M}}}}
\newcommand*{\xbox}{{\fboxsep 0pt%
  \framebox[\height]{\vphantom{M}$\times$}}}
```

If you want a bit bigger box, like ☐, you could use this larger `\Tickbox` instead of `\tickbox`.

```
\newcommand*{\Tickbox}{\framebox{\phantom{M}}}
```

The length `\fboxsep` is the space between the frame of a `\framebox` and its contents, so you can adjust the size of this kind of box by changing `\fboxsep` or by using a different phantom character.
    Or you might prefer ☐, made with `\TickBox`:

```
\newcommand*{\TickBox}{{\fboxsep 0pt%
  \fbox{\rule{0em}{1em}\rule{1em}{0em}}}}
```

This definition uses invisible rules (a `\rule` with zero height or width cannot be seen) to control the size of the tightly fitting `\fbox`. In this case, as the rules are the same length, the box is square.

2.2 Blanks, dashes and rules

Could we teach taste or genius by rules, they would be no longer taste or genius.

Discourses on Art, JOSHUA REYNOLDS

Along the lines of checkboxes, another regular component of a form is _____.
    The last sentence ended with `\hrulefill{}`. to give a rule that stretched to margin. You can use `\hrulefill` more than once in a line, such as in the next line where it is used twice.

Last name: _____ First: _____

Which was coded as:
`Last name: \hrulefill{} First: \hrulefill`
    Or, you may want to have a rule of a particular length. The rule in the following line is just long enough for the word 'something' to be typeset:

Put _____ here.
Put something here.

The previous two lines were input as:

```
Put \underline{\phantom{something}} here. \\
Put something here.
```

Here is a variety of rules and blanks. In each case I've shown the code of the interesting part of the sentence above the typeset result.

1. `... in \rule{10mm}{0.4pt} the ...`
   Fill in _____ the blank.

2. `... in \hrulefill{} the ...`
   Fill in _____ the blank.

3. `... in \xfill[0.5ex] the ...`
   Fill in ——————————— the blank.

4. `... in \srule{something} the ...`
   Fill in _____ the blank.

5. ... in `\srule[0.5ex]{something}` the ...
Fill in ——————— the blank.

6. ... in `\phantom{something}` the ...
Fill in   the blank.

The macros used above are part of LaTeX with the exceptions of `\xfill` and `\srule` which are defined below.

The `\xfill[⟨len⟩]` macro is like `\hrulefill` in that it draws a rule in the available space but you can use the optional ⟨len⟩ length argument to raise or lower the rule with respect to the baseline.

```
\newcommand*{\xfill}[1][0pt]{%
  \cleaders
    \hbox to 1pt{\hss
      \raisebox{#1}{\rule{1.2pt}{0.4pt}}%
    \hss}\hfill}
```

`\srule[⟨len⟩]{⟨text⟩}` draws a rule that is the same length as ⟨text⟩, but does not typeset ⟨text⟩. You can use the optional ⟨len⟩ argument to alter the height of the rule with respect to the baseline.

```
\newcommand*{\srule}[2][0pt]{%
  \setbox0\hbox{#2}%
  \rule[#1]{\wd0}{0.4pt}}
```

The `\rule` command has an optional argument, which is the amount to raise (lower) the rule from its normal position at the baseline.

LaTeX provides two dashes, the en-dash (–), input as --, and the em-dash (—), input as ---. En-dashes are used as the separator in a number range, like 2–4. Depending on your country's typesetting tradition an en-dash or an em-dash may be used instead of a comma as a phrase separator in normal text. Longer dashes may be used to indicate that something is missing; a 2em dash (`\iiemdash`) for missing letters in a word and a 3em dash (`\iiiemdash`) to indicate a missing word. You can use `\rule` as a basis for longer dashes; for instance

```
\newcommand*{\iiemdash}{%    2em dash
  \rule[0.5ex]{2em}{0.4pt}}
\newcommand*{\iiiemdash}{%   3em dash
  \rule[0.5ex]{3em}{0.4pt}}
```

2.3 Forms

> I own I like a definite form in what my eyes are to rest upon ...
>
> *Travels with a Donkey,*
> ROBERT LOUIS STEVENSON

Customs Declaration			CD 44
May be opened officially			

☒ Gift		☐ Commercial sample	
☐ Documents		☐ Other	

Quantity and detailed description of contents	Weight lb. oz.		Value
Toy			15
Scarf			12
For commercial items only *If known*, HS tariff number and country of origin of goods	Total Weight		Total Value

I, the undersigned, whose name and address are given on the item, certify that the particulars given in this declaration are correct and that this item does not contain any dangerous article or articles prohibited by legislation or by postal or customs regulations.

Date and sender's signature

PS Form **1234**, March 2004

I have found that often the easiest way for me to define a form is to use the `picture` environment as this lets me place things just where I want them. Here is a possibly boring example for a customs declaration form; the real form is about 10% smaller than the example.

```
\newcommand{\form}{%
\setlength{\unitlength}{1mm}
\begin{picture}(79,80)
\sffamily \scriptsize \thicklines
\put(0,0){\line(1,0){80}}
\put(0,5){\line(1,0){80}}
\put(2,4){\makebox(0,0)[tl]{\normalsize PS Form
        \textbf{1234}, March 2004}}
\put(0,14){\line(1,0){80}}
\put(2,13){\makebox(0,0)[tl]{Date and sender's
        signature}}
\put(0,26){\line(1,0){80}}
\put(2,25){\makebox(0,0)[tl]{%
  \begin{minipage}{76mm}
  I, the undersigned, ... regulations
  \end{minipage}}}
\put(0,30){\line(1,0){48}}
\put(0,39){\line(1,0){80}}
\put(2,38){\makebox(0,0)[tl]{%
  \begin{minipage}{44mm}
  \textbf{For commercial items only} \\
  \textsl{If known,} ... \end{minipage}}}
\put(56,38){\makebox(0,0)[t]{Total Weight}}
\put(72,38){\makebox(0,0)[t]{Total Value}}
\put(0,53){\line(1,0){80}}
\put(2,52){\makebox(0,0)[tl]{%
  \begin{minipage}{40mm}
  \CONT \end{minipage}}}
\put(0,60){\line(1,0){80}}
```

```
\put(2,59){\makebox(0,0)[tl]{%
  \begin{minipage}{40mm}
  Quantity ... \end{minipage}}}
\put(49,59){\makebox(0,0)[tl]{%
  \begin{minipage}{14mm}
  \hfill Weight \hfill \mbox{}\\
  lb. \hfill oz. \end{minipage}}}
\put(72,58){\makebox(0,0)[t]{Value}}
\put(65,52){\makebox(0,0)[tl]{%
  \begin{minipage}{14mm}
  \CVAL \end{minipage}}}
\put(0,68){\line(1,0){80}}
\put(14,61){\makebox(0,0)[bl]{\DBX\ Documents}}
\put(14,66){\makebox(0,0)[tl]{\GBX\ Gift}}
\put(34,61){\makebox(0,0)[bl]{\OBX\ Other}}
\put(34,66){\makebox(0,0)[tl]{\CBX\ Commercial
                             sample}}
\put(0,80){\line(1,0){80}}
\put(2,79){\makebox(0,0)[tl]{%
  \begin{minipage}{76mm}\normalsize
  \textbf{Customs Declaration} ...
  officially \end{minipage}}}
%% vertical lines
\put(48,26){\line(0,1){34}}
\put(64,26){\line(0,1){34}}
\thinlines
\put(56,26){\line(0,1){9}}
\put(56,39){\line(0,1){14}}
\end{picture}
\setlength{\unitlength}{1pt}
}% end of \form
```

The variable parts of the form (i.e., the non-commercial answers) are represented by the uppercase commands, which have to be defined for any specific instance of the \form. For the example shown the code to complete and display it is:

```
\let\GBX\xbox    \let\DBX\tickbox
\let\OBX\tickbox \let\CBX\tickbox
\newcommand{\CONT}{\normalsize\rmfamily
Toy \\ Scarf}
\newcommand{\CVAL}{\normalsize\rmfamily
\centering 15 \\ 12}

\begin{figure}
\centering
\form
\end{figure}
```

2.4 Readers' input

I received the following[1] from Michael Barr regarding string comparisons. Perhaps someone can help?

Following your column in the recent issue of *TUGboat* [138] (Chapter 1) I have a problem in string comparisons that I don't think is solvable. At least I couldn't. Suppose you want to decide if an argument ultimately expands to nothing. Or if two arguments have the same ultimate expansion. What I was finally led to was similar to your \strcfstr on page 1 [Ed. reproduced here],

```
\newif\ifsame
\newcommand{\strcfstr}[2]{%
  \samefalse
  \begingroup
    \def\1{#1}\def\2{#2}%
    \ifx\1\2\endgroup \sametrue
    \else    \endgroup
  \fi}
```

except with \def replaced by \edef. This worked until the day that the argument (I was actually testing for being empty, but the difficulty is the same) happened to be a matrix. At this point, I got a curious error message about misplaced &. It turns out that while you can put a matrix (or any alignment) into a \def, you cannot put one into an \edef.

Michael Barr

[Ed.: For other approaches by Michael and others to this problem, see § 23.3, page 92.

In addition, the question was investigated at tex.stackexchange.com/questions/59565, with answers involving the extended primitive \pdfstrcmp (functionality available in all engines except the original TeX), and the \romannumeral-`0 construct, which is explained in Joseph Wright's article "Exploring \romannumeral and expansion" published in *TUGboat* 37:1, tug.org/TUGboat/tb37-1/tb115wright.pdf.]

---

[1] I have exercised editorial privilege on the original.

CHAPTER 3

> All that glisters is not gold —
> Often have you heard that told.

Merchant of Venice, Act II scene 7
WILLIAM SHAKESPEARE

One issue that has cropped up recently on the `comp.text.tex` (ctt) newsgroup is what can be done when two packages clash by defining the same macro.

> And we are here as on a darkling plain
> Swept with confused alarms of struggle
> and flight,
> Where ignorant armies clash by night.

Dover Beach
MATTHEW ARNOLD

3.1 Package/package clashes

A very simple method of undefining a macro, let's say `\amacro`, is to let it be undefined, as:

```
\let\amacro\undefined
```

Of course, `\undefined` must never be defined. You might feel safer if instead you used, say

```
\let\amacro\uNdEFiNed
```

or some other unlikely name.

If two packages are being used, say packA and packB, which both create `\amacro` then, provided the second has used `\newcommand` and not the TeX `\def` macro which will silently replace any prior definition, it will complain that `\amacro` is already defined. If the definitions in packA and packB are identical then the following resolves the problem.

```
\usepackage{packA}
\let\amacro\undefined
\usepackage{packB}
```

Life being what it is, the definitions are usually different. In this case both definitions can be used but the name of the first definition has to be altered.

```
\usepackage{packA}
\let\Aamacro\amacro
\let\amacro\undefined
\usepackage{packB}
```

Following this, you use `\Aamacro` when you want packA's version and `\amacro` for the packB version.

Of course, life gets even more awkward if packA uses `\amacro` as part of another macro that you might use. At some point you have to hope that the author of at least one of the packages will change it to eliminate the clash.

3.2 Class/package clashes

A slightly different version of the same problem is when there is some clash between the code in a class and the code in a package. I came across this when I was developing the memoir class [142] which incorporates code from many[1] packages. In some cases I needed to make sure that a particular package was not used with the class. I came up with this macro that fooled LaTeX into thinking that a package had been loaded, even though it hadn't been. The argument to the macro is the package name.

```
\newcommand*{\@memfakeusepackage}[1]{%
  \@namelet{ver@#1.sty}\@empty}
\newcommand*{\@namelet}[1]{%
  \expandafter\let\csname #1\endcsname}
```

(The code must be put where @ is treated as a letter.)

The LaTeX kernel has two useful macros for composing and using macro names which do not necessarily consist only of letters, namely:
`\@namedef{⟨text⟩}{⟨def⟩}`, and
`\@nameuse{⟨text⟩}`.
The first of these lets you define a macro called `\⟨text⟩` and the second lets you call a macro called `\⟨text⟩` As an example, the result of the next piece of code is shown afterwards; note that you can't directly call a macro whose name includes analphabetic characters.

```
\makeatletter
\newcommand*{\ru}{are you}
\@namedef{ru4me}#1{#1, are you for me?}
'\ru4me{Fred}' he asked. \\
'\@nameuse{ru4me}{Fred}' he asked.
\makeatother
```

---

[1] Mostly written by me.

'are you4meFred' he asked.
'Fred, are you for me?' he asked.

In the same vein the macro
`\@namelet{⟨text⟩}`
defined above is for `\leting`. Thus, calling

`\@memfakeusepackage}{pack}`

effectively expands to

`\let\ver@pack.sty\@empty`

which appears to be the magic incantation to make
LaTeX believe it has already used the pack package.

The memoir class includes[2] code similar, but not
identical, to the array, dcolumn, delarray and tabularx
packages and I used `\@memfakeusepackage` to make
sure these were not loaded again.

The memoir class also includes code corresponding
to Heiko Oberdiek's ifpdf package [96] but I did not
do anything to prevent loading the package. This
resulted in a thread on ctt where the poster was
using

```
\documentclass{memoir}
\usepackage{ps4pdf}
```

only to be told that `\ifpdf` was already defined.
It turns out that the ps4pdf package uses the ifpdf
package which defines `\ifpdf` which was also defined
in memoir.

Heiko Oberdiek [97] gave the simple 'let to undefined' solution and the following more complex one:

```
\documentclass{memoir}
    %% memoir defines \ifpdf
\makeatletter
    %% save memoir's \ifpdf
\let\saved@ifpdf\ifpdf
    %% then undefine it
\let\ifpdf\@undefined
    %% use ifpdf package (defines \ifpdf)
\usepackage{ifpdf}
    %% is \ifpdf undefined?
\@ifundefined{ifpdf}{%
    %% yes, used the saved memoir version
  \let\ifpdf\saved@ifpdf
}{%
    %% no, check for matching definitions
  \ifx\ifpdf\saved@pdf
  \else
    %% mismatch, write error message
  \latex@error{Different meaning
              of \@backslash ifpdf}\@ehc
```

```
  \fi
}
\makeatother
    %% use ps4pdf which uses \ifpdf
\usepackage{ps4pdf}
```

This scheme can be applied to similar situations.
Note that it produces an error if the second and
first definitions are different, which could very well
be useful.

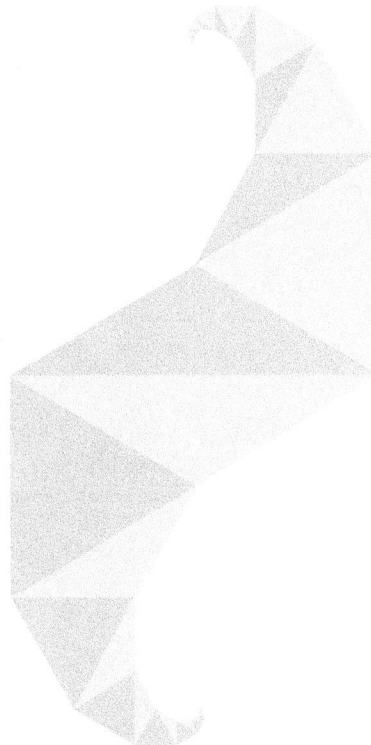

---

[2]The 2018 release of memoir no longer includes these as
they are readily available as packages.

Seagulls scream upon the shorelines' wrack
And seals abound
Amid the setting sun's glistering track
Across the Sound.

Puget Sound, PETER WILSON

The three topics which are the subject of this month's column have all been suggested by readers.

4.1 Empty arguments

They cannot scare me with their empty spaces
Between stars — on stars where no human race is.

Desert Places, ROBERT FROST

In an earlier column [138] (Chapter 1) I talked about how to check if two strings were the same, that is, that they consisted of the same characters in the same order. A recent query on the `texhax` mailing list [43] asked about how to check if an argument was empty, which on the face of it is just a check comparing a string with an empty string. However the earlier approach does not work in this case.

In LATEX there is often a need to check if an optional argument is present or not. The typical form for this is:

```
\newcommand{\amacro}[1][\@empty]{...
  \ifx\@empty#1 ... % no optional
  \else ...         % optional not \@empty
```

The question at hand, though, is what is the proper replacement for the pseudo-code in the second line below?

```
\newcommand{\amacro}[1]{...
  \if(#1 is empty) ... % no argument
  \else ...            % argument not empty
```

where 'empty' means zero or more spaces. Thus `{}` and `{   }` both qualify as 'empty'. If you are a LATEX user then the ifmtarg package on CTAN provides a solution. For TEX users here is the equivalent code, noting that all the macro definitions before the `\begingroup` are a regular part of LATEX.

```
\def\makeatletter{\catcode`\@11\relax}
\def\makeatother{\catcode`\@12\relax}
\makeatletter
\long\def\@gobble #1{}
```

```
\long\def\@firstofone#1{#1}
\long\def\@firstoftwo#1#2{#1}
\long\def\@secondoftwo#1#2{#2}
\begingroup
\catcode`\Q=3
\long\gdef\@ifmtarg#1{%
  \@xifmtarg#1QQ\@secondoftwo\@firstoftwo\@nil}
\long\gdef\@xifmtarg#1#2Q#3#4#5\@nil{#4}
\long\gdef\@ifnotmtarg#1{%
  \@xifmtarg#1QQ\@firstofone\@gobble\@nil}
\endgroup
\makeatother
```

The useful parts of this are:

$\verb|\@ifmtarg{|\langle arg\rangle\verb|}{|\langle empty\ code\rangle\verb|}{|\langle not\ empty\ code\rangle\verb|}|$

$\verb|\@ifnotmtarg{|\langle arg\rangle\verb|}{|\langle not\ empty\ code\rangle\verb|}|$

For example, these could be used like

```
\def\isempty#1{\@ifmtarg{#1}{EMPTY}{FULL}}
\def\isnotempty#1{\@ifnotmtarg{#1}{FULL}}
\def\mt{}
\isempty{}          -> EMPTY
\isempty{   }       -> EMPTY
\isempty{\mt}       -> FULL
\isempty{ E }       -> FULL
\isnotempty{}       ->
\isnotempty{   }    ->
\isnotempty{ \mt }  -> FULL
```

The ifmtarg package originally had a much simpler approach until Donald Arseneau pointed out the error of my ways. The perils of empty were discussed in the late Michael Downes' *Around the Bend* series; the one in question is available from `ctan.org/tex-archive/info/aro-bend/answer.002`.

Postscript: Eplain provides an `\ifempty` macro with a completely different implementation, but basically the same behavior; interested readers may like to compare. See the sources at `https://tug.org/eplain`.

4.2 The usefulness of nothing

Faultily faultless, icily regular, splendidly null,
Dead perfection, no more.

Maud, ALFRED, LORD TENNYSON

Another correspondent on `texhax` [33] wanted an even-page version of LATEX's `\cleardoublepage`. It might appear that a `\cleardoublepage`, which will get you to the next odd-numbered page, followed by a `\clearpage` or `\newpage` will end up at an even-numbered page, but this is not so as you will find that you can't move on from a page with nothing on it (excepting headers and footers). What is required is something that appears to be a nothing or a null but which is not, so far as TeX is concerned. For the purposes at hand an empty box will do. TeX has a `\null` command, which is shorthand for an empty horizontal box, but we can use something with wider applicability which I will name `\nowt`:[1]

```
\newcommand*{\nowt}{\leavevmode\hbox{}}
%% \nowt <==> \mbox{}
\newcommand{\cleartoevenpage}[1][\@empty]{%
  \clearpage
  \ifodd\c@page
    \nowt\ifx\@empty#1\else #1\fi
    \newpage
  \fi}
```

The macro `\cleartoevenpage` clears the current page and if the next is not an odd one then the task is finished. Otherwise we put (the invisible) `\nowt` on the odd page we have reached and move on to the next one, which will be even. The optional argument can be used to put some text or illustration on the skipped over odd page. For instance:

```
\cleartoevenpage[%
\vfill\centering THIS PAGE LEFT BLANK\vfill
\thispagestyle{empty}]
```

where the phrase 'THIS PAGE LEFT BLANK' will be centered on the odd page, and there will be neither a header nor a footer.

If you have ever tried something like this

```
\begin{description}
\item[Nothing] \\
  Also known as \ldots
...
```

then you probably got an error message saying: `There's no line to end here.` This can be resolved by putting `\nowt` just before the `\\` newline command.

4.3 Picking characters

> We may be in some degree whatever character we choose.
>
> *London Journal*, JAMES BOSWELL

A `texhax` reader [136] wanted a macro that would ensure that the first letter of a string would be in uppercase. Various answers were supplied and I'm providing a couple of my own. All the solutions depend on the fact that a TeX macro takes as a single argument either braced text or a single token, where a token is either a command name (the name of a macro) or a single character. Further, when defining a TeX macro the argument list is ended by a token, which is usually the initial opening brace of the definition.

Here's my first, long winded solution.

```
\def\gettwo#1#2\nowt{%
  \gdef\istchar{#1}\gdef\restchars{#2}}
\def\splitoff#1{\gettwo#1\nowt}
\def\Upfirst#1{\splitoff{#1}%
  \MakeUppercase{\istchar}\restchars}
```

`\gettwo` expects two arguments with the end of the second denoted by '`\nowt`' (I have chosen this on the assumption that it will not be part of either argument; any other command name that would not be in the arguments would serve as well). The macro `\splitoff` takes a single (string) argument and passes it on to `\gettwo`, which then takes the first character in the string as its first expected argument, and the rest of the string as its second argument. It globally defines `\istchar` and `\restchars` as the two arguments. `\Upfirst` takes a string argument, calls `\splitoff`, and hence `\gettwo`, and then ensures that `\istchar` is typeset in uppercase, followed by the rest of the characters.

This does not work if the argument to `\Upfirst` is a macro that is defined as a string (for example `\def\arg{string}`). This can be resolved by using TeX's `\expandafter` macro to make sure that `\Upfirst`'s argument is expanded[2] before being used by `\splitoff`:

```
\def\Upfirst#1{%
  \expandafter\splitoff\expandafter{#1}%
  \MakeUppercase{\istchar}\restchar}
```

The second version, below, is not as versatile as the first as the string is consumed internally instead of being made available in the form of the `\istchar` and `\restchars` macros.

```
\def\upperfirst#1#2\nowt{%
  \MakeUppercase{#1}\MakeLowercase{#2}}
\def\Upfirst#1{\expandafter\upperfirst#1\nowt}
```

The basic idea is the same as the first proposal. It has the added function of ensuring that only the first

---

[1] 'Nowt' is a Northern English dialect word meaning naught or nothing as in "Y' can't get owt fer nowt" — You cannot get something for nothing.

[2] To one level only.

character in the string is uppercase (it lowercases the remainder). Neither solution can handle the case where the first character is a ligature (e.g., \oe) or accented (e.g., \^{a}), or other commands.

Uwe Lück [74] provided a more complete but more complex solution.

```
\DeclareRobustCommand{\Upfirst}[1]{%
  \protected@edef\upfirst@rg{#1}%
  \expandafter\upit\upfirst@rg\nowt}
```

Using \DeclareRobustCommand instead of \def or \newcommand ensures that \Upfirst can be used in a moving argument without having to be protected. The \protected@edef is used to expand the argument while maintaining any \protects. In order to handle an accented initial character the string has to be split into three parts: the first element (which may be a character or an accent command), the second (which may be the argument to an accent command), and the third is the remainder of the string. The string, by the way, must have at least two characters.

```
\def\upit#1#2#3\nowt{%
  \let\@uptokone#1%
  \let\@xuptoktwo\@empty
  \def\@yuptoktwo{#2}%
  \expandafter\test@ccent\@ccentlist\@sentinel
  \MakeUppercase{#1\@xuptoktwo}%
  \MakeLowercase{\@yuptoktwo#3}}
```

The \upit macro takes three arguments, which are then the three portions of the initial string, and stores the first two in \@uptokone and \@yuptoktwo respectively. The macro \test@accent determines if the first token is an accent, changing \@xuptoktwo and \@yuptoktwo if it is.

```
\def\@ccentlist{'>\"\'\`\b\c}% plus the rest
\def\test@ccent#1{%
  \ifx#1\@sentinel\else
    \ifx\@uptokone#1
      \let\@xuptoktwo\@yuptoktwo
      \let\@yuptoktwo\@empty
    \fi
    \expandafter\test@ccent
  \fi}
```

\@ccentlist is a list of the accent commands; if a string is likely to start with an analphabetic character, such as an opening quote ('), then these characters should also be included in the list.

The \test@ccent macro iterates through the list of accent commands and characters supplied as its argument and if there is a match with \@uptokone then it swaps the \@xuptoktwo and \@yuptoktwo

values. The end result is that if the initial string starts with an accent then \@xuptoktwo has the accented character and \@yuptoktwo is empty, otherwise \@xuptoktwo is empty and \@yuptoktwo has the second character in the string.

Here are some examples using the last definition of \Upfirst:

```
\def\stuff{rAnDoM 26 sTuFf}
low UP \& \Upfirst{low UP} ->
low UP & Low up

\stuff{} \& \Upfirst{\stuff} ->
rAnDoM 26 sTuFf & Random 26 stuff

\oe{}rstead \& \Upfirst{\oe{}rstead} ->
œrstead & Œrstead

\c{c}edilla \& \Upfirst{\c{c}edilla} ->
çedilla & Çedilla

\emph{strong} \& \emph{\Upfirst{strong}} ->
strong & Strong

'quote' \& \Upfirst{'quote} ->
'quote' & 'Quote

>que? \& \Upfirst{>que?} ->
>que? & >Que?
```

As always, if you are doing things with macros that include @ in their name, either put the code into a package (.sty) file or enclose the code in a \makeatletter ... \makeatother pair.

Perhaps next time I'll take a look at going through a string character by character and other kinds of looping macros but on the other hand, perhaps not.

5.1 Address lists

Addresses are given to us to conceal our whereabouts.

Reginald in Russia, SAKI

For many a year I have been promising my wife that I would print labels for the envelopes for our Christmas cards. I even went as far as buying some software to run on an OS that went out of date in the last century. This year (2005) I have at last salved this part of my conscience with the aid of LaTeX and Boris Veytsman's envlab package [132].

After some experiments I created a package file, myenvlab, that gave me the setup that I wanted. I found that I had to use the envlab's \SetLabel command to adjust the address spacing to match the sheets of labels that I was planning to use. I also organised things so that each label could be framed by an \fbox and I could then print a page of addresses onto an ordinary sheet of paper to check if the spacing was correct for the real label sheets. For further information consult the package documentation.

```
% file myenvlab.sty
\usepackage[avery5160label,
            noprintbarcodes,
            nocapaddress]{envlab}
%% Subtract 0.1 inch from vertical dimensions!!
\SetLabel{4.19in}{1.23in}{0.73in}{0.16in}%
         {0.19in}{2}{7}
\newif\ifboxlabel
\let\oldPrintLabel\PrintLabel
\renewcommand{\PrintLabel}[1]{%
  \ifboxlabel
    \fbox{\oldPrintLabel{#1}}%
  \else
    \oldPrintLabel{#1}%
  \fi}
\boxlabeltrue
\endinput
```

The myenvlab package could then be used in a file like the one below to print out a set of address labels, where the \add macro defined the name and address for a label.

```
% file xmas.tex
\documentclass[12pt]{letter}
\usepackage{myenvlab}
%%\boxlabelfalse
\newcommand{\add}[1]{%
  \mbox{}\mlabel{\mbox{}}{#1}}
\newcommand{\UK}{UNITED KINGDOM}
\startlabels
\begin{document}
\add{John Doe \\
    98765 931st St \\ Someplace YN 12345}
\add{A N Other \\
    The House \\ The Road \\ Town \\ \UK}
% etc., etc.
\end{document}
```

Having printed out sheets of labels it occurred to me that probably other labels would be required at other times. My wife was also talking about starting a new address book because the current one was becoming illegible due to many deletions, changes, and additions. I was toying with the idea of subverting BibTeX into an address database but fortunately hesitated before having the joy of programming with the BibTeX language. I now keep all the addresses in a file that looks like this, where I specify a macro for each name and address, and any other personal details that might be of interest:

```
% file addresslist.tex
%%% \add{name}{address}{telephone}{email}{notes}
\newcommand*{\UK}{UNITED KINGDOM}
\newcommand*{\DoeJ}{\add{John Doe}%
  {98765 931st St \\ Someplace YN 12345}%
  {(981) 123--4567}%
  {\url{jd576@email.moc}}%
  {birthday 01/01/01}}
\newcommand*{\OtherAN}{\add{A N Other}%
  {The House \\ The Road \\ Town \\ \UK}%
  {+44 1273 5798 8975}%
  {\url{ano@ano.org}}%
  {dog: Fido}}
% etc., etc.
\endinput
```

Using a suitable definition for \add, which in this case puts the various arguments into a minipage, I can print an address book by:

```
% file addressbook.tex
\documentclass[12pt,twocolumn]{article}
\usepackage{url}
```

```
\newcommand{\add}[5]{%
  \begin{minipage}{\linewidth}\raggedright
  #1 \\ #2 \\ #3 \\ #4 \\ #5 \end{minipage}%
  \\[\baselineskip]}
\begin{document}
\input{addresslist}
\DoeJ
\OtherAN
% etc., etc.
\end{document}
```

With a different definition for \add, which here just uses the first two arguments, namely the name and address, I can print labels by:

```
% file xmas.tex
\documentclass[12pt]{letter}
\usepackage{url}
\usepackage{myenvlab}
\newcommand{\add}[5]{%
  \mbox{}\mlabel{\mbox{}}{#1\\#2}}
\startlabels
\begin{document}
\input{addresslist}
\DoeJ
\OtherAN
% etc., etc.
\end{document}
```

5.2 Animated books

> Now, *here*, you see, it takes all the running *you* can do, to keep in the same place. If you want to go somewhere else, you must run at least twice as fast as that.
>
> *Through the Looking Glass*,
> LEWIS CARROLL

While sorting through some old files I found a piece written by Jeremy Gibbons for his Hey — it works! *column but which was not published before he handed his baton over to me. Jeremy kindly gave me permission to include it here.*

When I was a child, my father used to make little booklets, each page with a slightly different picture; flicking through the booklet quickly makes a 'movie'. Recently James Willans from York asked on comp.text.tex how to achieve this effect in LaTeX, and Michael Liebling answered. Here I show a simpler version of Liebling's approach.

First you need a collection of little pictures; the following assumes that they are all the same size. I used METAPOST to generate a running man in different positions. Here is a representative sample:

The METAPOST file running.mp to create these figures is linked from https://tug.org/TUGboat/Contents/contents27-1.html and is also shown at the end of this section.

Next we compute the page number modulo the number of different pictures:

```
\def\compute@modulus#1#2{%
  \@tempcnta=#2\relax
  \divide\@tempcnta by #1\relax
  \multiply\@tempcnta by #1\relax
  \multiply\@tempcnta by -1\relax
  \advance\@tempcnta by #2\relax}
```

So for example \compute@modulus{12}{\thepage} computes the page number modulo twelve.

We also work out how far to move the image on each page, dividing the difference between the text width and the image width by the number of pages:

```
\newcount\pagecount
\pagecount=100
\setbox0=\hbox{%
  \includegraphics[scale=0.5]{running.0}}
\newdimen\distance
\distance\textwidth
\advance\distance by -\wd0
\divide\distance by \pagecount
```

Finally, we use the plain page style, and put the right image in the right place on each page:

```
\newdimen\offset
\def\@oddfoot{%
  \offset=\distance
  \multiply\offset by \thepage
  \hskip\offset
  \compute@modulus{12}{\thepage}%
  \includegraphics[scale=0.5]%
    {running.\the\@tempcnta}%
  \hfil}
\let\@evenfoot\@oddfoot
```

All that remains is to generate the right number of pages:

```
\loop
  \mbox{} \newpage
\ifnum \pagecount>0
  \advance\pagecount by -1
\repeat
```

As promised earlier, here is the code for the METAPOST file running.mp but please don't ask me to try and explain it.

```
torsoLength = 40;
upperLegLength = 30;
lowerLegLength = 25;
footLength = 10;
upperArmLength = 25;
lowerArmLength = 20;
headDiam = 15;

def leftHipRange(expr r) =
  if r<=1: r[225,360] else: (r-1)[360,225] fi
enddef;

def leftKneeRange(expr r) =
  if r<=1:
    if r<=0.5: (2*r)[150,180]
    else: (2*(r-0.5))[180,330] fi
  else:
    if r<=1.5: (2*(r-1))[330,240]
    else: (2*(r-1.5))[240,150] fi
  fi
enddef;

def leftAnkleRange(expr r) =
  leftKneeRange(r) + 90
enddef;

def leftShoulderRange(expr r) =
  if r<=1: r[210,315] else: (r-1)[315,210] fi
enddef;

def leftElbowRange(expr r) =
  leftShoulderRange(r) + 90
enddef;

def rightHipRange(expr r) =
  leftHipRange(if r<=1: r+1 else: r-1 fi)
enddef;

def rightKneeRange(expr r) =
  leftKneeRange(if r<=1: r+1 else: r-1 fi)
enddef;

def rightAnkleRange(expr r) =
  leftAnkleRange(if r<=1: r+1 else: r-1 fi)
enddef;

def rightShoulderRange(expr r) =
  leftShoulderRange(if r<=1: r+1 else: r-1 fi)
enddef;

def rightElbowRange(expr r) =
  leftElbowRange(if r<=1: r+1 else: r-1 fi)
enddef;

def man(expr phase) =
  pair pelvis;
  pelvis = (0,0);

  pair neck;
```

```
neck = pelvis + torsoLength*dir 75;

numeric leftHipAngle;
leftHipAngle = leftHipRange(phase / 180);
pair leftKnee;
leftKnee = pelvis + upperLegLength*dir
           leftHipAngle;

numeric leftKneeAngle;
leftKneeAngle = leftKneeRange(phase / 180);
pair leftAnkle;
leftAnkle = leftKnee + lowerLegLength*dir
            leftKneeAngle;

numeric leftAnkleAngle;
leftAnkleAngle = leftAnkleRange(phase / 180);
pair leftToes;
leftToes = leftAnkle + footLength*dir
           leftAnkleAngle;

numeric leftShoulderAngle;
leftShoulderAngle =
  leftShoulderRange(phase / 180);
pair leftElbow;
leftElbow = neck + upperArmLength*dir
            leftShoulderAngle;

numeric leftElbowAngle;
leftElbowAngle = leftElbowRange(phase / 180);
pair leftWrist;
leftWrist = leftElbow + lowerArmLength*dir
            leftElbowAngle;

numeric rightHipAngle;
rightHipAngle = rightHipRange(phase / 180);
pair rightKnee;
rightKnee = pelvis + upperLegLength*dir
            rightHipAngle;

numeric rightKneeAngle;
rightKneeAngle = rightKneeRange(phase / 180);
pair rightAnkle;
rightAnkle = rightKnee + lowerLegLength*dir
             rightKneeAngle;

numeric rightAnkleAngle;
rightAnkleAngle = rightAnkleRange(phase/180);
pair rightToes;
rightToes = rightAnkle + footLength*dir
            rightAnkleAngle;

numeric rightShoulderAngle;
rightShoulderAngle =
  rightShoulderRange(phase / 180);
pair rightElbow;
rightElbow = neck + upperArmLength*dir
             rightShoulderAngle;

numeric rightElbowAngle;
```

```
  rightElbowAngle = rightElbowRange(phase/180);
  pair rightWrist;
  rightWrist = rightElbow + lowerArmLength*dir
               rightElbowAngle;

  draw neck -- pelvis;
  draw fullcircle shifted (0.5*up)
       scaled headDiam shifted neck;
  draw neck -- leftElbow -- leftWrist;
  draw pelvis -- leftKnee -- leftAnkle
               -- leftToes;
  draw neck -- rightElbow -- rightWrist;
  draw pelvis -- rightKnee -- rightAnkle
               -- rightToes;

  drawdot neck + headDiam*up
    + (upperLegLength+lowerLegLength)*left
    withcolor white;
  drawdot neck + headDiam*up
    + (upperLegLength+lowerLegLength)*right
    withcolor white;
  drawdot pelvis
    + (upperLegLength+lowerLegLength)*down
    withcolor white;
enddef;

n = 12;
for i := 0 upto n-1:
  beginfig(i); man(i*180/n); endfig;
%  beginfig(i.ps); man(i*180/n); endfig;
endfor

end.
```

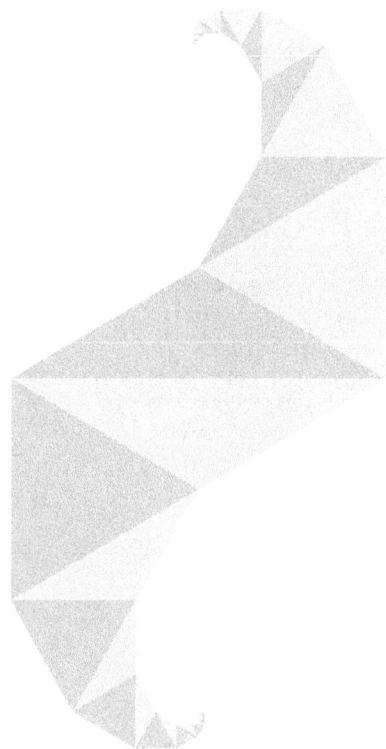

'Tis better to be lowly born
And range with humble livers in content
Than to be perked up in a glist'ring grief
And wear a golden sorrow.

Henry VIII, WILLIAM SHAKESPEARE

6.1 Stringing along

To no one but the Son of Heaven does it belong
to order ceremonies, to fix the measures, and
to determine the written characters.

The Analects, CONFUCIUS

In an earlier column [143] (Chapter 4) I mentioned
that I might continue looking at character strings.
Here is some basic `\allchars` code that can be used
for examining each character in a simple string:

```
\catcode'\^^?=12
\newcommand*{\allchars}[1]{%
  \def\stuff{#1}\ifx\stuff\@empty\else
  \@llchars#1^^?\fi}
\def\@llchars#1#2^^?{%
  \def\letter{#1}
  \def\others{#2}%
  \ifx\letter\@empty
    \let\next\@gobble
  \else
    \doachar{#1}%
    \ifx\others\@empty \let\next\@gobble
    \else \let\next\@llchars \fi
  \fi
  \next#2^^?}
\catcode'\^^?=15
```

Here I have used the special character `^^?` as a
marker for the end of the string. This is normally
an invalid character but I temporarily changed its
catcode to make it an 'other' character (as, say, !
normally is). The `\@gobble` macro is part of the
LaTeX kernel; it takes one argument and does nothing with it. Buried inside the code `\allchars` calls
a macro `\doachar{⟨char⟩}` for each character in the
string. With this definition

```
\newcommand*{\doachar}[1]{\textit{#1}}
```

some examples of `\allchars` are:

```
\allchars{allchars} -> allchars
\allchars{{\oe}rstead's} -> œrstead's
\allchars{} ->
\allchars{with spaces} -> withspaces
```

The special case of an empty argument is handled
in the `\allchars` macro itself, while everything else
is dealt with by `\@llchars`. This keeps calling itself, grabbing one character from the initial string
each time until all are used up, via a process called
tail recursion, meaning that the last thing that it
does is call itself (or effectively do nothing if all the
characters have been processed).

Remember that with LaTeX, if you put any code
that includes macros with @ in their names it either
has to go in a package file (a `.sty` file) or be sur-
rounded by the `\makeatletter` and `\makeatother`
pair of commands.

One unfortunate property of `\allchars` is that it
discards all spaces in the original string. Spaces can
be handled by a two-part process. The first part
goes through the string word by word, where a word
is a set of characters followed by a space. The second part then goes through each word character by
character.

First some preliminaries and the main user command `\Upeach`.

```
\newif\if@newword
\def\checkrelax{\relax}
\catcode'\^^?=12
\newcommand*{\Upeach}[1]{%
  \@upeach#1^^?}
\def\@upeach#1^^?{%
  \def\stuff{#1 }%
  \expandafter\getaword\stuff ^^?}
```

`\getaword` extracts the next word from the string
(note the argument delimited by a space). It then
calls `\getachar` with the word as its argument.

```
\long\def\getaword#1 {%
  \@newwordtrue
  \expandafter\getachar#1\relax}
```

`\getachar` gets the next 'letter' in the word. If
it is `^^?` then the string is finished. If the letter is
the same as `\relax` then it is a space and the macro
must call `\getaword` to repeat the cycle. Otherwise

it has a letter, calls \doUpeach to do something with it, and calls itself again to get the following letter.

```
\def\getachar#1{%
  \def\letter{#1}%
  \if\letter^^?\let\next\relax
  \else
    \ifx\letter\checkrelax
      \let\next\getaword
    \else
      \doUpeach{#1}%
      \let\next\getachar
    \fi
  \fi
  \next}
\catcode`\^^?=15
```

\getachar is another example of tail recursion.

The macro \doUpeach checks if a new word has just started. If so, it converts its argument into italic uppercase and sets \@newwordfalse. If its argument is not the first letter in a word, the argument is typeset in a bold font. Of course this is not a realistic thing to do — it's merely to demonstrate that all the characters in the string have been examined.

```
\newcommand*{\doUpeach}[1]{%
  \if@newword
    \space\textit{\MakeUppercase{#1}}%
    \@newwordfalse
  \else \textbf{#1}\fi}
```

Here are a couple of examples:

```
\Upeach{string with spaces} ->
        String With Spaces
\Upeach{{\oe}rstead's rule} ->
        Œrstead's Rule
```

These macros work for simple strings but are likely to fail if there are accents or anything else to disturb the even tenor of simple characters. The earlier column [143] gave an indication of how such problems might be resolved. On the other hand, it could be a lot simpler and quicker to change the strings by hand using your normal text editor.

6.2 Loops

> Here we go loop de loop.
> Here we go loop de li.
> Here we go loop de loop
> On a Saturday night.

> *Loop de loop*, JOHNNY THUNDER?

There are occasions when you need to perform a repetitive action that does not involve string processing. TeX provides a \loop ... \repeat which can be useful in some circumstances. The general scheme is like this:

```
\loop
  <lots of useful commands>
\if<some condition>
  <more code>
\repeat
```

TeX processes the commands following the \loop and then performs the \if test (without any closing \fi). If the test is true TeX will then process the <more code> and start again with the first batch of commands. If the condition is false it will do whatever comes after the \repeat.

LaTeX, among other internal facilities, provides a mechanism for going through a list of things that are separated by commas (like the option list for a class or package). This scheme looks like:

```
\@for\scratch:=<list>\do{%
    <something with \scratch>}
```

where \scratch is some command name and <list> is a comma-separated list. It takes each element of the list in turn, defines \scratch as that element and then does whatever you tell it to do with it. This continues until the list is exhausted.

It is easier to see how these work with a real example. The following is a very stripped down version of some code from the memoir class [142]. It provides a means of putting a list of things into a tabular form without having to worry about signifying the end of each row. The command is:

$$\fillrows\{\langle width \rangle\}\{\langle numcols \rangle\}$$
$$\{\langle comma\text{-}separated\ list \rangle\}$$

\fillrows creates a centered tabular form of overall width $\langle width \rangle$ and $\langle numcols \rangle$ columns, with the elements from $\langle comma\ separated\ list \rangle$ filling up the tabular row by row (i.e., left to right, top to bottom). I got the initial idea from *TeX for the Impatient* [2] which gave a TeX version, filling top to bottom and left to right.

First some counters and lengths, etc., that we need. Be warned, much of the code below you won't want to know about and I'm not going to try and explain it. In LaTeX this is the kind of stuff that is hidden within the tabular environment.

```
\newcount\CT@cols      % number of cols
\newcount\@cellstogo   % columns left
\newdimen\CT@col@width % column width
\newtoks\crtok
  \crtok = {\cr}%
```

Now we can start on \fillrows itself, which takes three arguments—the overall width, the number of columns, and the list of entries. The first part sets up counters based on the number of columns.

```
\newcommand{\fillrows}[3]{\par\begingroup
  \CT@cols=#2\relax
  \@cellstogo=\CT@cols
```

The next bit defines code that will be called after each entry is put into the tabular; it will insert either a & (we'll let there be normal word spaces ending and beginning our columns, that is, around our & markers), or the internal form of \\.

```
\def\@endcolactions{%
  \global\advance\@cellstogo\m@ne
  \ifnum\@cellstogo<\@ne
    \global\@cellstogo=\CT@cols
    \the\crtok
  \else
    &
  \fi}%
```

Calculate the column widths and start off the tabular by defining the preamble (the general layout of the tabular).

```
\CT@col@width=#1
\divide\CT@col@width \CT@cols
\penalty 10000\relax
\noindent
\vskip -\z@
\def\@preamble{}%
\begingroup
  \let\@sharp\relax
```

Now comes a \loop...\repeat going over all but one of the columns, and for each column extending the \@preamble by adding some spacing and a &.

```
\ifnum\CT@cols>\@ne
  \loop
    \g@addto@macro{\@preamble}{%
      \hb@xt@ \CT@col@width
        {\strut\relax\@sharp\hfil} &}%
    \advance\CT@cols\m@ne
  \ifnum\CT@cols>\@ne
  \repeat
\fi
```

The & is not required for the last column.

```
\g@addto@macro{\@preamble}{%
  \hb@xt@ \CT@col@width
    {\strut\relax\@sharp\hfil}}%
\endgroup
```

(The above code sets each column to a fixed width (\CT@col@width). Commenting out the two lines that start with \hb@xt@ will result in each column being set to its natural width, just wide enough for the widest entry in the column.) Now finish up the preliminaries.

```
\let\@sharp ##
\tabskip\fill
\halign to\hsize \bgroup
  \tabskip\z@
  \@preamble
  \tabskip\fill\cr
```

The entries are added to the tabular, using a \@for loop to extract each entry from the comma-separated list.

```
\@for\@tempa:=#3\do{%
  \@tempa\unskip\space\@endcolactions}%
```

All the entries have been dealt with, so wrap everything up.

```
\the\crtok \egroup \endgroup \par}
```

As a simple example, the code below creates the following tabular:
```
\fillrows{0.7\textwidth}{3}{ one, two,
        three, four, five, six, seven}
```

one	two	three
four	five	six
seven		

And here is the result of another \fillrows, this time with five columns set to their natural width.

```
\renewcommand*{\setcols}{}
\fillrows{0.7\linewidth}{5}{ That's, all,
  folks!, Until, we, meet, again, \ldots}
```

That's	all	folks!	Until	we
meet	again	...		

Whose waves do glister by the Queen's
bright beams.
Which makes them murmure as they
passe away.

———

Poems and Fancies,
MARGARET CAVENDISH

This year (2006) there seems to have been a spate of
questions on the `comp.text.tex` newsgroup about
controlling paragraphs.

7.1 Paragraphs regular

for life's not a paragraph
and death I think is no parenthesis.

———

since feeling is first, EE CUMMINGS

The typical paragraph in a LaTeX document is typeset like:

The typical paragraph in a LaTeX document
looks like this, with the first line indented otherwise lines are set left and right justified except for
the last line which is set ragged right.

The indent at the start of a paragraph is given by
the length `\parindent`. To temporarily achieve a
paragraph with no indentation of the first line put
`\noindent` at the start of the paragraph.

The other regular available paragraph shapes are
ragged left (flush right), ragged right (flush left) and
centered (each line is centered).

On occasions it is useful to be able to set a 'hanging paragraph' where more than one line is indented.
TeX provides two commands for specifying such a
paragraph (the hanging package [141] provides these
in a more LaTeX-like manner).

`\hangindent`⟨*length*⟩ specifies a 'hanging indentation' and `\hangafter`⟨*num*⟩ specifies the number of
hung lines. If ⟨*num*⟩ is positive hanging indentation
is applied to lines ⟨*num*⟩+1, ⟨*num*⟩+2, ..., while if
negative hanging indentation is applied to the first
⟨*num*⟩ lines of the paragraph. When ⟨*length*⟩ is positive the indentation applies to the left-hand end of
the lines and when it is negative the right-hand ends
are indented.

```
\hangindent=3pc\hangafter=-2
```
Following the above incantation the first
two lines of this paragraph are indented at
the left by the given amount. You can use these
commands in a LaTeX document.

At the end of the paragraph, these values are reset to
their defaults. Thus you have to repeat the hanging
specification for each hung paragraph.

LaTeX has an internal command `\@hangfrom` that
it uses for several purposes, such as in the internal
code for section titles. An author-friendly version of
this is:

```
\makeatletter % unless in a .cls or .sty file
\newcommand*{\hangfrom}[1]{%
  \setbox\@tempboxa\hbox{{#1}}%
  \hangindent \wd\@tempboxa
  \noindent\box\@tempboxa}
\makeatother  % unless in a .cls or .sty file
```

Using `\hangfrom{`⟨*text*⟩`}` at the start of a paragraph
produces a paragraph where the second and further
lines are indented with respect to the first by the
width of ⟨*text*⟩. For instance, the code below produces the result following.

```
\hangfrom{$\Longrightarrow$\space}Here
we get a paragraph that is hung in
relation to its first element, which can
sometimes be useful.
```

⟹ Here we get a paragraph that is hung in re-
lation to its first element, which can sometimes
be useful.

Much more exotically, you can achieve very odd
looking paragraphs with the `\parshape` primitive or
the shapepar package.

For more symbolic para-
graph shapes like this one,
TEX provides the \parshape
command. For LATEX users this is
provided in a   more friendly
fashion via   Donald Arseneau's   shapepar
package [10].   Use this kind
of paragraph   very,   very
rarely,   and   only   then
if you really   cannot avoid
it as it is a typesetting curiosity.
This one has been made using
the shapepar package and the
\nutshape specification.

The shapepar package provides several shape specifications, and there are programs which will automatically generate shape specifications.

7.2 Paragraphs particular

> For precept must be upon precept; precept
> upon precept; line upon line; line upon
> line; here a little, and there a little.

Isaiah, ch. 28, v. 10

In addition to \hangafter, \hangindent and
\parshape, TEX provides four parameters[1] for controlling the shape of regular paragraphs. The length
\parindent sets the initial indentation of the first
line. \leftskip and \rightskip are inserted at the
start and end of each line, and \parfillskip is put
at the end of the last line; these last three parameters
take rubber length values, in LATEX terminology. By
changing these you can obtain some particular kinds
of paragraph shapes. Assuming that:

```
\Zeroskip = 0pt plus 0pt minus 0pt
\Flushglue = 0pt plus 1fil
```

then LATEX's settings for its regular paragraph styles
are given in Table 7.1. By adjusting the parameters

---

[1] There are really five parameters, the fifth being
\everypar which is inserted between the indent and the
start of the first line. Only change this if you really know
what you are doing.

you can arrange that the middle lines of a paragraph
have a particular shape, while the first and/or last
lines can have different forms. For instance:

```
\newcommand*{\justlastragged}{%
  \leftskip  =0pt plus 1fil
  \rightskip =-\leftskip
  \parfillskip=\leftskip
  \parindent=0pt }
```

Following a \justlastragged declaration para-
graph(s) will look like the example below.

The shape of this paragraph is not too strange. It is
flush left and right, except for the last line which is
ragged left.

Another particular paragraph shape is one where
the lines are flush left and right, except for the last
which is to be centered, as in:

The lines in this paragraph, with the normal indentation of the first line, should be flush left and
right except for the last line which should be centered.

This can be achieved by using the declaration
\centerlastline before the paragraphs(s) in question:

```
\newcommand{\centerlastline}{%
  \leftskip  =0pt plus 1fil
  \rightskip =0pt plus -1fil
  \parfillskip=0pt plus 2fil\relax}
```

For no initial indentation put \noindent at the start
of the paragraph's text.

```
\newcommand*{\raggedrightthenleft}{%
  \leftskip  =0pt plus 1fill
  \rightskip =0pt plus 1fil
  \parfillskip=0pt
  \everypar{\hskip 0pt plus -1fill\relax}%
  \parindent=0pt\relax}
```

After a \raggedrightthenleft declaration the
first line of any paragraph will be ragged right and
all the other lines will be set ragged left. This looks
odd to me.

	regular	raggedleft	raggedright	centered
\leftskip	\Zeroskip	\Flushglue	\Zeroskip	\Flushglue
\rightskip	\Zeroskip	\Zeroskip	\Flushglue	\mindxFlushglue
\parfillskip	\Flushglue	\Zeroskip	\Zeroskip	\Zeroskip

Figure 7.1: LATEX's paragraph settings

> This is a strangely shaped paragraph. The paragraph's first line is ragged right and all the remaining lines are ragged left.

One way or another the paragraph layouts depend on the amount of what Knuth terms 'glue' (I think, though, that 'spring' would be a more evocative term) at the start and end of each line (the values of `fil`). For fuller explanations of glue see *The TEXbook* [71, ch. 12] or, in my view, more accessibly by Victor Eijkhout [38, ch. 8, 16–18].

In the definition of the last macro the `\leftskip` has a glue (spring) of strength `1fill`, which is infinitely stronger than the `\rightskip` with strength `1fil`, so normally a line will get pushed to the right. The last line has a `\parfillskip` of `0pt`, which will not affect the end of the line. The first line of the paragraph has a springiness of `-1fill` from the `\everypar` and a springiness of `1fill` from the `\leftskip`, which cancel each other out, leaving the spring of `1fil` at the right of the line, and consequently the line gets pushed to the left.

Nikos Platis [108] wanted to ensure that some words at the end of a paragraph were right justified — if there was not enough space on the current line for them then they should be moved to the next line while leaving the current line ragged right. That is either:

> A short line.   Text at right

or

> A very much longer line than the first one above.
>   Text at right

Several solutions were given but the one initially proposed by Knuth in *The TEXbook* [71, p. 106] and submitted by Dirk Schlimm turned out to be the most robust according to Nikos' tests. In LaTeX terms this is:

```
\newcommand*{\atright}[1]{{%
  \unskip\nobreak\hfil\penalty50
  \hskip2em\hbox{}\nobreak\hfil#1
  \parfillskip=0pt\finalhyphendemerits=0\par}}
```

and putting `\atright{⟨text⟩}` at the end of a paragraph ensures that ⟨text⟩ is flush right.

Another often-occurring request is how to ensure that the last line of a paragraph is 'not too short'.

Following the declaration `\nottooshort`, which I have defined as

```
\newdimen\parabout
\newdimen\about
\about=2em
\newcommand*{\nottooshort}{%
```

```
\parabout=\hsize
\advance\parabout -\about
\leftskip=0pt plus 0pt minus 0pt
\rightskip=\leftskip
\parfillskip=\parabout minus \parabout
\parindent=2em }
```

then the last lines of paragraphs will be at least approximately `\about` long.

> The last line in this paragraph should not be too short, for a suitable definition of short. 1 2 3 4

> The last line in this paragraph should not be too short, for a suitable definition of short. 1 2 3 4 5

With short paragraphs, like the examples, the overall effect might not look as well as you might expect. The situation improves with more lines.

Peter Flynn [47] answered Mark's question posed below by providing code for what he termed a 'spring margin', noting that very few systems provided it.

> Hi, I'd like   ...and some text over here.
> left- and   I've tried `tabularx` and
> right-justified   `TabularC`, but they are not
> text on the   precise enough to line up with
> same line. e.g.,   the margins. Any
> some text   suggestions? Thanks, Mark
> here...

The above was produced, with appropriate replacements for the ..., by

```
\spring{0.3}{0.6}%
    {Hi, I'd like left- ...}%
    {\dots and some text ...}
```

where `\spring` is a slight extension of Peter's code. The first two arguments are the fractions of the overall line allocated to the left and right texts; the sum of these must be less than 1. The second pair of arguments is the left and right texts.

```
\newcommand{\spring}[4]{%
\par\noindent\hbox to\columnwidth{\vtop{%
\hsize=#1\columnwidth\flushleft#3\par}\hss
\vtop{\hsize=#2\columnwidth\flushright#4\par}%
}}
```

> I have seen legal documents where each line must be filled at the right so that no extra words can be added later. ————————

This last example was created based on the following code.

```
\let\origpar\par
\newcommand*{\parrule}{%
  \hrule height 2.2pt depth -1.8pt\relax}
\newcommand*{\lastlinerule}{%
  \unskip\nobreak\space
  \leaders\parrule\hskip\Flushglue
  \vadjust{}{\parfillskip=0pt\origpar}}
```

If you have many paragraphs of this kind then following a

```
\let\par\lastlinerule
```

all paragraphs will potentially have the last line filled with a rule. Be aware that LaTeX considers many things to be paragraphs so you could be in for some surprises. To revert back to the regular paragraphs specify:

```
\let\par\origpar
```

Alternatively, do something along these lines:

```
\begingroup
\let\par\lastlinerule
A ruled paragraph ...

Another one...

Even more...

\endgroup
```

The end of a paragraph is normally signalled by either a blank line or the `\par` command. For an isolated ruled paragraph, just end the text with `\lastlinerule` instead of `\par` or a blank line.

7.3 Paragraphs Russian

> On Nevski Bridge a Russian stood
> Chewing his beard for lack of food.
> Said he, 'It's tough stuff to eat
> But a darn sight better than shredded wheat!'

ANONYMOUS

A while after I had completed this column I was going through old papers, trying to winnow those that were no longer useful. Doing this I came across an old issue of *Baskerville — The Annals of the UK TeX Users' Group* which included an article about Russian style paragraphs [29]. Apparently in the Russian typographic tradition the last line of a multiline paragraph must be either at least as long as the `\parindent` and have at least `\parindent` space at the end, or it must be flush left and flush right.

This requirement can't be fulfilled by any simple adjustment of the paragraph setting parameters.

The *Baskerville* article ended with two solutions. The first, shown below, was by Peter Schmitt. The basic technique is to end each paragraph by (glue + hbox + glue), where the empty `hbox` spans `\parindent`, the (glue+hbox) ranges from `\parindent` to (`\hsize−\parindent`) and the (hbox+glue) covers (`\hsize−\parindent`) to `\hsize`, where `\hsize` is the line length. According to TeX rules a line break may occur either before the `glue+hbox` or just after the `\hbox`, in either case giving the paragraph a final blank line, which has to be backed up over.

```
\def\Srussianpar{\ifhmode \unskip
  \hskip-2\parindent minus -2\parindent
  \hskip\hsize minus\hsize
  \hbox{\hskip\parindent}%
  \hskip0pt \hbox{\strut}%
  \hskip-\parindent
  \hskip\hsize plus\parindent
  \vadjust{\nobreak\vskip-\baselineskip}%
  \parfillskip0pt
  \origpar
  \fi}
```

How this works in practice is shown below, where the `\parindent` has been set to 2em, together with `\let\par\Srussianpar`.

The last line in this paragraph should conform to the Russian typesetting tradition. 1 2 3 4
 The last line in this paragraph should conform to the Russian typesetting tradition. 1 2 3 4 5
 The last line in this paragraph should conform to the Russian typesetting tradition. 1 2 3 4 5 6
 The last line in this paragraph should conform to the Russian typesetting tradition. 1 2 3 4 5 6 7
 The last line in this paragraph should conform to the Russian typesetting tradition. 1 2 3 4 5 6 7 8
 The last line in this paragraph should conform to the Russian typesetting tradition. 1 2 3 4 5 6 7 8 9
 The last line in this paragraph should conform to the Russian typesetting tradition. 1 2 3 4 5 6 7 8 9 0

The second solution was by Donald Arseneau as `\Arussianpar`:

```
\def\Arussianpar{\ifhmode \unskip
  \strut\vadjust{}\nobreak
  \discretionary{}%
    {\hbox{\hskip2\parindent
           \vrule depth 273sp
               width 0sp height \ht\strutbox}}%
    {\hbox{\hskip\parindent}}%
  \hskip-2\parindent minus 2\parindent
```

```
\hskip\hsize minus\hsize
\kern0pt\parfillskip0pt
\origpar
\ifdim\prevdepth=273sp
  \nobreak
  \vskip-2\baselineskip
  \hbox{\strut}%
\fi
\fi}
```

This works in approximately the same manner as Peter Schmitt's but it does not always produce an unwanted extra blank line. A rule with a unique depth small enough to be invisible on the page is inserted with the glue items. If the break is such that this is left on the last line, which will be otherwise empty, it can be detected from the \prevdepth value and the line backed up.

[Editor's note: Long after this was published, a question on tex.stackexchange.com asked how to set a rectangular paragraph. The following was proposed: ... xxx{\parfillskip=0pt \par} followed by a blank line. This could be made into a command for more frequent use:

```
\newcommand{\squarepara}
  {\unskip{\parfillskip=0pt \par}}
```

Of course, this works best if the paragraph in question has a last line that is nearly full. Just don't leave a blank line before issuing the command; \unskip works only in horizontal mode.]

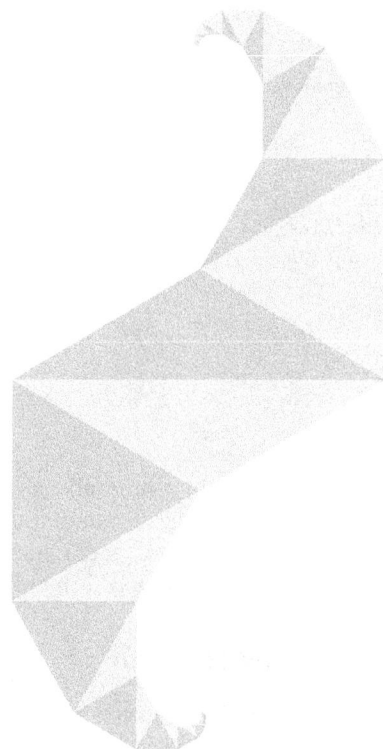

The raging waves doth belching upwardcast
The wretched wrackes that round about doe fleete,
The silken sayles and glistering golden Mast,
Lies all to torne and trodden under feete.

The Ship of Safegarde, BARNABE GOOGE

This main topic this time is macro definition. Questions about this, particularly with respect to LaTeX, are fairly regular on the `comp.text.tex` newsgroup. But first...

8.1 More on paragraphs

Prose is where all the lines except the last go on to the end. Poetry is where some fall short of it.

Jeremy Bentham, quoted in *The Life of John Stuart Mill*, M ST J PACKE

Donald Knuth sent me a version of the following code saying

'I've found this macro to be useful for checking out a `\parshape` specification before cluttering it up with actual text.'

```
% parshape.tex, featuring a possibly useful
%    macro by Don Knuth, April 2007
% \parshapetest{n} will typeset n lines of
%    horizontal rules using the current
%    paragraph shape (as specified by
%    \hangindent, \hangafter, \parshape, or
%    none of the above)
\def\parshapetest#1{%
  \leavevmode%% DEK originally had \indent here
  \count255=1 \loop
    \ifnum\count255<#1
    \null\leaders\hrule\hfil\null\break
    \advance\count255 by 1   \repeat
  \null\leaders\hrule\hfil\hskip-\parfillskip
  \null\par}
```

Unfortunately it was too late to incorporate it into the last column [146] (Chapter 7) which was about how to typeset variously shaped paragraphs. It was doubly unfortunate because when I tried using `\parshapetest` on some of the examples I found that I had misunderstood some aspects of paragraph setting.

`\parshapetest{`⟨*num*⟩`}` draws ⟨*num*⟩ lines according to the current paragraph shape specification, which doesn't sound very exciting but can save a lot of fiddling trying to get the right number of words for a more realistic trial layout.

For instance, I tried this example from [146] (Chapter 7)

```
\begingroup
\hangindent=3pc \hangafter=-2
\parshapetest{4}
\endgroup
```

which, to my surprise, resulted in:

What I hadn't realised that even with specifying `\hangindent` and `\hangafter`, `\parindent` was applied to the first line of the shaped paragraph. The effect that I had expected is obtained as below.

```
\begingroup
\parindent=0pt
\hangindent=3pc \hangafter=-2
\parshapetest{4}
\endgroup
```

which results in:

Following this I tried the `\hangfrom` example from the same column which demonstrated a hanging paragraph. The macro was defined as:

```
\newcommand*{\hangfrom}[1]{%
  \setbox\@tempboxa\hbox{{#1}}%
  \hangindent \wd\@tempboxa
  \noindent\box\@tempboxa}
```

And a demonstration is:

```
\hangfrom{$\Rightarrow$\space}
\parshapetest{3}
```

⇒ _____
  _____
  _____

Here's a more interesting paragraph shape, and the result of testing it:

```
\newdimen\zide
  \zide=\baselineskip
\newcommand*{\aparshape}{%
\parshape=10 0pt 10\zide % 1
              0pt 10\zide % 2
              9\zide \zide % 3
              8\zide \zide % 4
              6\zide \zide % 5
              4\zide \zide % 6
              2\zide \zide % 7
              \zide \zide % 8
              0pt 10\zide % 9
              0pt 10\zide % 10
}
\aparshape
\noindent\parshapetest{10}
```

Try using this paragraph shape with a text of 76 'z' characters with spaces between each, like this:

```
\aparshape
\noindent
z z z z z z z z z z z z z z z z z z
etc
\par
```

which should result in:

```
z z z z z z z z z z z z z
                         z
                       z
                     z
                   z
                 z
               z
z z z z z z z z z z z z z
z z z z z z z z z z z z z
z z z z z z z z z z z z z
z z z z z z z z z
```

Following a request on the `comp.text.tex` newsgroup by Stephen Moye, Paul Vojta [134] posted the following code[1] for setting the first line of a paragraph flushleft, the following lines centered but the final line flushright.

```
\newcommand*{\leftcenterright}{%
  \leftskip=0pt plus 1fil
  \rightskip=0pt plus 1fil
  \parfillskip=0pt plus -1fil
  \parindent=0pt
  \everypar={\hskip0pt plus -1fil\relax}}
```

`\leftcenterright` should either be used in a group, or you can use the following macro `\regularpar` to return to the regular paragraph style, where you have previously specified `\myparindent` as the normal value of `\parindent`.

```
\newcommand*{\regularpar}{%
  \leftskip=0pt plus 0pt minus 0pt
  \rightskip=\leftskip
  \parfillskip=0pt plus 1fil
  \parindent=\myparindent
  \everypar{}}
```

Following is an example of a `\leftcenterright` paragraph, typeset from:

```
\begingroup
\leftcenterright
First line \\ Second line \\
Third line \\ Last line \par
\regularpar
\endgroup
```

First line
                    Second line
                     Third line
                                     Last line

---
[1] For convenience I have put Paul's code into a macro.

8.2 LATEX's defining triumvirate

> Who will change old lamps for new? ...
> new lamps for old ones?
>
> *Arabian Nights: The History of Aladdin*

The basic macro provided by LATEX for defining new commands is somewhat simpler than the TEX macro upon which it is based. This is the LATEX one:

\newcommand{⟨*cmd*⟩}[⟨*num*⟩][⟨*arg1*⟩]{⟨*defn*⟩}

where ⟨*cmd*⟩ is the name, including the backslash (e.g., \amacro), of the new macro being defined and ⟨*defn*⟩ is the definition of the new macro, which may be simply some text to be typeset or something very complex. The optional ⟨*num*⟩ argument specifies the number of arguments that the new macro will take; if given this must be at least one and at most nine. The new macro will take an optional argument if ⟨*arg1*⟩ is given, where ⟨*arg1*⟩ is the default value of the first argument. The macro resulting from \newcommand is, in TEX terms, a *long* macro, meaning that an argument may consist of more than one paragraph or, equivalently, include a \par. The star form of the command, \newcommand*, creates a macro where paragraph(s) are *not* allowed in an argument to the new macro. If ⟨*cmd*⟩ has been defined previously LATEX will give an error message.

The LATEX macro

\renewcommand{⟨*cmd*⟩}[⟨*num*⟩][⟨*arg1*⟩]{⟨*defn*⟩}

and its companion \renewcommand*, are similar to \newcommand except that they change the definition of ⟨*cmd*⟩, which *must* have been defined earlier, otherwise LATEX will complain.

The third member of LATEX's macro definition triumvirate is:

\providecommand{⟨*cmd*⟩}[⟨*num*⟩][⟨*arg1*⟩]%
    {⟨*defn*⟩}

which acts like \newcommand if ⟨*cmd*⟩ has not been defined, otherwise it silently does nothing. Again, there is a starred version of the command.

If you want to make sure that your definition for ⟨*cmd*⟩ is used regardless of whether or not it has been defined before you can do this:

```
% ensure \amacro is defined
\providecommand{\amacro}{}
% change the definition
\renewcommand{\amacro}...
```

Within the ⟨*defn*⟩ argument to the macros the use of the first argument, if any, is denoted by #1, the second by #2, and so on up to the ninth which is denoted by #9. The arguments can be used as many times as needed and in any order.

A question that pops up now and then on the comp.text.tex newsgroup is how to define a macro

that takes more than 9 arguments. The answer is to split it up into two or more macros each of which handles a portion of the required number. For, say, 11 arguments:

```
\newcommand{\xiargs}[9]{%
  % 9 args used here then
  \xtrargs}
\newcommand{\xtrargs}[2]{%
  % use last 2 args here
  % #1 and #2 are the apparent 10th & 11th args
}
```

The user calls \xiargs with the 11 arguments, and \xiargs processes the first 9 of these. It then calls \xtrargs, which is effectively hidden from view, to process the remaining 2 arguments. If you need to use, say, the 4th argument within \xtrargs this can be easily accomplished:

```
\newcommand{\xiargs}[9]{%
  % 9 args used here then
  \xtrargs{#4}}
\newcommand{\xtrargs}[3]{%
  % #1 here is #4 of from \xiargs and
  % #2 and #3 are the apparent 10th & 11th args
}
```

As a lead-in to the next section, here is another way of getting the 4th argument into \xtrargs:

```
\newcommand{\xiargs}[9]{%
  % 9 args used here including
  \def\ivarg{#4}%
  % then
  \xtrargs}
\newcommand{\xtrargs}[2]{%
  % #1 and #2 are the apparent 10th & 11th args
  % call \ivarg for original 4th arg
}
```

where \def is the TEX command for defining a command, as we'll discuss next.

This kind of code can obviously be extended to handle as many arguments as you wish, but after a while it might be easier to use the keyval package [28], or the later extension called xkeyval [4], which provide a very different approach. You name each argument and the user can use as many or as few of these as he deems necessary.

8.3 TEX's dictator

> He who can properly define and divide is to be considered a god.
>
> *Novum Organum*, FRANCIS BACON
> quoting PLATO

TeX has an all-purpose command for defining new macros, namely `\def`. There are too many aspects to this to cover them all in a short article; Knuth [71, ch. 20] provides the definitive explanation, but you may find that Eijkhout [38, ch. 11] or Abrahams *et al.* [2, chs. 4 and 9] are more accessible or helpful.

The syntax of the `\def` command is unlike anything you see in an author's view of LaTeX.

`\def⟨cmd⟩⟨paramspec⟩{⟨defn⟩}`

As in the LaTeX formulation, ⟨*cmd*⟩ is the name, including the backslash (e.g., `\amacro`), of the new macro being defined and ⟨*defn*⟩ is the definition of the new macro, just as with LaTeX. Note that there are no braces around ⟨*cmd*⟩.

The ⟨*paramspec*⟩ is where you specify the appearance of any arguments to ⟨*cmd*⟩. Each argument is denoted by #1, #2, etc., in ⟨*paramspec*⟩; these must be in numerical order, and spaces within ⟨*paramspec*⟩ (but not before, unless a control symbol is being defined) are significant. Below are two (almost) equivalent pieces of (LA)TeX code:

```
\newcommand*{\amacro}[2]{....} % LateX
\def\amacro#1#2{....}          % TeX
... \amacro{foo}{bar} ...      % (La)TeX
```

They are only "almost" equivalent because while `\newcommand` complains if `\amacro` is already defined, `\def` does not — it just throws the old definition away. Be careful of this as it is not a good idea to inadvertently redefine some vital macro that you did not know existed.

If you need an argument to consist of one or more paragraphs, by including a blank line or a `\par` (as `\newcommand` provides for by default), then the macro must be made *long*, by preceding the `\def` with `\long`.

Here are two more almost (for the analogous reason) equivalent pieces of code:

```
\renewcommand{\amacro}[2]{....}        % LateX
\long\def\amacro#1#2{....}             % TeX
... \amacro{A paragraph\par}{bar} ... % (La)TeX
```

When the ⟨*paramspec*⟩ consists only of parameters (the #1 etc.) they are said to be *undelimited*; simplistically these correspond to LaTeX's mandatory arguments. On the other hand, if any non-parameter tokens (that is, anything except a #n or the opening { of the {⟨*defn*⟩}) occur after a #n then that parameter is said to be *delimited*. When the new macro is called, the argument for a delimited parameter does not end until TeX encounters the delimiting character(s). Internally, LaTeX uses delimited parameters to implement optional arguments.

Suppose we need a macro that looks like this:

`\where{foo}(x,y)`

where `foo`, `x` and `y` are the arguments to `\where`. The LaTeX commands described above can't handle this, but TeX can:

```
\def\where#1(#2,#3){#1 in #2 #3}
```

and calling

```
\textit{%
\where{A nightingale sang}
(Berkeley,Square)}
```

results in

A nightingale sang in Berkeley Square

Perhaps you need a command that comes in two versions, like the `\newcommand` does. The LaTeX kernel includes a macro called `\@ifnextchar`, whose syntax is like this:

`\@ifnextchar⟨char⟩{⟨yes⟩}{⟨no⟩}`

It looks to see if the next non-space character in the input text is ⟨*char*⟩. If so, it executes the ⟨*yes*⟩ argument, otherwise it executes the ⟨*no*⟩ argument. The kernel also provides this convenient test command:

`\@ifstar{⟨yes⟩}{⟨no⟩}`

which looks to see if the next character is a * and if it is it gobbles up the * and executes the ⟨*yes*⟩ argument, otherwise it executes the ⟨*no*⟩ argument. It is defined as follows:

```
\long\def\@firstoftwo#1#2{#1}
\def\@ifstar#1{%
  \@ifnextchar*{\@firstoftwo{#1}}}
```

Now you can define your own (un)starred command pair, like this:

```
\makeatletter  % if not in a .cls or .sty file
\def\maybestar{%
  \@ifstar{\@maybestarS}{\@maybestar}}
  % handle starred version
\def\@maybestarS#1#2{Star (#1) and (#2).}
  % handle plain version
\def\@maybestar#1#2{(#1) and (#2).}
\makeatother   % if not in a .cls or .sty file
```

The end result is a macro with both starred and unstarred versions that takes two arguments. A pair of example results are:

```
\maybestar*{1st}{2nd} -> Star (1st) and (2nd).
\maybestar{1st}{2nd}  -> (1st) and (2nd).
```

If you would like to use another character, say a ?, in place of the *, here's a way of doing it.

```
\def\maybeQ{%
  \@ifnextchar ?{\@maybeQ}{\@maybe}}
\def\@maybeQ#1#2#3{Query (#2) and (#3).}
\def\@maybe#1#2{(#1) and (#2).}
```

Unlike the starring code where `\@ifstar` got rid of the * the `\@maybeQ` macro has to discard the ? which is the first character it will see; TeX treats a single character[2] as an argument so `\@maybeQ` is defined such that it throws away its first argument.

A pair of example results are:

```
\maybeQ?{1st}{2nd} -> Query (1st) and (2nd).
\maybeQ{1st}{2nd} -> (1st) and (2nd).
```

Maybe you would like a LaTeX command that takes two optional arguments and one required one. Heiko Oberdiek has produced a comprehensive package for creating such macros, namely twoopt [95], but as another TeX example, here is a simple method that might be useful for the odd occasion. The result will be a LaTeX macro, `\twoopt`, that takes one required and two optional arguments. The defaults for the two optional arguments are to be 'opt1' and 'opt2', respectively and unimaginatively.

```
\def\twoopt{%
  \@ifnextchar [{\@twoopt}{\@twoopt[opt1]}}
\def\@twoopt[#1]{%
  \@ifnextchar [%
     {\@@twoopt{#1}}{\@@twoopt{#1}[opt2]}}
\def\@@twoopt#1[#2]#3{%
  1 (#1) 2 (#2) 3 (#3)}
```

Don't forget that this has to be defined when LaTeX thinks that @ is a letter. Trying this out we get:

```
\twoopt{no opts} -> 1 (opt1) 2 (opt2) 3 (no opts)
\twoopt[foo]{one opt} -> 1 (foo) 2 (opt2) 3 (one
opt)
\twoopt[bar][baz]{two opts} -> 1 (bar) 2 (baz)
3 (two opts)
```

---

[2]More precisely, a token, but now is not the time to get into all that.

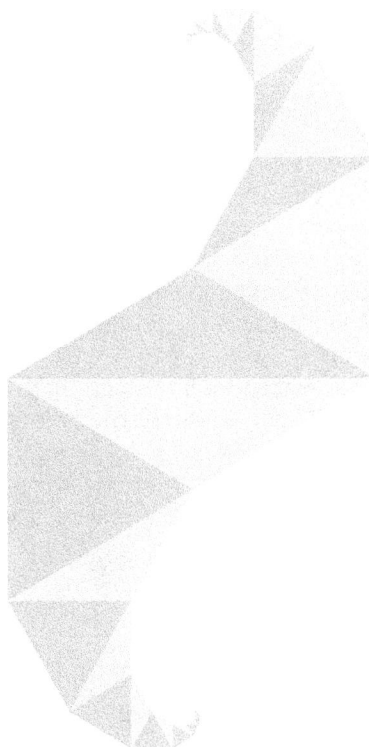

CHAPTER 9

TUGBOAT 30:1, 2009

Child! do not throw this book about!
Refrain from the unholy pleasure
Of cutting all the pictures out!
Preserve it as your chiefest treasure!

A Bad Child's Book of Beasts,
HILLAIRE BELLOC

9.1 METAPOST and pdfLATEX

The METAPOST program generates PostScript illustrations. These can easily be inserted into a document to be processed by (LA)TEX to produce a `dvi` file. Generally speaking, though, pdfLATEX cannot handle PostScript files. Fortunately it can handle the limited form of PostScript that METAPOST generates, and so METAPOST illustrations can be directly embedded into a pdfLATEX document. This, though, is not quite as straightforward as it might be.

Given a file called, say, `figs.mp`, which contains perhaps three pictures, we can process it with :

```
mpost figs
```

METAPOST will generate 3 files, `figs.1`, `figs.2` and `figs.3`, one for each picture. On the other hand, pdfLATEX expects METAPOST generated PostScript files to have an `.mps` extension. If you use the `graphicx` package you can get it to accept files with numeric extensions as though they had an `.mps` extension by specifying:

```
\DeclareGraphicsRule{*}{mps}{*}{}
```

which tells `\includegraphics` to treat any extension it does not recognise as though it were `.mps`.

LATEX, or rather programs like `dvips` or `xdvi`, can handle Encapsulated PostScript (`.eps`) files, and so you can perform similar magic for the `graphicx` package when using DVI output:

```
\usepackage{ifpdf}
\ifpdf
  \usepackage{graphicx}
  \DeclareGraphicsRule{*}{mps}{*}{}
\else
  \usepackage{graphicx}
  \DeclareGraphicsRule{*}{eps}{*}{}
\fi
```

If a METAPOST illustration might be used in a LATEX (as opposed to pdfLATEX) document, then put
```
prologues := 1;
```
at the start of the METAPOST file, which tells METAPOST to generate Encapsulated PostScript files. It seems to do no harm to use that same `prologues` value for pdfLATEX.

9.2 Spidrons

A mathematician, like a painter or a poet, is a maker of patterns. If his patterns are more permanent than theirs, it is because they are made with ideas.

A Mathematician's Apology, G. H. HARDY

The other week I was idly glancing through *Science News* when I came across a short article about spidrons [106]; try googling for 'spidron' to get more on the subject.

Spidrons, which were discovered and named by the Hungarian designer and graphic artist Dániel Erdély while doodling with hexagons, are made up of ever smaller connected triangles alternating between isosceles and equilateral in form.

It occurred to me that METAPOST could be used to draw these and after a little trial and error I came up with the following METAPOST program to support drawing spidrons.

```
%% semispid.mp  MP macro to draw a semi-spidron
% semispid(center, vertex, iterations,
%          color1, color2, clockwise)
def semispid(suffix $$, $)%
        (expr iter, shadea, shadeb, clock) =
if clock: hxa := -60; else: hxa := 60; fi
pair v[];
path phex[];
v0 := z$$;
v1 := z$;
% enclosing hexagon
for i := 2 upto 6:
  v[i] := v1 rotatedaround(v0,(i-1)*hxa);
endfor
z$a = v1; z$b = v2; z$c = v3;
z$d = v4; z$e = v5; z$f = v6;
phex0 := v1--v2--v3--v4--v5--v6--cycle;
if showverts:
  dotlabels.lft($a,$b,$c,$d,$e,$f);
fi
```

```
if showlines:
  draw v1--v3--v5--cycle;
  draw v2--v4--v6--cycle;
fi
% construct triangles
for n:= 1 upto iter:
  k  := 10(n-1);
  j  := 10n;
  v[1+j] := (v[1+k]--v[3+k])
            intersectionpoint
            (v[2+k]--v[6+k]);
  for i := (2+j) upto (6+j):
    v[i] := v[1+j]
            rotatedaround
            (v0, (i-1-j)*hxa);
  endfor
  if showlines:
    draw v[1+j]--v[3+j]--v[5+j]--cycle;
    draw v[2+j]--v[4+j]--v[6+j]--cycle;
  fi
  phex[n]   := v[1+j]--v[1+k]--v[2+k]--cycle;
  phex[n+1] := v[1+j]--v[2+j]--v[2+k]--cycle;
  fill phex[n] withcolor shadea;
  fill phex[n+1] withcolor shadeb;
  if showcells:
    draw phex[n]; draw phex[n+1];
  fi
  if showedges:
    draw v[1+k]--v[1+j];
    draw v[2+k]--v[2+j];
  fi
endfor
if showedges: draw v[1+j]--v[2+j]; fi
if showhex: draw phex0; fi
enddef;
```

As its name implies, the routine `semispid` generates and draws half of a spidron, which Erdély called a semi-spidron, and this is contained within a hexagon. The location arguments are the center point of the enclosing hexagon and the location of one of the vertices. The other arguments control the number of triangles and two colors for coloring alternate triangles. The routine uses booleans, specified elsewhere, to control the display of various aspects of the construction method.

I used the next METAPOST program to create the spidron shown in Figure 9.1.

```
% glstr9.mp  MP spidron figures
prologues := 1;
input semispid
%%% define the boolean flags and defaults
% show the initial hexagon
boolean showhex; showhex := false;
% label vertices
boolean showverts; showverts := false;
% draw construction lines
boolean showlines; showlines := false;
```

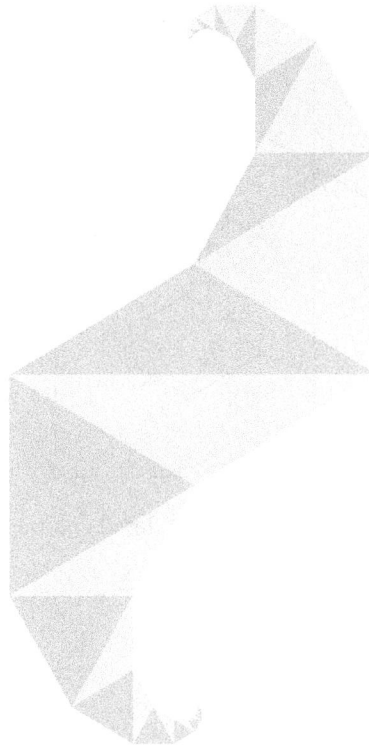

Figure 9.1: A spidron

```
% draw triangle cell boundaries
boolean showcells; showcells := false;
% work clockwise (yes = true)
boolean rh; rh := false;
% draw sem-spidron outline
boolean showedges; showedges := false;
% shading
color light,dark;
light := 0.1[white,black];
dark := 0.2[white,black];

beginfig(1); % a spidron
  u := 1in;  % units
showhex := false;
showverts := false;
showlines := false;
showcells := false;
rh := false;
showedges := false;
% center & initial vertex
z0 = (0,0);
z1 = (x0-2u,y0) rotatedaround(z0,60);
semispid(0, 1, 9, dark, light, rh);
y0-y1a = y1a-y10; x10=x0;
z11 = z1b;
semispid(10, 11, 9, light, dark, rh);
endfig;
%% more pictures here
end
```

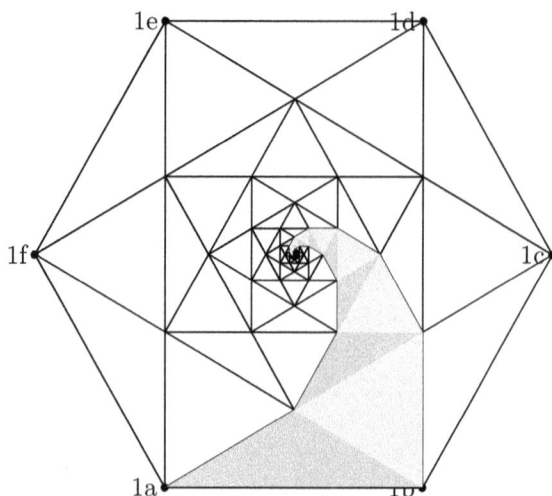

Figure 9.2: Construction details of a spidron

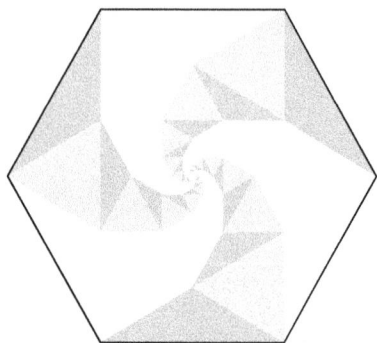

Figure 9.3: Three semi-spidrons in a hexagon

Figure 9.4: A hornflake

The construction details of a semi-spidron are illustrated in Figure 9.2. The `semispid` routine generates the vertices of a hexagon, labelling the given one as 'a', then the others in turn as 'b', 'c', etc. The hexagon is repeatedly partitioned by joining alternate vertices, which creates a smaller interior hexagon, which is then partitioned into a smaller one again, and so on until it all gets 'too small'. The shaded triangles form a semi-spidron, starting on the 'a-b' side of the hexagon, and finishing close to the center. The second half of the complete spidron is a rotation of the first semi-spidron about the midpoint of the 'a-b' edge of the hexagon, with the colors reversed.

Spidrons are space-filling; that is, they can be assembled to completely cover, or tile, a plane surface. You can get a hint about this from Figure 9.3 which shows three semi-spidrons constructed in a single hexagon. The empty spaces can be exactly filled by three more semi-spidrons. A plane can be completely tiled using hexagons; in this particular case it happens that it can also be completely tiled by spidrons. Interesting effects can be achieved by changing the coloring of the spidrons. An example is shown in Figure 9.5. For much, much, more on tilings see *Tilings and Patterns* [58], although it doesn't include spidrons as they hadn't been discovered when the book was published.

There is an associated figure that can also be made out of two semi-spidrons. In a spidron the two semi-spidrons are rotations of each other. In the shape that Erdély calls a *hornflake*, shown in Figure 9.4, the two halves are mirror images of each other. Unlike spidrons, hornflakes are not space-filling but can be used for tiling if they are suitably combined with spidrons, as can be seen in Figure 9.5.

In his article Peterson says that

> [Erdély's] insight was to start with an array of hexagons drawn on a sheet of paper and laid as if they were bathroom tiles. By creasing the pattern in the right combinations of mountains and valleys at the lines within each spidron arm and leaving a small hole at the center of each hexagon, he crinkled the whole array into a dramatic three-dimensional relief.

It turns out that spidron patterns can also be assembled into novel three-dimensional crystal-like forms with spiral polygonal faces.

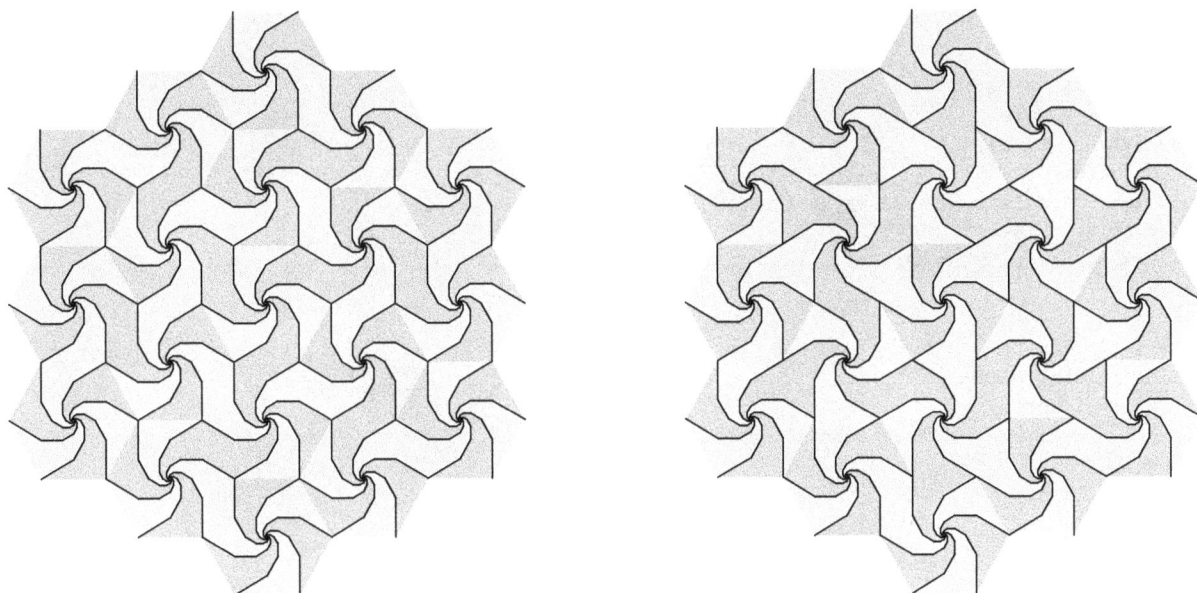

Figure 9.5: Tilings: (left) Spidrons can do it alone; (right) Hornflakes need spidrons

What was missing from this article was any hint as to what those 'right combinations' of folds might be to create these effects. After some searching on the web I found the following remarks by Erdély [40].

> I folded every second edge, reaching to the centre of the created hexagon in the given Spidron system, as a spine and folded every first edge as a groove. The resulting relief-like surface, under the impact of an external deforming force, does not show simple linear displacements, such as those produced with an accordion; instead, the edges between the vertices and the centres of the original hexagonal system move in a vortex within each hexagon.

After a lot of cogitation and physical experimentation I came to believe that among the 'right combinations' are the ones shown in Figure 9.6, which shows half a hexagon with three semi-spidrons. The dotted lines indicate 'valley' folds (paper on either side of the fold, or crease, is bent upwards) and the full lines indicate 'mountain' folds (paper on either side of the crease is bent downwards).

If you want to create a large construct for folding, here is the code for generating the spidron tiling shown in Figure 9.5. You can, of course, modify this to meet your needs.

```
% glstr9.mp  MP spidron figures
% earlier pictures
beginfig(5); % spidron tiling
```

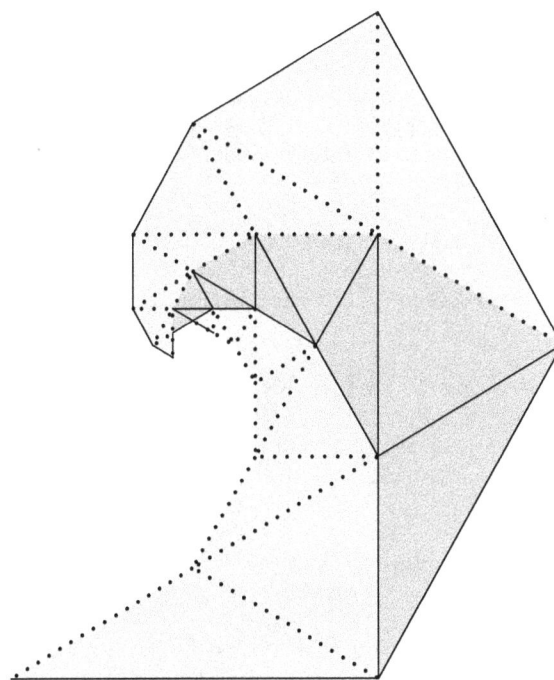

Figure 9.6: Folding. [Editor's note: We gratefully acknowledge Jeremy Gibbons' paper "Dotted and dashed lines in METAFONT", *TUGboat* 16:3 (1995), https://tug.org/TUGboat/tb16-3/tb48gibb.pdf, which aided us in finalizing this figure, and a fascinating read in itself.]

```
    u := 0.175in;
showhex := false;
showverts := false;
showlines := false;
showcells := false;
rh := false;
showedges := false;  showedges := true;
color cola, colb;
cola := light; colb := dark;
depth := 7;
rad := 2u;
z0 = (0,0);
% fill initial hexagon
for kn := 1 upto 6:
z[kn] = (x0-2u,y0) rotatedaround(z0,60*(kn-1));
if odd kn:
  cola := light;
else:
  cola := dark;
fi
 colb := cola;
semispid(0, [kn], depth, cola, colb, rh);
endfor
% copy (in circles) the filled hexagon
% to make the tiling
shd := (sqrt 3)/2*rad; % shift up/down
shr := 3rad;           % shift left/right
picture pic[];
pic100 := currentpicture;
pic0 := pic100 shifted (0,2shd);
for kn := 1 upto 6:
  pic[kn] := pic0 rotatedaround(z0,60kn);
  draw pic[kn];
endfor
pic10 = pic100 shifted (0,4shd);
for kn := 1 upto 6:
  pic[10+kn] := pic10 rotatedaround(z0,60kn);
  draw pic[10+kn];
endfor
pic20 = pic100 shifted (3rad, 0);
for kn := 1 upto 6:
  pic[20+kn] := pic20 rotatedaround(z0,60kn);
  draw pic[20+kn];
endfor
endfig;
% more pictures
end
```

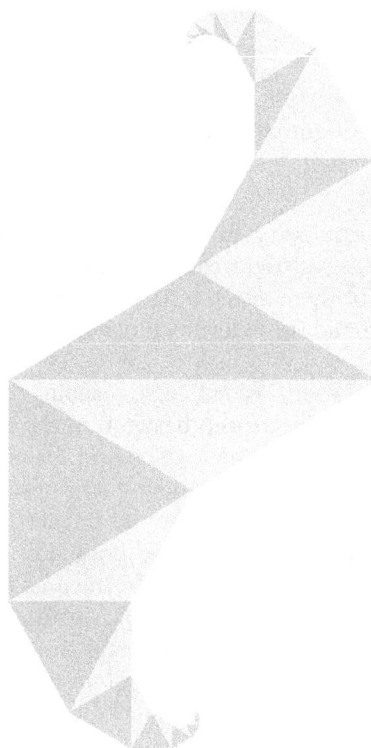

However, I found that it was difficult enough to properly fold even a single large filled hexagon e.g., one that just fitted onto a typical sheet of paper, such as letter paper or A4. I decided that the best way was to use single spidrons, fold them appropriately, and then hinge them together with sticky tape. I then concluded that it was much more pleasurable to look at pictures of what others had accomplished (most of which, I suspect, were done using computer graphics instead of using physical methods and photographing the results).

Yet in his feverish mind
He still could find
The miraging domes of Samarkand
Glistering through the roiling sand.

Doubt

10.1 Repetition

There was an old man named Michael Finnegan
Grew some whiskers on his chinnegan.
The wind came out and blew them innegan.
Poor old Michael Finnegan.
Beginnagen.
There was an old man named Michael Finnegan
. . .

TRADITIONAL

There are occasions when an author wants to repeat some text that occurred in a document at some later place, perhaps in an Appendix.

If the original is plain text then this is simple enough — define a macro holding the text and use it in each place the text is to appear. A variation on this is when there is some boilerplate text that will be used in many documents. If the text is short, then define a macro to hold it. If the text is longer, say a page or two, then put the text into a `.tex` file and define a macro that `\input`s that file. I used both these schemes when I was writing class [139] and package [140] files for some ISO International Standard documents which tended to have much boilerplate text, both short and long.

Life gets more complicated if you need to repeat something that is automatically numbered by LaTeX, as requested by David Romano [117] in this partial quote from his posting to `texhax`, which was passed on to me by Barbara Beeton.

> *Here is the problem I'm trying to solve. I'd like to have a particular theorem appear twice in a paper, and I'd like its appearance to be identical in both, the numbering in particular, without having to set the section and theorem counters by hand.*

For the following examples I have specified:

```
\newtheorem{again}{Repetitive}[subsection]
\newsavebox{\Tsaved}
\newcounter{savesub}\newcounter{savethm}
```

```
\newcounter{restoresub}\newcounter{restorethm}
\newcommand*{\fox}{The slow old fox readily
  leaped over the quick brown dog.}
\newcommand*{\party}{All the good men came
  to the party.}
\newcommand*{\boring}{Some things get very
  boring when repeated too often.}
```

10.1.1 Box it

Here is one theorem:

> **Repetitive 10.1.1.1** *All the good men came to the party.*

and the next one is the one that is to be repeated. One way of repeating some typeset text is to save it in a box and then use that box wherever the text is to be repeated. The typeset theorem (10.1.1.2) below is produced by the following code:

```
\savebox{\Tsaved}{%
\begin{minipage}{\linewidth}
\begin{again}\label{th1}
\boring
\end{again}
\end{minipage}}
\vspace{\topsep}
\noindent\usebox{\Tsaved}
\vspace{\topsep}
```

> **Repetitive 10.1.1.2** *Some things get very boring when repeated too often.*

I discovered that I had to put a vertical space of `\topsep` before and after the box to match the normal spacing around theorems.

And we can use the box again to obtain a repetition of the theorem:

```
\vspace{\topsep}
\noindent\usebox{\Tsaved}
\vspace{\topsep}
```

> **Repetitive 10.1.1.2** *Some things get very boring when repeated too often.*

Using this technique a theorem has to be put into a minipage inside the box in order to get the correct line breaking, but minipages don't break across page boundaries. Provided the theorem is short and the stars are aligned then this won't be a problem. On the other hand, for long theorems and normal alignment the repetition will make a page too long.

Here is another theorem (10.1.1.3) to be repeated. This time, for use later, I save the values of the current \subsection and the current **again** theorem counters before typesetting the theorem:

```
\setcounter{savesub}{\value{subsection}}
\setcounter{savethm}{\value{again}}
\begin{again}\label{th2}
\party
\end{again}
```

> **Repetitive 10.1.1.3** *All the good men came to the party.*

10.1.2 Save the numbers

Any **again** theorem in this subsection will normally have a number starting **10.1.2**.

Having saved the relevant numbers for the first appearance of theorem 10.1.1.3 we can now typeset it again. The process is:

1. Save the current values of the \subsection and the **again** theorem counters.

2. Set the current values of those counters to those for the original **again** theorem.

3. Repeat the theorem.

4. Restore the values of the \subsection and the **again** theorem counters.

Here, then, is a repetition of theorem 10.1.1.3.

```
\setcounter{restoresub}{\value{subsection}}
\setcounter{restorethm}{\value{again}}
\setcounter{subsection}{\value{savesub}}
\setcounter{again}{\value{savethm}}
\begin{again}
\party
\end{again}
\setcounter{section}{\value{restoresub}}
\setcounter{again}{\value{restorethm}}
```

> **Repetitive 10.1.1.3** *All the good men came to the party.*

Show another theorem here:

```
\begin{again}
This is a new theorem.
\end{again}
```

> **Repetitive 10.1.2.1** *This is a new theorem.*

And for the third time display theorem 10.1.1.2:

```
\vspace{\topsep}
\noindent\usebox{\Tsaved}
\vspace{\topsep}
```

> **Repetitive 10.1.1.2** *Some things get very boring when repeated too often.*

If the theorem to be repeated is complex then you could either define a macro for it, or put it into a file to be input.

```
\newcommand*{\foxy}{%
\begin{again}
\fox
\end{again}}
\foxy
```

> **Repetitive 10.1.2.2** *The slow old fox readily leaped over the quick brown dog.*

10.2 Rectangular text

> A work that aspires, however humbly, to the condition of art should carry its justification in every line.
>
> *The Nigger of the Narcissus,*
> JOSEPH CONRAD

In an earlier column [146] Chapter 7 I discussed how to create paragraph shapes of various kinds. One that I had not considered was sought after by Brad Cooper who asked on comp.text.tex:

> *I am trying to do something ... whereby two lines of large text are justified on the right and left without any hyphenation occurring.*

Several solutions were posted and I give some of them below, in alphabetic order of the respondents.

Donald Arseneau [12] said that the solution was to use a 'stretch' tabular column type, but that unfortunately there isn't one. Instead he suggested

```
\noindent\begin{tabular}{@{}r@{}}
\hfilneg A SHORT LINE \\
\hfilneg A LITTLE LONGER LINE \\
\hfilneg Donald Arseneau
\end{tabular}
```

```
A        SHORT        LINE
A LITTLE LONGER LINE
Donald               Arseneau
```

Or, using the array package, like this:

```
\newcolumntype{s}{>{\hfilneg}r}
\enskip\begin{tabular}{s}
A SHORT LINE \\
...
```

where I have used the \enskip space, as well as the regular paragraph indent, to set off the text from the left margin:

```
 A        SHORT        LINE
 A LITTLE LONGER LINE
 Donald               Arseneau
```

Enrico Gregorio [55] posted the following solution, defining a new center-like environment:

```
\newenvironment{stretchcenter}%
{$$\let\\\cr\vbox\bgroup\ialign\bgroup%
  \unskip##\unskip\cr}%
{\crcr\egroup\egroup$$}
```

The stretchcenter environment is used just like the regular center environment. The result is:

```
       A        SHORT        LINE
       A LITTLE LONGER LINE
       Enrico               Gregorio
```

Dan Luecking [75] posted further solutions. The first simply involves measuring the longest line and putting the others into boxes to match.

```
\newlength\gxx
\settowidth{\gxx}{A LITTLE LONGER LINE}
\noindent\makebox[\gxx][s]{A SHORT LINE}\par
\noindent\mbox{A LITTLE LONGER LINE}\par
\noindent\makebox[\gxx][s]{Dan Luecking}\par
```

This results in:

```
A        SHORT        LINE
A LITTLE LONGER LINE
Dan                  Luecking
```

That was the kind of method I had thought of but it does require some manual work. Dan also provided a more elegant solution to match the others, as:

```
\halign{#\cr
A SHORT LINE\cr
A LITTLE LONGER LINE\cr
Dan Luecking\cr}
```

which results in no indentation of the text from the left margin:

```
A        SHORT        LINE
A LITTLE LONGER LINE
Dan                  Luecking
```

To have the text indented, add space (\quad in the example below) inside the \halign like:

```
\halign{\quad#\cr
A SHORT ...
```

Note that the \halign and \ialign commands used by Dan and Enrico are usually hidden from LaTeX users but are used by the LaTeX kernel in defining environments like tabular, for example.

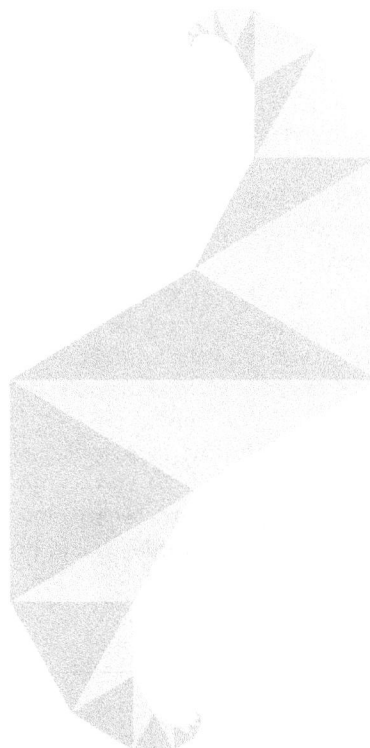

CHAPTER 11

His eye, which scornfully glisters like fire,
Shows his hot courage and his high desire.

Venus and Adonis,
WILLIAM SHAKESPEARE

11.1 Counting

Words are wise men's counters, they do
but reckon with them, but they are the
money of fools.

Leviathan, THOMAS HOBBES

11.1.1 Number of words

Some publications put word limits on manuscripts,
and the question often arises as what is the (best)
way to count them. This is answered in detail in
the FAQ [42] but my answer is to simply count the
number of words on one page of your manuscript and
multiply by the number of pages. This is essentially
the technique used by book designers and publishers
when confronted with a manuscript in the process
called *casting off* (see, for example, [87, ch. 8]). The
publishers are not particularly interested in the exact number of words but are very much interested
in the number of pages in the final production.

If you are writing a thesis the powers-that-be may
specify a word limit, but it is probably safe to assume that they will not actually check the number of words themselves, unless there is an obvious mismatch between your number and the size of
the thesis. In any event, what counts as a 'word'?
Is 'powers-that-be' one word or three? How many
'words' are the equivalent of a table or a figure?
If different sized fonts will be used, are all 'words'
equal. What about footnotes, mathematical equa-
tions, verse — how many 'words' should be allocated
to them?

11.1.2 Lua

By the time you read this LuaTeX should be available, and perhaps you have used it. At the time of
writing it is still being developed and I have not tried
it. However, assuming that Lua [65] will be available
on all TeX platforms, I thought that I would try and
use it for its own sake.

I have been fortunate in being able to use lead type
and a hand-operated press, much as Gutenberg did

in the 15th century. Unlike digital typesetting where
you can have an unlimited number of characters of
any particular kind, the number of available characters is strictly limited — if the font you are using
has only 23 'e' sorts (a *sort* is a single piece of lead
type), then in one go you can only set text that has
no more than 23 'e' characters. It is therefore important to know how many of each sort is required to set
a page of text. For example, I wanted to print a 16th
century poem — only two verses on one page — in a
particular font but I couldn't do so as I was one 'h'
short (there were a lot of thee, thou, thine, ...eth,
etc., words compared to modern English). I work on
a GNU/Linux system which provides programs for
counting the number of words and the total number
of characters in a piece of text; presumably other
systems provide the equivalent. But what I wanted
was a program to count the numbers of the individual characters — the number of 'A' characters, the
number of 'a' characters, and so on.

I managed to extend a Lua program that would
do this for me. Here it is, in a file that is called
`gwc.lua`:

```
#!/usr/local/bin/lua5.1
-- gwc.lua Lua program to count characters, etc
-- (see Lua Manual p.198)
-- call as: gwc.lua file

local BUFSIZE = 2^13        -- 8k
local f = io.input(arg[1])  -- open input file
local cc = 0        -- count of chars
local lc = 0        -- count of lines
local wc = 0        -- count of words
local ct = {}       -- table of char counts
local k, v          -- table key and value
for i = 32,126 do   -- initialise ASCII slots
  ct[i] = 0
end
local T = 0         -- my total chars
local tc = 0        -- actual total chars
                    -- (no newlines, etc)
while true do
  -- read a chunk of text
  local lines, rest = f:read(BUFSIZE, "*line")
  if not lines then break end
  if rest then
    lines = lines .. rest  .. "\n" end
  cc = cc + #lines
  -- count words in the chunk
  local _, t = string.gsub(lines, "%S+", "")
```

```
   wc = wc + t
   -- count newlines in the chunk
   _, t = string.gsub(lines, "\n", "\n")
   lc = lc + t
-- make a list of character frequencies
   local K
   for i = 1, string.len(lines) do
     K = string.byte(lines,i)
     if K > 32 then
      if K < 126 then
       ct[K] = ct[K] + 1
       T = T + 1
      end
     end
   end
end

-- strip off input (e.g., fin.ext) file's
-- extension and make output file fin.gwc
base, ext = string.match(arg[1],
             "(%w+)%.(%w+)")
ofile = base..".gwc"

-- cc includes newlines, so T = (lc + wc)
tc = cc - lc - wc
io.output(ofile)
io.write("Character counts in file ",
        arg[1], "\n")
io.write("", "lines =", lc, "\n",
            "words =", wc, "\n",
            "characters = ", tc, "\n\n")

io.write("Character total\n")
for k,v in pairs(ct) do
  if v > 0 then
    print(string.char(k),v)
    io.write("  ", string.char(k), "        ",
            string.format("%4d",v), "\n")
  end
end
print("Output saved in: ", ofile)
```

That ends the Lua program. In this case a 'word' is a sequence of characters followed by one or more spaces. I was only interested in characters corresponding to the sorts in the fonts that were available to me. Being English this fortunately restricted the characters to the ASCII printable character set. If you need to count other characters then you will have to extend the program. The Lua manual [65, p. 198] describes how the word and line count part of the program works in more detail.

11.2 Changing the layout

Change is not made without inconvenience, even from worse to better.

A Dictionary of the English Language: Preface,
SAMUEL JOHNSON

A question that pops up from time to time is 'How do I change the layout for a particular page?', where the layout includes items like the size and location of the textblock, and different headers and footers.

11.2.1 The shape of the page

You can do many things, but one that you cannot do is to change the text width in the middle of a paragraph. For instance if the textblock is 30pc wide on one page and 25pc wide on the following page, then a paragraph that starts on the first page and continues onto the next will be 30pc wide on both pages. This is because TeX internally typesets paragraph by paragraph according to the current textwidth. Having set a paragraph it then decides if there should be a page break in it. If so, it puts the beginning of the already laid out paragraph on the first page and the remainder, which is already set internally, goes on the following page(s) with the *same* text width.

The general page layout parameters are diagrammed in Figure 11.1.

To change the height of the textblock on a particular page use the LaTeX \enlargethispage macro. This takes a single length argument which is added to the text height for the page on which it occurs — a positive length increases the textheight and a negative one decreases it. The change is made at the bottom of the textblock; the location of the top of the textblock is unchanged.

The quote and quotation environments temporarily change the margins and width of the textblock, and you can do the same by using, for example, the adjustwidth environment provided by the changepage package [147].

> The adjustwidth environment takes two length arguments, and increases the left and right margins by the given amounts. For example, I used
>
> \begin{adjustwidth}{3em}{1.5em}
>
> at the start of this paragraph, and will end adjustwidth at the end of the paragraph.

The page layout parameters used are those in effect at the start of a page when the first item (e.g., a character, a box, etc.) is put onto the page. Layout changes after that will not be effective until the start of the next page. You can, though, change the text

The circle is at 1 inch from the top and left of the page. Dashed lines represent
(\hoffset + 1 inch) and (\voffset + 1 inch) from the top and left of the page.

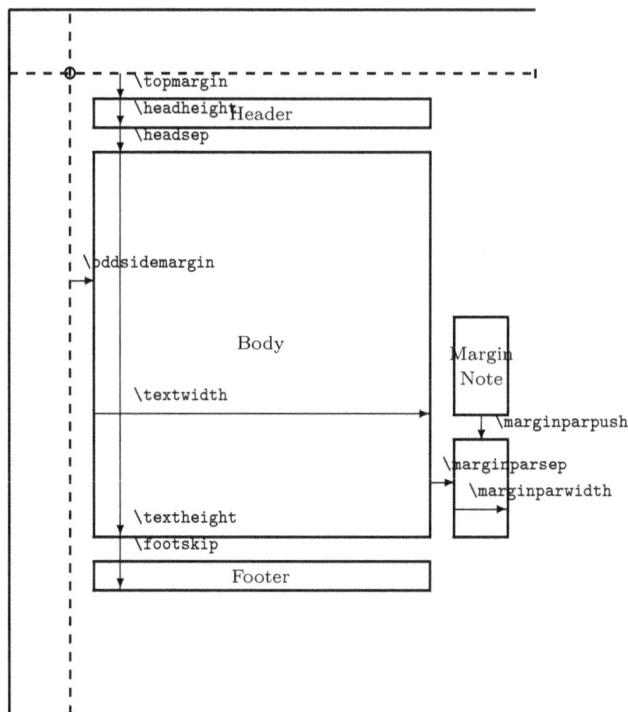

Figure 11.1: LaTeX page layout parameters for a recto page

width *between* pages. The trick here is that when you change from one column to two columns, or vice versa, LaTeX recalculates its view of the layout. The general scheme is to clear the page, change the layout parameters, then set the number of columns which starts the same new page again but with the layout changes implemented. Assuming a one column document, the general procedure is:

```
\clearpage
% change textblock, margins, ...
\onecolumn
```

If you need them, the changepage package provides macros to 'change textblock, margins, ...'.

Just so you can see what happens, the kernel definition of \onecolumn is:

```
\def\onecolumn{%
  \clearpage
  \global\columnwidth\textwidth
  \global\hsize\columnwidth
  \global\linewidth\columnwidth
  \global\@twocolumnfalse
  \col@number \@ne
  \@floatplacement}
```

The code for \twocolumn is similar but does a bit more, especially as it takes an optional argument, although that has no effect on the various width settings.

As an example, if you needed to have different text heights and widths for one set of pages, those in the frontmatter perhaps, than for another set, say the rest of the work, you could define

```
\newcommand*{\addtotextheightwidth}[2]{%
  \clearpage
  \addtolength{\textheight}{#1}
  \addtolength{\textwidth}{#2}
  \onecolumn}
```

and use it when you need to make a change.

11.2.2 Headers and footers

Another kind of layout change that I have seen requested is to add 'Page' above the page numbers in the Table of Contents or List of Figures, etc. As an example say that the requirement is that for the List of Figures (LoF) the word 'Figure' should be placed flushleft at the start of the column of figure titles and the word 'Page' flushright above the page numbers;

if the LoF continues for more than one page, these should be repeated at the start of each page. The page number(s) of the LoF itself should be centered at the bottom of the page (i.e., the plain pagestyle). There are similar requirements for the Table of Contents (ToC) and List of Tables (LoT), but I'll just show how the LoF requirements can be met.

Changing pagestyles can be accomplished with the fancyhdr package [130] but I will assume that the memoir class [142] is being used which includes similar facilities.

The memoir class lets you define as many pagestyles as you want. We need a pagestyle for any LoF continuation pages (and others for the ToC and LoT). Here's the one for the LoF, which I have called the lof pagestyle. This puts the page number centered in the footer and 'Figure' at the left in the header and 'Page' at the right.

```
\makepagestyle{lof}% a new pagestyle
  \makevenfoot{lof}{}{\thepage}{} % like plain
  \makeoddfoot{lof}{}{\thepage}{} % like plain
  \makeevenhead{lof}{Figure}{}{Page}
  \makeoddhead{lof}{Figure}{}{Page}
```

When we start the LoF we need to make sure that the lof pagestyle will be used for any continuation pages. We can do this by adding the necessary code to the \listoffigures command, and memoir provides the \addtodef command for doing this. It takes three arguments; the first is the name of a macro, the second is code to be added at the start of the macro's definition and the third is code to be added at the end of the macro's definition.

```
\addtodef{\listoffigures}{%
  \clearpage\pagestyle{lof}}{}
```

The memoir class also provides a command that is called before setting the title of the LoF and another that is called after the title. You can redefine these to do what you want. In this case we just need to extend what happens after the title.

```
\renewcommand*{\afterloftitle}{%
  \thispagestyle{plain}%
  \par\nobreak
  {\normalfont\normalsize Figure \hfill Page}%
  \par\nobreak}
```

The above makes the first page of the LoF use the plain pagestyle, and then puts a line containing 'Figure' at the left and 'Page' at the right. The actual listing of titles and page numbers will start after these preliminaries.

Setting up the ToC and LoT is almost identical to the above, but with names changed.

One thing to watch for is that after the LoF has been processed the lof pagestyle is still in effect. After the LoF has finished it will be necessary to revert back to the regular pagestyle which, for the sake of argument, let's say is heads. To be on the safe side the general scheme, then, is:

```
\documentclass[...]{memoir}
%% define heads pagestyle
%% ToC, LoF, ToC changes
%% more preamble
\addtodef{\mainmatter}{}{\pagestyle{heads}}
\pagestyle{heads}
\begin{document}
%% title pages
%% maybe Preface and such
%% \tableofcontents\clearpage\pagestyle{heads}
%% \listoffigures\clearpage\pagestyle{heads}
%% \listoftables\clearpage\pagestyle{heads}
%% other prelims
\mainmatter
...
\end{document}
```

which ensures that at the start of the main matter the regular heads pagestyle is in effect, no matter what games were played beforehand.

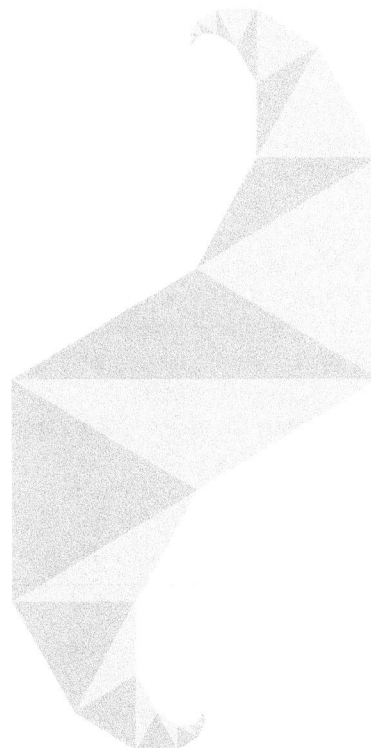

If our understanding have a film of
ignorance over it, or be blear with gazing on
other false glisterings, what is that to truth?

Of reformation in England, JOHN MILTON

12.1 Meandering

When true simplicity is gained,
To bow and bend, we will not be ashamed.
To turn, turn, will be our delight
'Til by turning, turning, we come 'round right.

Simple Gifts, SHAKER HYMN

Some years ago William Adams produced a little eight page booklet called *One Typeface, Many Fonts* [3], which I encourage you to get if you do not already have it. Apart from the content and the various typefaces an interesting aspect was that it was printed on one side of a single sheet of letterpaper, which could then be cut and folded to make the final booklet. I found this the other month when I was clearing out old papers getting ready to move house and country.

A little earlier I had come across a class of books called *miniatures* [24], which are defined as books not more than 3 in, or 76 mm, in any dimension.[1] Some are shown in Figure 12.1. The largest is 3 by 2 1/8 inches and is a miniature book about miniature books. The two smallest in the group are 1 5/8 by 1 1/4 inches. One is John Kennedy's Inaugural Address in January 1961 and the other is Abraham Lincoln's speech at Gettysburg in November 1863. The type in these appears to be just a little smaller than that in the footnotes here.

These two events got me to wondering whether there were other methods like William's of creating a (miniature) booklet. I tried cutting and folding scrap paper in many ways with not much success until I remembered that I had a book by Cherryl Moote [89] which had been advertised as:

This book features book forms perfect for creating small editions of art books with your photocopier or computer printer.

[1]In 2000 the record for the smallest miniature was held by *The Twelve Horary Signs — Chinese Zodiac* published in an edition of 100 by the Toppan Printing Company, Tokyo, Japan. It measured just 0.95 mm square!

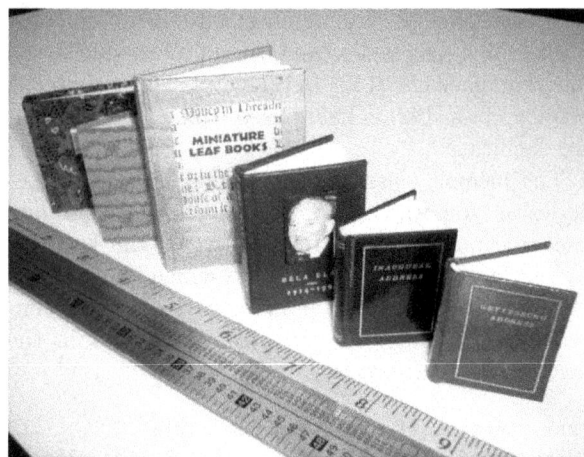

Herries Collection

Figure 12.1: Some miniature books; the scales are marked in inches, points, and picas

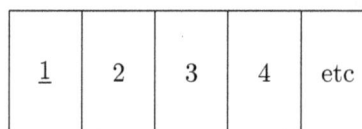

1	2	3	4	etc

Figure 12.2: Accordion layout

...Standard size papers are used for most projects ...

There are several ways in which you can print on one side of a single sheet and by folding and cutting make acceptable small works. The simplest is an accordion book where the pages on the sheet are laid out as in Figure 12.2. In this and later diagrams the numbers correspond to the page ordering and text orientation, with potentially ambiguously oriented numbers underlined, such as 1, 6, and 8. Thin lines are where the paper is to be folded, and thick lines where it is to be cut. In the accordion form the folds are alternately up and down (or down and up). Many Japanese and Chinese books use this basic form. One example is illustrated in Figure 12.3 which shows one quarter of a book whose English title is *Biographies of Twelve Chinese Great Scholars*; the text is in both Chinese and a form of English.

Another simple form is one that is called *French Folds* where the paper is folded in half one way then folded in half again the other way. This is often used

Herries Collection

Figure 12.3: A Chinese book in the accordion style, showing one quarter of the overall work which measures 8 1/4 inches by 14 feet

Figure 12.4: French Folds layout

for greetings cards, and is illustrated in Figure 12.4.

William Adams refers to his booklet form as a *Stroke Book* and is called a *Two-Minute Book* by Cherryl Moote [89]. The general layout for such a work is shown in Figure 12.5. William's instructions for 'binding' the booklet are:

> After printing fold in half (top to bottom), unfold, fold in half lengthwise, then fold in half and open, and fold each resulting panel in half, unfold and restore to the original fold, then cut along the inner half of the lengthwise fold, open and fold lengthwise. Then all the pages should be folded within the front and back covers and *voila!* a single signature booklet.

Another way of describing the procedure is:

> Fold in half, short side to short side (1/2 to 6/5) with text exposed; this is called a *mountain fold*. Fold each half in half again (6/5 to 7/4 and 1/2 to 8/3) with text hidden; these are both *valley folds*. Unfold to original flat sheet. Fold in half lengthwise (1/8/7/6 to 2/3/4/5) with text exposed (i.e., a mountain fold). Cut along the inner half of the lengthwise fold (the thick line in the diagram). Refold lengthwise, push the two pairs of end pages (1/2 and 6/5) towards each other and the center pages should fold outwards. Finally, fold the result so that the pages are in the prescribed order.

Figure 12.5: Layout for a Two-Minute book

I didn't know how William imposed his eight pages onto the one sheet but I suspected that he typeset each page on separate sheets then used some imposition software like psnup to arrange these on a single sheet. I have since learnt from him[2] that:

> I composed *One Typeface Many Fonts* in Altsys Virtuoso (a drawing program) on my NeXT Cube — I saved out .eps files (a nifty facility of a pdf viewing program I was using in NeXTstep) and then arranged and rotated the bits by hand working up from a folded "dummy" (you're a dummy if you don't make a dummy).

I know of some pure LaTeX methods for imposition. There is the booklet package [145] for creating a booklet of half-size pages from full size originals, and Nicola Talbot's flowfram package [123] which lets you define 'frames' on a page and the text will automatically flow from one frame to the next; Andreas Matthias' pdfpages package [85] provides imposition facilities if you are using pdfLaTeX. As separate processes Angus Duggan's PSUtils suite [36] has several programs, such as psnup, for imposition of ps files, while Tom Phelps' Multivalent suite of tools [107] provides similar programs for dealing with pdf files. I was, though, particularly interested using LaTeX to create miniature books from a single sheet of paper, printed on one side only, of short poems or epigrams without using any packages. For this kind of work it seemed reasonable to do 'page breaking' by hand rather than automatically, as the flowfram package would provide.[3]

Cherryl presented several layouts that, applied to the most common size[4] of paper, would result in a miniature book. These are illustrated in Figure 12.6 to Figure 12.10. To create a book from one of these, cut along the thick lines and then start folding starting with pages 1 and 2, where 1 will be the first one

---

[2]Personal email, 2008/06/25.

[3]Also, I couldn't work out how to automatically put a 'page number' in the frames.

[4]Either letter or A4 size.

in the book, and proceeding along until page 16 is reached. The folds should be alternately mountain and valley. The diagrams show the initial orientation of the text 'pages' to give a reasonable orientation after the folding. The orientation sequence does depend on whether the first fold is a mountain or a valley.

I don't know if there are any commonly accepted names for these layouts so I have used my own.

You can design your own layout if you prefer. For instance Figure 12.8 is one that I made up; I make no claim regarding either its usefulness or its aesthetics, nor how the folds or page numbering should be configured. The shape of the cuts vaguely reminds me of stoking a wood burning stove, hence the name.

Perhaps you have been wondering how I produced these diagrams? But even if you haven't, I did it by using the graphicx package and the picture environment. For example, here is the essence of the code for Figure 12.6, which does get tedious after a while.

```
%% turn its argument upside down
\newcommand*{\rupd}[1]{%
  \rotatebox[origin=c]{180}{#1}}
%% save some typing
\let\ul\underline

%% the diagram
\begin{figure}
\centering
\setlength{\unitlength}{0.003\textwidth}
\begin{picture}(100,120)
  %% draw the boxes
  \thinlines
  \put(0,0){\framebox(100,120){}}
  \put(25,0){\line(0,1){120}}
  \put(50,0){\line(0,1){120}}
  ...
  \put(0,90){\line(1,0){100}}
  %% draw the cutting lines
  \linethickness{2pt}
  \put(0,90){\line(1,0){75}}
  \put(75,90){\line(0,-1){60}}
  \put(75,30){\line(-1,0){50}}
  \put(25,30){\line(0,1){30}}
  \put(25,60){\line(1,0){25}}
  %% insert the page numbers
  \linethickness{0pt}
  \put(0,90){\framebox(25,30){\ul{1}}}
  \put(25,90){\framebox(25,30){2}}
  ...
  \put(0,30){\framebox(25,30){\rupd{\ul{11}}}}
  \put(25,30){\framebox(25,30){\rupd{16}}}
  \put(50,30){\framebox(25,30){\rupd{15}}}
  \put(75,30){\framebox(25,30){\ul{6}}}
  \put(0,0){\framebox(25,30){\rupd{10}}}
  \put(25,0){\framebox(25,30){\rupd{\ul{9}}}}
  \put(50,0){\framebox(25,30){\rupd{\ul{8}}}}
```

```
  \put(75,0){\framebox(25,30){7}}
\end{picture}
\caption{Spiral layout (mountain)}
\label{fig:lay1M}
\end{figure}
```

Cherryl Moote described other layouts that led to more complex results after cutting and folding, one of which is illustrated in Figure 12.11. Essentially this consists of two Two-Minute layouts (see Figure 12.5) joined together. By folding this in one way you can produce a Dos-a-Dos book which is two Two-Minute books conjoined back to back, and in folding another way you can interleave pages from the left and right halves.

With all these layouts you have to experiment to see what is best for the particular project you have in mind.

As an aid to seeing how miniature books can be based on one or other of the presented layouts I offer Figure 12.12 and Figure 12.13. You can photocopy these and cut and fold the copies to see what the result(s) look like. Both of the offerings are based on the Serpent layout, with the first following Figure 12.9 which starts off with a mountain fold. In this case the title is on the very first page and the colophon is on the last.

The second is meant to start off with a valley fold, and the first and last pages after folding are both blank. This is so you can use these pages as endpapers and attach cover boards to them to give a more finished look to the booklet.

If you would like to try something similar, here is the code for the layout in Figure 12.13.

```
%% The miniature page sizes
\newlength{\across}
\newlength{\down}
\setlength{\across}{0.2\textwidth}
\setlength{\down}{0.2\textheight}
%% no space between an \fbox and contents
\setlength{\fboxsep}{0pt}
\let\fbx\fbox

%% vplace environment is in memoir class
%% vertical placement of contents,
%% centered by default
\providecommand{\vplace}[1][1]{%
  \par\vspace{\stretch{#1}}}
\def\endvplace{\vspace*{\stretch{1}}\par}

%% Put one minipage centered inside another
\newcommand{\portion}[1]{\fbx{%
\begin{minipage}[c][\down][t]{\across}
#1
\end{minipage}}}
\renewcommand{\portion}[1]{\fbx{%
```

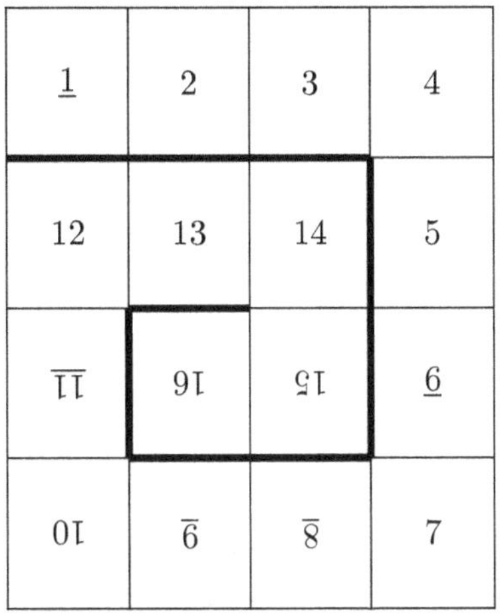

Figure 12.6: Spiral layout (mountain)

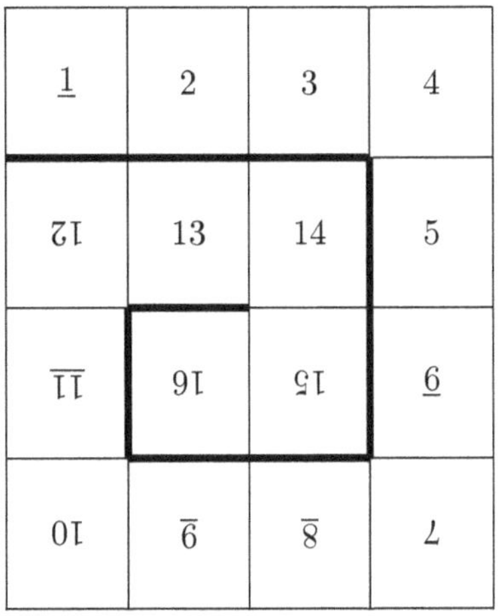

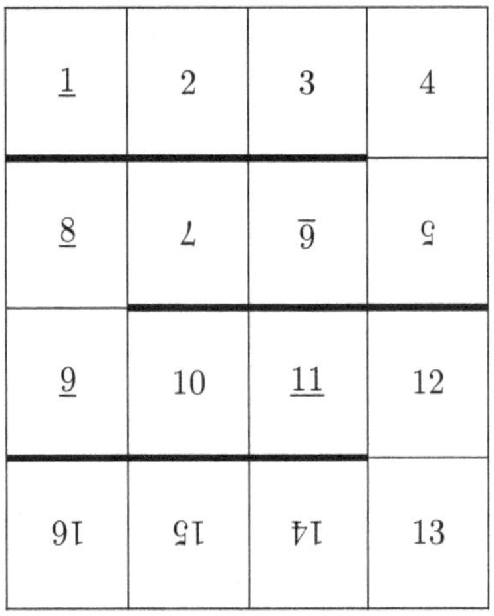

Figure 12.9: Snake layout (mountain)

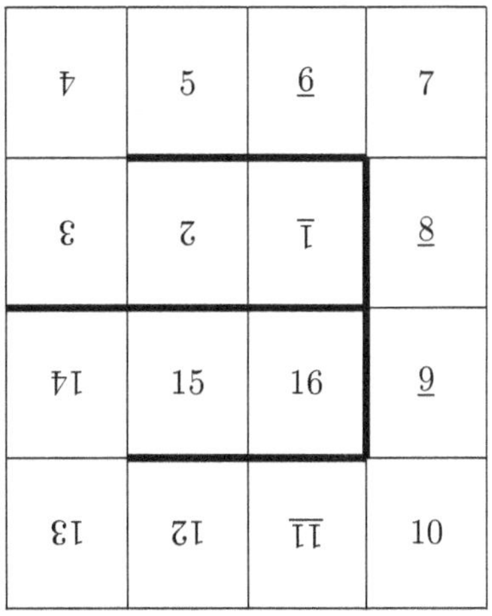

Figure 12.7: Spiral layout (valley)

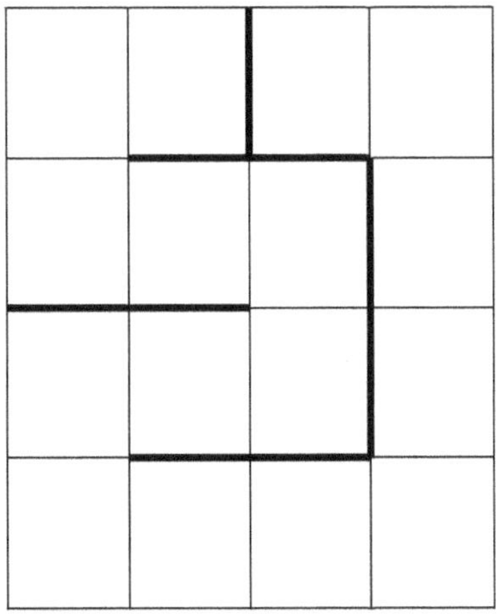

Figure 12.10: T layout (valley)

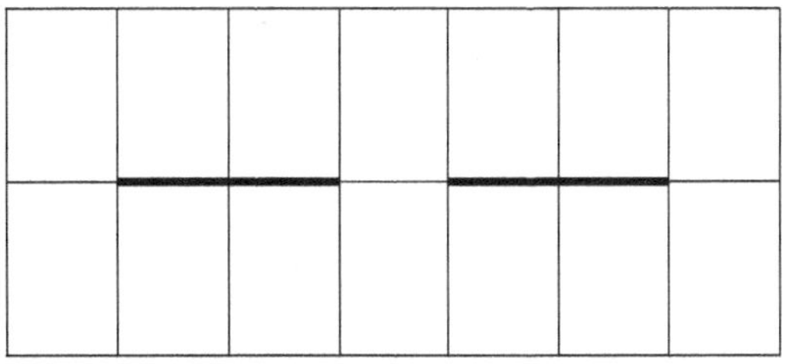

Figure 12.8: Stove layout

Figure 12.11: Interleaved or Dos-a-Dos layout

```
\begin{minipage}[c][\down][t]{\across}
  \centering
  \begin{minipage}[c][\down][t]{0.8\across}
  #1
  \end{minipage}
\end{minipage}}}

%% Vertically center the contents of a portion
\newcommand{\vcp}[3][1]{%
\portion{\centering%
  \begin{vplace}[#1]#2\end{vplace}#3%
  \vspace*{\onelineskip}}}
%% turn contents of a \vcp upside down
\newcommand{\rvcp}[3][1]{%
  \rotatebox[origin=c]{180}{%
    \vcp[#1]{#2}{#3}}}
%% for typeseting page numbers
\newcommand*{\pgn}[1]{{\tiny #1}}

%%%%% Typeset
\noindent
%% top row
\vcp{\mbox{}}{}
\vcp{%
  \Large \textit{Vitae Summa Brevis} \\[5mm]
  \large  Ernest Dowson}{}
\vcp{They are not long,}{\pgn{3}}
\vcp{The weeping and the laughter,}{\pgn{4}}

%% second row
\noindent
\rvcp{We pass the gate.}{\pgn{8}}
\rvcp{in us after}{\pgn{7}}
\rvcp{I think they have no portion}{\pgn{6}}
\rvcp{Love and desire and hate:}{\pgn{5}}

%% third row
\noindent
\vcp{They are not long,}{\pgn{9}}
\vcp{the days of wine and roses:}{\pgn{10}}
\vcp{Out of a misty dream}{\pgn{11}}
\vcp{Our path emerges for a while,}{\pgn{12}}

%% bottom row
\noindent
\vcp{\mbox{}}{}
\rvcp{{\footnotesize The Herries Press\\[1cm]
      2008}}{}
\rvcp{Within a dream.}{\pgn{14}}
\rvcp{then closes}{\pgn{13}}
```

I have not used the whole of the printed sheet in producing the miniatures, but rather the extent of the typeblock (see the definitions of \across and \down which I used in the specification of the size of the final pages). If you are using the memoir class you can easily change the size of the typeblock, otherwise you can use the geometry package. I also boxed, using \fbox (via \fbx), each final page. If

you do not want to do that then change \fbx, for example:

```
\renewcommand*{\fbx}[1]{#1}
```

May you have much pleasure in creating your own unique miniature books.

Acknowledgements

William Adams was kind enough to review the column and I have incorporated many of his suggestions. One that I didn't, but will now, is to say that he felt that another possible source for folding techniques would be the literature on Origami. Though perhaps not directly related, he said that *The Folding Universe* [39] is a fascinating book regardless and well worth looking at.

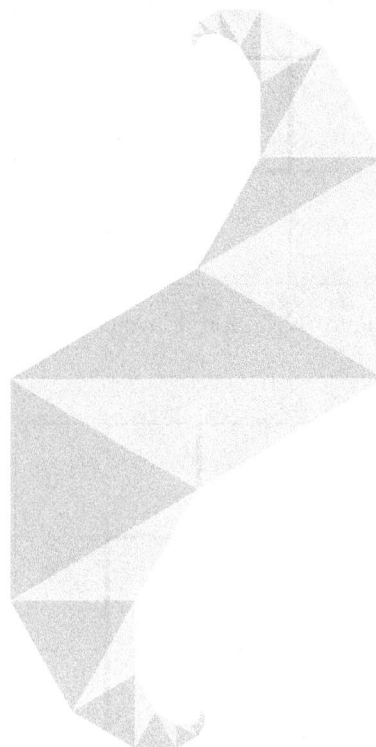

Vitae Summa Brevis Ernest Dowson		They are not long, 3	The weeping and the laughter, 4
We pass the gate. 8	7 in us after	6 no portion I think they have	Love and desire and hate: 5
They are not long, 9	the days of wine and roses: 10	Out of a misty dream 11	Our path emerges for a while, 12
2008 The Herries Press		14 Within a dream.	then closes 13

Figure 12.12: Layout of a miniature book based on that shown in Figure 12.9, starting with a mountain fold

Vitae Summa Brevis

Ernest Dowson

They are not long,

3

The weeping and the laughter,

4

8

7

6

5

We pass the gate.

in us after

I think they have no portion

Love and desire and hate:

They are not long,

9

the days of wine and roses:

10

Out of a misty dream

11

Our path emerges for a while,

12

2008

The Herries Press

14

13

Within a dream.

then closes

Figure 12.13: Layout of a miniature book based on that shown in Figure 12.9, starting with a valley fold

CHAPTER 13

TUGBOAT 32:1, 2011

Fame is no plant that grows on mortal soil,
Nor in the glistering foil
Set off to the world, nor in broad rumour lies:
But lives and spreads aloft by those pure eyes
And perfect witness of all-judging Jove;
As he pronounces lastly on each deed,
Of so much fame in heaven expect thy meed.

Lycidas, Elegy on a Friend drowned in the
Irish Channel, 1637, JOHN MILTON

13.1 Framing

I wuz framed!

Traditional criminal defence

Variously people ask on `comp.text.tex` about putting boxes around some text, or how to put a background colour behind some text. An `\fbox` puts a frame round its contents and a `\colorbox`, from the color or xcolor package, puts in a coloured background. However, boxes don't continue across page breaks and on occasions the text for framing will have a page break in the middle. Donald Arseneau's framed package [11] is often the solution for this. The package provides four environments as demonstrated below.

> The `framed` environment from the framed package puts a frame around its contents. Unlike the usual box commands or environments, `framed` continues over page breaks.

The `shaded` environment, also from the framed package, puts a colour (or a shade of gray) behind its contents which may continue across page breaks. Before using this environment you have to define a colour called `shadecolor`. In this case I have used the xcolor package and
`\definecolor{shadecolor}{gray}{0.75}`

The `snugshade` environment is similar to `shaded` and puts a colour (or a shade of gray) behind its contents which may continue across page breaks. Unlike the `shaded` environment, though, the colour does not bleed into the margins. This time I set `shadecolor` as

---

FRAMED ILLUSTRATION

Figure 13.1: Example framed figure

`\definecolor{shadecolor}{gray}{0.9}`
to give a look not so arresting as with the setting for the `shaded` example.

> The `leftbar` environment, also from the framed package, puts a vertical line at the left side of its contents, which may continue across page breaks.

The package can be useful even if you know that there won't be a page break. For instance a `figure` is constrained to be on one page, but you may want to set off some illustrations from the text.

Figure 13.1 is produced from the code below, where only the illustration is framed but not the caption.

```
\begin{figure}
\centering
\begin{framed}\centering
FRAMED ILLUSTRATION
\end{framed}
\vspace*{-0.5\baselineskip}
\caption{Example framed figure}
\label{fig:framef}
\end{figure}
```

Figure 13.2, where the entire `figure` environment including the caption is framed, is produced from the code below:

```
\begin{figure}
\begin{framed}\centering
FRAMED ILLUSTRATION \& CAPTION
\caption{Example framed figure and caption}
\label{fig:framefcap}
\end{framed}
\end{figure}
```

If a full frame seems a bit of an overkill then using rules might be appropriate. Figure 13.3 is produced from the following code, and no package is needed. For illustrative purposes I have used very thick rules above and below the illustration; normally I would not have them so bold.

```
┌─────────────────────────────────────────┐
│                                           │
│   FRAMED ILLUSTRATION & CAPTION           │
│                                           │
│   Figure 13.2: Example framed figure and caption │
│                                           │
└─────────────────────────────────────────┘
```

RULED ILLUSTRATION & CAPTION

Figure 13.3: Ruled figure and caption (2)

SHADED ILLUSTRATION & CAPTION

Figure 13.4: Example shaded figure and caption

```
\begin{figure}
\centering
\rule{\linewidth}{2pt}\\
\vspace*{0.5\baselineskip}
RULED ILLUSTRATION \& CAPTION
\vspace{0.5\baselineskip}
\hrule
\caption{Ruled figure and caption (2)}
\label{fig:ruledfcap}
\rule{\linewidth}{2pt}
\end{figure}
```

Depending on its contents, using shading to delineate an illustration may be an option. Figure 13.4 is produced by the following code, which uses the framed package's **shaded** environment.

```
\begin{figure}
\begin{shaded}\centering
SHADED ILLUSTRATION \& CAPTION
\caption{Example shaded figure and caption}
\label{fig:shadefcap}
\end{shaded}
\end{figure}
```

The framed package does have some limitations on what can be within its environments. Floats, footnotes, marginpars and header entries will be lost. Further, the package does not work with the multicol package's page breaking, or other code that perform multicolumn balancing. Some of the restrictions may be lifted in later versions of the package.

Using the package you can create your own new cross-page environments, based on the **MakeFramed** environment defined in the package and specifying a \FrameCommand macro which should draw the frame. The **MakeFramed** environment takes one argument which should contain any adjustments to the text width, applied to \hsize, and some

form of a *restore* command, such as the package's \FrameRestore macro or the LaTeX internal macro \@parboxrestore, that restores the text attributes to their normal state. The length \width is the width of the frame itself. Some examples are given later. But first...

The frame in the **framed** environment is implemented as an \fbox via:

```
\providecommand{\FrameCommand}{%
  \setlength{\fboxrule}{\FrameRule}%
  \setlength{\fboxsep}{\FrameSep}%
  \fbox}
```

where \FrameRule and \FrameSep are lengths defined by the package. By changing these you can change the rule thickness and spacing of the frame. Here is the definition of the **framed** environment itself, which uses the default \FrameCommand defined above.

```
\newenvironment{framed}{%
  {\MakeFramed {\advance\hsize-\width
   \FrameRestore}}%
  {\endMakeFramed}
```

where \FrameRestore restores some text settings, but not as many as have to be done at the end of a **minipage**.

The other environments are defined similarly. Both **shaded** and **snugshade** use a \colorbox as the framing mechanism.

```
\newenvironment{shaded}{%
  \def\FrameCommand{\fboxsep=\FrameSep
  \colorbox{shadecolor}}%
  \MakeFramed {\FrameRestore}}%
  {\endMakeFramed}
\newenvironment{snugshade}{%
  \def\FrameCommand{%
  \colorbox{shadecolor}}%
  \MakeFramed {\FrameRestore\@setminipage}}%
  {\par\unskip\endMakeFramed}
```

The **leftbar** environment simply uses a vertical rule.

```
\newenvironment{leftbar}{%
  \def\FrameCommand{\vrule width 3pt
              \hspace{10pt}}%
  {\MakeFramed {\advance\hsize-\width
   \FrameRestore}}%
  {\endMakeFramed}
```

Note that in the **framed** and **leftbar** environments the text is narrower than the normal measure, while in the shade environments the text width is unaltered and the shading extends into the margins.

13.2 New frames

> Tyger, tyger, burning bright
> In the forests of the night,
> What immortal hand or eye
> Could frame thy fearful symmetry?
>
> *Songs of Experience*, WILLIAM BLAKE

In some cases it is relatively easy to define your own framing environment based on the framed package, but I have found that some experimentation is often required.

Perhaps you would like to center and frame some text. Here's how.

```
\newenvironment{narrowframe}[1][0.8\hsize]%
  {\MakeFramed{\setlength{\hsize}{#1}
  \FrameRestore}}%
  {\endMakeFramed}
```

> This is the narrowframe environment where you can adjust the width with the environment's optional length argument. This example is set with the default width.

Or perhaps you would like something a little smoother:

> This is the roundedframe environment. It requires the fancybox package. Perhaps you could use something other than the \ovalbox box from that package to give a different frame.

This is the definition I have used for the environment. You can, of course, change the lengths to suit.

```
\newenvironment{roundedframe}{%
  \def\FrameCommand{%
    \cornersize*{20pt}%
    \setlength{\fboxsep}{5pt}%
    \ovalbox}%
  \MakeFramed{\advance\hsize-\width
             \FrameRestore}}
  {\endMakeFramed}
```

Another request that pops up from time to time on comp.text.tex is for an environment to show off examples or questions. Robert Nyqvist [94] answered one of these by providing code based on the framed package, that was basically as follows. An example of the ruledexample environment is shown as Ruled Example 1.

```
\makeatletter
\definecolor{rulecolor}{gray}{0.65}
\newcounter{ruledexample}
\newlength{\releftgap}
  \setlength{\releftgap}{4pt}
\newlength{\rerightgap}
  \setlength{\rerightgap}{1em}
\newlength{\rerule}
  \setlength{\rerule}{1.25pt}
\newlength{\Eheight}
\newenvironment{ruledexample}[1][Example]{%
  \settoheight{\Eheight}{\textbf{#1}}%
  \addtolength{\Eheight}{-\rerule}%
  \def\FrameCommand{\hspace{-\releftgap}%
    {\color{rulecolor}%
      \vrule width \rerule}%
    \hspace{\releftgap}\hspace{-\rerule}}%
  \MakeFramed{\advance\hsize-\width}%
  \refstepcounter{ruledexample}%
  \makebox[0pt][l]{%
    \hspace{-\parindent}%
    \hspace{\rerightgap}%
    {\color{rulecolor}\rule{1.5em}{\rerule}}%
    \quad
    \raisebox{-0.5\Eheight}[0pt]{%
      \textbf{#1\ \theruledexample}}%
  }\\[.5\baselineskip]%
  \noindent\ignorespaces}%
  {\@afterheading\\
  \makebox[0pt][l]{%
    \hspace{-\releftgap}%
    {{\color{rulecolor}
      \rule{\columnwidth}{\rerule}%
      \rule{\releftgap}{\rerule}}%
 }}
  \endMakeFramed}
\makeatother
```

Ruled Example 1

This is the ruledexample environment, which is titled and numbered and can be \labelled, and which will break across pages if need be. The code basis was originally posted to comp.text.tex by Robert Nyqvist in 2003 but I have added some extra means of controlling the rules and spacing.

- rulecolor is the color of the rules

- \rerule is the thickness of the rules

- \releftgap is the distance the vertical rule is moved into the margin

- \rerightgap is the indentation of the title rule

- You can use the optional argument to specify the title, which by default is 'Example'.

As you can see with this example, you can use code like itemize within a framed environment.

Some users have found that the behaviour of the `framed` environment within a list environment such as `quote`, or `adjustwidth` from the `changepage` package [147], is not quite what they expected. This is described in a little more detail below

This is the start of a `quotation` environment. You can use the `framed` environment within this, and also any other `list` based environment.

> We are now in the `framed` environment, and notice how the frame extends across the original textwidth. This is not always what you might want.

Donald Arseneau and I had an exchange of views, and code, on this and we each produced code that created a closer frame. As usual Donald's code was much better than mine.

> Now we are in the `qframe` environment based on Donald Arseneau's code and which I included in my memoir class [142]. The class also provides a 'shaded' version.

If you happen to use the `adjustwidth` environment, from the `changepage` package[1] [147] or the `memoir` class, then the `qframe` environment works better in it than does the `framed` environment.

Here endeth the `quotation` environment.

This is the definition of the `qframe` environment.

```
\makeatletter
\newenvironment{qframe}{%
  \def\FrameCommand##1{%
    \setlength{\fboxrule}{\FrameRule}%
    \setlength{\fboxsep}{\FrameSep}%
    \hskip\@totalleftmargin\fbox{##1}%
    \hskip-\linewidth
    \hskip-\@totalleftmargin
    \hskip\columnwidth}%
  \MakeFramed{\advance\hsize-\width
             \advance\hsize \FrameSep
             \@totalleftmargin\z@
             \linewidth=\hsize}}%
  {\endMakeFramed}
\makeatother
```

---

[1]`changepage` is the successor to the `chngpage` package which is being phased out.

If you put this code in a class (`.cls`) or package (`.sty`) file then you do not need the `\makeatletter` and `\makeatother` pairing, otherwise you do.

Another potentially useful sort of frame is where there is a title — one that gets repeated after a page break. The code for this is considerably more complicated than earlier, and I had to do quite a lot of experimentation to get it to work. First, though, an example.

> ### A 'framewithtitle'
>
> Using the `framewithtitle` environment, as we are doing here, you can put a title inside the frame. If the contents extend past a page break then a 'continued' title is put at the start of the frame on the succeeding pages. The code for `framewithtitle` is given in this chapter.
>
> The position of the title is set by the `\frametitle` command which is initially defined as below. If you would prefer the title to be centered, then change it like this:
>
> ```
> \newcommand*{\frametitle}[1]{%
>   \strut#1}%                    at left
> \renewcommand*{\frametitle}[1]{%
>   \centerline{\strut#1}}%       centered
> ```
>
> This example shows that you can include verbatim text in a framed environment.

Here is the code for the `framewithtitle` environment. It is based on hints from Donald Arseneau that applied to an earlier version of `framed`. Much of the code is concerned with handling the title so that the given text (the first argument) can be used initially, then after a page break a continuation title will be used instead. I have also extracted a lot of code from my original version as separate macros as I plan to reuse much of it later.

My most difficult problem was that internally the package keeps resetting the text to determine where any page breaking will occur, and only after that does it actually typeset. I couldn't assume that the initial title would be immediately set and had to reserve its typesetting until after all the internal resetting had been completed; I used `\ifcontframe` for this purpose.

The macro `\Fr@meSetup` does most of the work related to the titling while `\FrameTitle` actually typesets the title(s). The required argument to the `framewithtitle` environment is the initial title, and you can use the optional argument to override the default continuation title.

```
\makeatletter
\newcommand*{\frametitle}[1]{\strut#1}
\newif\ifcontframe

\newcommand*{\Fr@meSetup}[2]{%
  \fboxrule=\FrameRule \fboxsep=\FrameSep
  \global\contframefalse
  \def\Fr@meFirst{\textbf{#2}}%
  \def\Fr@meCont{\textbf{#1}}%
  \def\FrameCommand##1{%
    \Title@Fr@me{\Fr@meCurrent}{##1}%
    \global\let\Fr@meCurrent\Fr@meNext
    \ifcontframe
      \global\let\Fr@meNext\Fr@meCont
    \fi
    \global\contframetrue}%
  \global\let\Fr@meCurrent\Fr@meFirst
  \global\let\Fr@meNext\Fr@meFirst}

\newcommand*{\FrameTitle}[1]{%
  \nobreak \vskip -0.7\FrameSep
  \rlap{\frametitle{#1}}%
  \nobreak\nointerlineskip
  \vskip 0.7\FrameSep}

\newenvironment{framewithtitle}[2]%
             [\Fr@meFirst\ (cont.)]{%
  \def\Title@Fr@me##1##2{%
    \fbox{\vbox{\FrameTitle{##1}%
    \hbox{##2}}}}%
  \Fr@meSetup{#1}{#2}
  \MakeFramed{%
    \advance\hsize-\width
    \FrameRestore}}%
  {\global\contframefalse
   \endMakeFramed}
\makeatother
```

As an alternative to `framewithtitle` you can use the `titledframe` environment where the title is set outside the frame. The arguments to the two environments are the same, as is setting the title's horizontal position.

A 'titledframe'

> With the `titledframe` environment, which this is, you can put a title on top of the frame. If the contents extend past a page break then a 'continued' title is put at the start of the frame on the succeeding pages. The code for `titledframe` is given in this chapter.
>
> The position of the title is set by the `\frametitle` command which is initially defined as below. If you would prefer the title to be centered, then change it like:

A 'titledframe' (cont.)

```
\newcommand*{\frametitle}[1]{%
  \strut#1}%                at left
\renewcommand*{\frametitle}[1]{%
  \centerline{\strut#1}}% centered
```

which is what I have done for this example.

So, here is the code for `titledframe` which, as you can see, shares most of the code with its companion environment.

```
\makeatletter
\newenvironment{titledframe}[2]%
             [\Fr@meFirst\ (cont.)]{%
  \def\Title@Fr@me##1##2{%
    \vbox{\FrameTitle{##1}%
      \noindent\fbox{##2}}}%
  \Fr@meSetup{#1}{#2}%
  \MakeFramed{%
    \advance\hsize-\width
    \advance\hsize -2\FrameRule
    \advance\hsize -2\FrameSep
    \FrameRestore}}%
  {\global\contframefalse
   \endMakeFramed}
\makeatother
```

I admit that I have given little explanation of the code examples. The excuse that I would like you to believe is that adding all the explanatory material would make the article too long, but the real reason is that I do not really understand how the `framed` package performs its magic; hence the experiments (i.e., many trials and even more errors) that I did to create code that seemed workable.

What e're this youth of fire weares fair,
Rosy fingers, radiant hair,
Glowing cheeks, and glistering wings,
All those fair and flagrant things,
But before all, that fiery Dart
Had fill'd the Hand of this great Heart.

The Flaming Heart, RICHARD CRASHAW

14.1 Ornaments

The web, then, or the pattern; a web at
once sensuous and logical, an elegant and
pregnant texture: that is style, that is the
foundation of the art of literature.

The Art of Writing, ROBERT LOUIS
STEVENSON

One of the many free fonts available for use with
LaTeX is Web-O-Mints, a Type 1 font, from the Gala-
pagos Design Group, with LaTeX support provided
by Maurizio Loreti [73]. Both should be available on
your system. The font consists of a set of printers'
ornaments and flowers as displayed in the font table
in Table 14.1.

Before getting into how you might use the font,
one simple application is generating a pattern like

this, composed from the Web-O-Mints glyphs accessed as 'I', 'J', 'K', and 'L'.

You could use this, or something similar, to separate writings on different topics.

To make life simpler I've defined a few macros
which I'll be using a lot in this column. These first
two are from the samples that come with the LaTeX
support for Web-O-Mints.

```
\newcommand*{\wb}[2]{%
  \fontsize{#1}{#2}\usefont{U}{webo}{xl}{n}}
\newcommand*{\wbc}[3]{%
  \vspace*{#1}\begin{center}
  \wb{#2}{#2}#3
  \end{center}\vspace*{#1}}
\newlength{\wsp}\setlength{\wsp}{1ex}
```

The first, \wb, makes Web-O-Mints the current font
with the given size and \baselineskip. The second, \wbc, sets up a center environment around

32	33	34	35	36	37	38	39
40	41	42	43	44	45	46	47
48	49	50	51	52	53	54	55
56	57	58	59	60	61	62	63
64	65	66	67	68	69	70	71
72	73	74	75	76	77	78	79
80	81	82	83	84	85	86	87
88	89	90	91	92	93	94	95
96	97	98	99	100	101	102	103
104	105	106	107	108	109	110	111
112	113	114	115	116	117	118	119
120	121	122	123	124	125	126	127

Figure 14.1: Glyphs in the Web-O-Mints font

the third argument with Web-O-Mints as the font with the size and \baselineskip equal. The first argument is space before and after the environment. For example, for the previous glyph I used:

```
\wbc{\wsp}{24pt}{4}
```

which centered the glyph accessed as '4', size 24pt, with vertical space of \wsp (which has been set to 1ex) before and after.

For ease of seeing what is happening I am using a much larger glyph size than one would normally.

I will be assembling some glyphs to make more elaborate patterns. The next set of macros move or rotate their argument.

```
\newcommand*{\wupit}[2]{\raisebox{#1}{#2}}
\newcommand*{\rotpi}[1]{\rotatebox{180}{#1}}
\newcommand*{\rotrt}[1]{\rotatebox{90}{#1}}
\newcommand*{\rotlft}[1]{\rotatebox{-90}{#1}}
```

You can use them on this glyph ⚘ (accessed as the character '3') like so

```
\wbc{\wsp}{24pt}{%
  \wupit{26pt}{\rotlft{3}}% rotate left & lift
  3%                       normal position
  \llap{%                  overlap
      \wupit{36pt}{\rotpi{3}}}% rotate & lift
  \wupit{10pt}{\rotrt{3}}% rotate right & lift
}
```

to produce this rather charming device:

If you haven't come across \llap or its companion \rlap, these are TeX macros that let their argument overlap its surroundings. More precisely, \llap places its argument at the left of the macro but without taking up any space; \rlap is similar but puts its argument at the right, again without taking up any space. Knuth's example is typesetting a ≠ (neq) symbol by using either \rlap{/}= or /\llap{=} to create the neq symbol. On the other hand, the \kern command moves the current position rightwards (positive length) or leftwards (negative length) the given amount, but the following character takes up its normal space.

I do find it difficult to tell just from looking at a single glyph what a group of them will look like. For example:

doesn't look like much to me, but when put together with another member of the family by using
\wbc{\wsp}{24pt}{[] [] []}
the appearance is rather different.

Below is the set of four glyphs that I will be using for the first sets of patterns, specified by:
\wbc{\wsp}{24}{opqn}

Note that these are in their natural relationship with each other. We can make simple chains like:
\wbc{\wsp}{24pt}{qpqpqp}

Which, although attractive, isn't all that exciting. What I'm going to do is to 'attach' the single horns to the double ones and use these as the basis for a more complex pattern.

The simpler part is to move (and rotate) two single horns to join with the right hand double horn. First move the single horn to join the double by

\wbc{\wsp}{24pt}{q\kern-14pt\wupit{-19pt}{n}}

Then rotate and move a second horn, overlapping the construction we already have

\wbc{\wsp}{24pt}{q\kern-14pt\wupit{-19pt}{n}%
  \llap{\wupit{35pt}{\rotpi{o}}}}

Doing the other double horn is slightly more complicated because of the order of the operations:

```
\wbc{\wsp}{24pt}{\wupit{-19pt}{o}%
  \llap{\wupit{35pt}{\rotpi{n}}}\kern-14pt p}
```

Defining a macro for each assembly will let us mix and match.

```
\newcommand*{\qno}{q\kern-14pt\wupit{-19pt}{n}%
  \llap{\wupit{35pt}{\rotpi{o}}}}
\newcommand*{\onp}{\wupit{35pt}{\rotpi{n}}%
  \kern-14pt p}
```

Now,
`\wbc{\wsp}{24pt}{\onp\qno\onp\qno\onp\qno}`
produces

and
`\wbc{\wsp}{24pt}{\qno\onp\qno\onp}`
displays

I had to experiment to decide on the various distances to move things to create the `\onp` and `\qno` assemblies. These distances would have to be changed if something other than 24pt was used as the font size. However, it is always possible to use `\scalebox` from the graphicx package to appropriately size a pattern. This gives a half-size result compared with the previous ones.

```
\wbc{\wsp}{24}{\scalebox{0.5}{\qno\onp}}
```

Except for the simplest scheme of just putting the glyphs in a row, experimentation will nearly always be required to obtain sympathetic relationships among the elements of the pattern. They don't have to be mathematically exact but must look good to the eye.

Moving on, here is another set of four glyphs, which would normally be used at the corners of a page, that can be combined in interesting ways.
`\wbc{\wsp}{24pt}{E F G H}`

One simple way is just using two lines, which reminds me of a row of gilt mirrors.
`\wbc{\wsp}{24pt}{EFEFEF\\GHGHGH}`

We can add some further decorative elements, reducing the size at the same time:

```
\wbc{\wsp}{12pt}{HGHGHGHGHGHG\\[-3pt]
  EFEFEFEFEFEF\\GHGHGHGHGHGH\\[-3pt]
  EFEFEFEFEFEF}
```

and add more and more if desired. On the other hand, joining the four elements in a different manner can lead to something even fancier.

In the days of lead type, a sort (a single character) was a rectangular bar of lead with the glyph in relief on the end that was to be inked and printed. There was no way of stretching or shrinking a piece of type, and neither was there any way of getting one piece of type to overlap another, except by printing twice, once with one sort and then with the second sort. With digital fonts these restrictions no longer apply. In the next example, the bounding boxes of the glyphs overlap, although the glyphs themselves do not.

```
\newcommand*{\kl}{\kern-24pt}
\newcommand*{\ks}{\kern-4pt}
\newcommand*{\mir}{E\kl H\ks G\kl F}
\wbc{\wsp}{24pt}{\scalebox{0.75}%
    {\mir\ks\mir\ks\mir\ks\mir}}
```

Again, you can add to this basic scheme, embellishing it as much as you think bearable. For instance, by inserting another set of glyphs inside a mirror, although this may get complicated. The experimentally determined code below appears to produce a reasonable result.

First, here is a macro for producing a more vertically oriented version of the four leaves that I showed earlier.

```
\newcommand*{\leaves}{\wupit{32pt}{\rotlft{3}}%
    \kern-6pt3%
    \kern-9pt\wupit{17pt}{\rotrt{3}}%
    \kern-30pt\wupit{49pt}{\rotpi{3}}}
\wbc{\wsp}{24pt}{\leaves}
```

And secondly, this is the code for combining the mirror and leaves so that they will be centered:

```
\wbc{\wsp}{24pt}{\mbox{}\kern-24ptEF%
    \kern-43pt{\wupit{-22pt}%
    {\scalebox{0.6}{\leaves}}}%
    \\[-18pt]\mbox{}\kern0ptGH}
```

Moving on to a more organic feel, represented above by `\wbc{\wsp}{16pt}{m/m/m/m/m/m}`, many of the traditional ornaments were based on vines, although whether this was due to a proclivity towards wine by the type designers I couldn't say.

This is a typical scheme, mixing grapes and leaves.
`\wbc{\wsp}{15pt}{cedafbcedced}`

And here is another with major emphasis on the grapes:
`\wbc{\wsp}{15pt}{ghghghghghgh}`

And a third, back to the grapes plus leaves:
`\wbc{\wsp}{15pt}{gfgfgfgfgfgf}`

This one, you may have noticed, forms the top and bottom of the frame around page 54. The sides are also formed from similar grapes and leaves.

The method I used to frame was to create the frame as a zero sized picture and add that to the page footer; I could just as well have added it to the header. You would normally use the facilities provided by the fancyhdr package [130] or the memoir class [142] for doing this, both of which should be available on your system.

Here's the code I used for the picture of the frame.

```
%%% draws a (page) frame
\newcommand*{\goddfoot}{\begin{picture}(0,0)
\wb{10pt}{10pt}
\put(-29,-20){% change these to move the frame
    \begin{picture}(0,0)
    \multiput(0,0)(25,0){21}{fg}    % bottom

    \multiput(-5,5)(0,24){31}{i}    % left
    \multiput(-5,23)(0,24){31}{\rotpi{k}}

    \multiput(520,5)(0,24){31}{j}   % right
    \multiput(520,23)(0,24){31}{\rotpi{l}}

    \multiput(0,742)(25,0){21}{fg} % top
    \end{picture}}
\end{picture}}
\let\gevenfoot\goddfoot
```

The *TUGboat* class defines the odd- and even-headers. I created a new pagestyle using the *TUGboat* headers and adding my feet creating the frame (this is code that is normally hidden in a class or package).

```
\makeatletter
%% new 'glister' pagestyle
\newcommand*{\ps@glister}{%
  \def\@evenfoot{\gevenfoot}
  \def\@oddfoot{\goddfoot}}
\makeatother
```

Zero sized pictures have other uses as well. I put one containing a gray checkerboard pattern, composed from the Web-O-Mints 'z' and '7' glyphs, at the start of the previous paragraph to form a textured background. You may love or hate this particular result but the technique can be useful. The code for the background pattern is:

```
%%%%% the background for the rest of the text
\newcommand*{\bkp}{\begin{picture}(0,0)%
  \wb{10}{10}%
  \put(-20,2){\begin{picture}(0,0)% reposition
    \multiput(0,0)(0,-22){6}{% vertical repeat
      \begin{picture}(0,0)% horizontal repeats
        \multiput(0,0)(22,0){11}{\lw}
        \multiput(11,0)(22,0){11}{\dw}
        \multiput(0,-11)(22,0){11}{\dw}
        \multiput(11,-11)(22,0){11}{\lw}
      \end{picture}}
    \end{picture}}
  \end{picture}}
```

May you have many happy hours designing your own ornaments and embellishments, but consider that maybe simple and few are better than elaborate and many; it all depends on the feel you are trying to convey.

Note If you want to install Web-O-Mints then the easiest way is to use `tug.org/fonts/ getnonfreefonts` which will install Web-O-Mints as well as some dozen other fonts if desired.

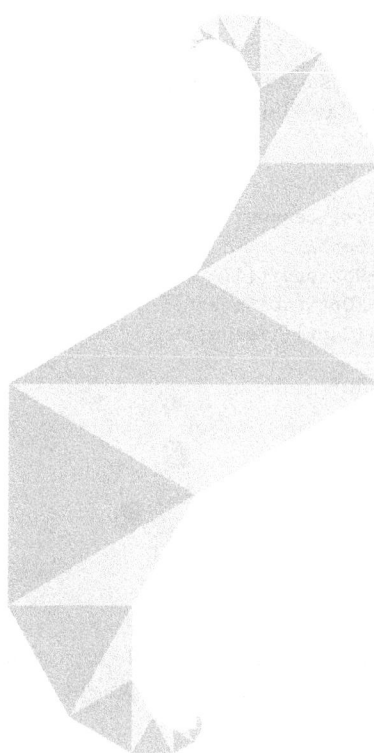

... Cloath'd all in glistering coats, which
made a shew ...

Poems and Fancies, MARGARET
CAVENDISH

15.1 Verbatim arguments

Sir, I have found you an argument,
but I am not obliged to find you an
understanding.

SAMUEL JOHNSON

I have been reminded recently that one problem with
verbatim material is that it cannot be used in an argument to a regular command (or environment). For
example to typeset something in a framed `minipage`
the obvious way is to use the `minipage` as the argument to the `\fbox` macro:

```
\fbox{\begin{minipage}{0.97\columnwidth}
    Contents of framed minipage
    \end{minipage}}
```

This works well until the contents includes some verbatim material and then you get nasty messages,
even though it appears to be wrapped inside the
`minipage`.

However, we can put material into a box, declared
by `\newsavebox` and output the typeset contents
later on via `\usebox`, which is how the framed text
below was processed.

This is the definition of the `framedminipage` environment which lets you put verbatim text into a
frame. All this is set within a `framedminipage` to
show that it does work.

```
\newsavebox{\minibox}
\newenvironment{framedminipage}[2][c]{%
  \begin{lrbox}{\minibox}
    \begin{minipage}[#1]{#2}}%
    {\end{minipage}\end{lrbox}
    \fbox{\usebox{\minibox}}}
```

I used `0.97\columnwidth` as the width of the environment like this:
```
\begin{framedminipage}%
    {\0.97\columnwidth}
```

An `lrbox` is an environment form of a `\savebox`
(or `\sbox`) and we can use it to solve the framed

minipage problem. The code displayed above, after getting a new save box (`\minibox`) defines a
`framedminipage` environment which is used just like
a regular `minipage`, including the optional positioning argument. It starts by opening an `lrbox` environment, then a `minipage` environment. At the
end it closes the `minipage` and `lrbox` environments,
then typesets an `\fbox` whose argument is the saved
box *the contents of which have already been typeset,
verbatims and all.*

In *The TₑXbook*, page 363, there is code for a
`\footnote` macro that can take verbatim material
in its argument. Knuth says that it is subtle and
requires trickery, and I don't understand it, but here
is the essence, in the form of a one argument macro
I've called `\verbtext`. I'm not sure, though, about
the location of the `\color@...` macros as there was
nothing comparable in Knuth's original code

```
\makeatletter
\long\def\verbtext{%
        \vtintro\futurelet\next\vte@t}
\def\vte@t{\ifcat\bgroup\noexpand\next
            \let\next\vt@@t
        \else \let\next\vt@t\fi \next}
\def\vt@@t{\bgroup\aftergroup\vtend\let\next}
\def\vt@t#1{%
  \color@begingroup
  #1\vtmid
  \color@endgroup}
\let\vtintro\relax
\let\vtmid\relax
\let\vtend\relax
\makeatother
```

The macros `\vtintro` and `\vtend` are called before
and after the argument is read and you can try and
define them to do something you think is useful.
Defining `\vtmid` may, on occasion, be helpful.

Here is an example of the `\verbtext` command,
which can take verbatim text as part of its argument.

```
\verbtext{'The argument to \verb?\verbtext?
        can include some \verb?\verb? text.'}
```

'The argument to `\verbtext` can include some
`\verb` text.'

The following code is a simple example of using
`\vtintro` and `\vtend` to specify a small caps font.

```
\makeatletter
\newcommand*{\fred}[1][\@empty]{Frederick%
        \ifx\@empty #1\else\ #1\fi}
\makeatother
\def\vtintro{\begingroup\scshape}
\def\vtend{\endgroup}
\verbtext{The macro \verb?\fred[III]?
        produces \fred[III], while
        \verb?\fred? results in \fred.}
```

THE MACRO \fred[III] PRODUCES FREDERICK III, WHILE \fred RESULTS IN FREDERICK.

Actually this could have been done as easily as:

```
{\scshape\verbtext{...}}
```

without bothering to redefine \vtintro and \vtend, but perhaps you may come across occasions when they can help in solving a particular problem.

15.2   Cut off in its prime

> Wickedness is always easier than virtue;
> for it takes a short cut to everything.

SAMUEL JOHNSON

Changing the subject, there was a question posed on comp.text.tex asking if there was any way of cutting a long text short, such as after two or three lines.

Donald Arseneau's truncate package [9] is available for truncating text to a specified width. By default ... (\ldots) is typeset at the end of the truncated text to indicate that something is missing. For instance

```
\truncate{0.9\columnwidth}{The%
 \texttt{truncate}
  package provides a macro for cutting off text
  so that it does not exceed a given length.}
```

will result in:

The truncate package provides a macro for ...

However, in response to the query Donald came up with a vertical equivalent to \truncate which he called \vtruncate [13], as follows:

```
\newsavebox\descbox
\newsavebox\partialbox
\newcommand{\vtruncate}[2]{%
   \setbox\descbox\vbox{{#2\par}}%
   \setbox\partialbox\vsplit\descbox to #1\relax
   \vtop{\unvbox\partialbox}%
```

```
% or use
%    \par\unvbox\partialbox
}
```

The first argument is the vertical space and the second is the text.

Will Robertson also responded, but with an environment, cutlines, that would truncate its contents if it exceeded a certain height [112]. His definition was:

```
\makeatletter
\newbox\cut@desc
\newenvironment{cutlines}[1][2]{%
   \@tempcnta=#1\relax
   \setbox\cut@desc\vbox\bgroup
   \parskip=0pt}{%
   \egroup
   \vsplit\cut@desc to \@tempcnta\baselineskip}
\makeatother
```

The argument is the number of lines (default 2).

I tried both of these, and found potential problems with each:

1. The text argument to the \vtruncate could not include any verbatim material (but this might not be of any concern).

2. If the number of lines specified for the cutlines environment was more than the lines in the original text, then the text was padded out with blank lines to make up the specified number.

3. In both cases the final truncated text was not always the specified height, but it was always to within plus or minus a line. However cutlines seemed to be more precise than \vtruncate.

4. The truncated text ends up in a box that cannot be split across a page boundary.

After some fiddling around[1] I came up with code for a truncate environment that was a mixture of Donald's and Will's code that seemed to avoid the first two of the four problems, and possibly the third as well. The fourth potential problem is inherent in all the proposals.

```
\newsavebox\descbox
\newsavebox\partialbox
\newlength{\vcutl}% for the limit height
\newlength{\Vcutl}% height of full text
\newenvironment{vcutlines}[1][2][\baselineskip]{%
   \setlength{\vcutl}{#1}%
   \setbox\descbox\vbox\bgroup
   \parskip=0pt%
```

---

[1]Quite a lot in fact.

```
}{%
\egroup
\Vcutl=\ht\descbox
\advance\Vcutl \dp\descbox
\setbox\partialbox\vsplit\descbox to
        \vcutl\relax
\vtop{\unvbox\partialbox}
\ifdim \vcutl<\Vcutl \vtruncont \fi}
\newcommand*{\vtruncont}{\noindent\strut\ldots}
```

In the following examples, the test text is:

```
{\itshape
Donald Arseneau created the \verb?\vtruncate?
command and Will Robertson the
\texttt{cutlines} environment to truncate text
if it requires more than a specified height.
This is an example, though, of the new
\texttt{vcutlines} environment\Dash a merge
of Donald's and Will's work.}
```

which does include a little verbatim material.

Let's give vcutlines a whirl with a limit of 20 lines (i.e., [20\baselineskip]).

Donald Arseneau created the \vtruncate *command and Will Robertson the* cutlines *environment to truncate text if it requires more than a specified height. This is an example, though, of the new* vcutlines *environment — a merge of Donald's and Will's work.*

And now the same text but with a limit of 3 lines (i.e., [3\baselineskip]).

Donald Arseneau created the \vtruncate *command and Will Robertson the* cutlines *environment to truncate text if it requires more than a spec-*
...

If the text is truncated, as in this example, then the environment finishes by calling the \vtruncont macro which by default outputs a final line consisting simply of ... (i.e., \ldots) to indicate that the original text continued. A comparison of the height of the original text with the specified height is used to decide if there was truncation.

You can change \vtruncont to typeset a different marker, or simply
\renewcommand*{\vtruncont}{}
to not do anything. Here's a repeat of the last example with that:

Donald Arseneau created the \vtruncate *command and Will Robertson the* cutlines *environment to truncate text if it requires more than a spec-*

However, eliminating the marker this way seems to lead to a slight problem with the spacing after the end of the environment. Defining instead
\renewcommand*{\vtruncont}{\noindent}}

Donald Arseneau created the \vtruncate *command and Will Robertson the* cutlines *environment to truncate text if it requires more than a spec-*

may give better spacing after the environment, as the \noindent starts a new paragraph, effectively resulting in a blank line, as shown here. Try both and see which works better for you.

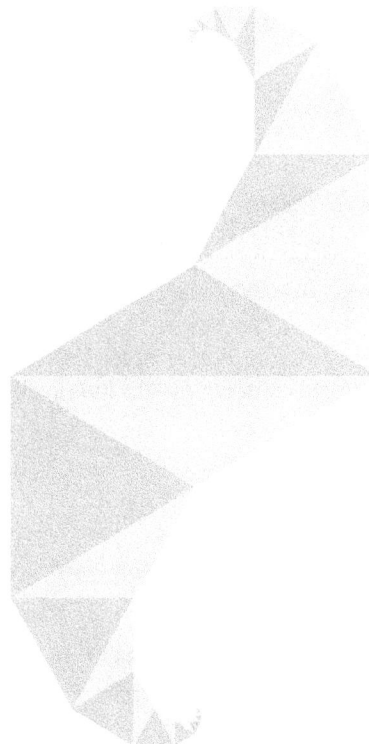

Sound like bels, and shine like lanternes.
Thunder in words and glister in works.

School of Abuse, STEPHEN GOSSON

This month's column relies heavily on work that others have done which I feel has either been lost to view or is likely to be, much of which I noticed on ctt.

16.1 Timelines

I didn't go to the moon, I went much further — for time is the longest distance between two places.

The Glass Menagerie, TENNESSEE
WILLIAMS

This is a slightly edited version of an article that Don Hosek wrote for TeXMaG, titled *Timelines with plain TeX and LaTeX* [64].

In the most recent issue of *TUGboat* as of this writing (Vol. 8 No. 2), there was a query for a macro to draw timelines in TeX. At the time, I had just finished writing DVIview and was waiting for bugs to surface and my paycheck to arrive with little else to do, so I decided to tackle the problem.

To make the problem more interesting, I decided to make the macro work in both LaTeX *and* plain TeX. A sample input file should look like:

```
%%% LaTeX sample
\documentclass{article}
\usepackage{timeline}
\def\TeXMaG{\TeX
   M\kern-.1667em\lower.5ex\hbox{A}%
   \kern-.2267emG}
\begin{document}
This is a timeline of the history of
the first year of \TeXMaG.
\begin{timeline}{2in}(0,180)
\optrule
\item[12]{Jan. 24}{No. 1}
\item[33]{Mar. 6}{No. 2}
\item[43]{Mar. 25}{No. 3}
\item[81]{May. 13}{No. 4}
\item[102]{Jun. 25}{No. 5}
\item[132]{Aug. 24}{No. 6}
\item[160]{Oct. 10}{No. 7}
```

```
\item[179]{Dec. 31}{To be}
\end{timeline}%% Must be a comment here!!!
If text immediately follows the end of the
timeline then a comment is required
otherwise there is an extraneous space at the
start of the text. A blank line following the
end behaves normally, whether or not there has
been a comment.
\end{document}
```

And something similar in plain TeX. In the example above, I used sort keys to control the spacing between entries. I also could have had a timeline whose entries looked like this:

```
\begin{timeline}{1.5in}(1750,1900)
\optrule
\item{1773}{The Boston Tea Party}
\item{1812}{War of 1812}
\item{1849}{Gold rush of '49}
\item[1862]{1862--5}{Civil War}
\item{1876}{Little Big Horn} % added by PW
\end{timeline}
```

where the dates themselves control the placement. Note that the entry for the Civil War uses a sort key to allow the year to be 1862–5. This was a pretty big problem. The comments in the code below give a fair idea of how to *use* the macro; the remainder of this section will deal with how the macros themselves *work*.

First of all, it helps to have some idea of how \begin{...} and \end{...} work in LaTeX. To view it in a simplified form, when the command \begin{FOO} is invoked, LaTeX issues the commands \begingroup followed by \FOO; similarly, \end{FOO} issues the commands \endFOO followed by \endgroup. Therefore, to allow an environment to function in plain TeX, all we need to do is include an extra grouping with \FOO...\endFOO and provide copies of any LaTeX internal macros used by the environment. Both of these tasks are fairly simple, and in the timeline macros, the only LaTeX internal macro called is \@ifnextchar (this is a very handy macro for many reasons, and gives some insight into the mysteries of LaTeX).

\@ifnextchar is called with a general form of:
\@ifnextchar X{YES}{NO}

The timeline macros use this for \item to check to see if the optional argument (enclosed in []s) is

present. If the next character after `\@ifnextchar`
matches X (X cannot be a space) then YES is executed, otherwise NO is executed. In the specific case
here, this is done with the call
`\@ifnextchar[\@item\@itemnosrtkey`
which calls `\@item` if the optional argument is
present, and `\@itemnosrtkey` if it isn't. In addition, the character that is tested remains in the input stream, so `\@item` has a parameter list that looks
like
`\@item[#1]#2#3`
rather than
`\@item#1]#2#3`.

The definition of `\item` for the timeline macros is
kept local so it won't interfere with other uses of that
control sequence name by either plain or LaTeX. The
main work of this is done by `\@item`, which takes
three arguments: the first argument is used to determine the vertical placement of the timeline item,
the second argument is the nominal date and the
third a description. `\@itemnosrtkey` calls `\@item`
using the nominal date as the first argument as well.

The placement of the item on the timeline is determined by taking the date number (first parameter)
and converting to a number between 0 and the length
of the timeline as specified with the arguments to the
`\timeline` (`\begin{timeline}`) macro. This number is then multiplied by 1/65536 times the length of
the timeline as specified by the user. The factor of
1/65536 prevents an arithmetic overflow from occur-
ring at the cost of reducing accuracy (measurements
are only kept accurate to one point). Finally, this
number is divided by the length of the range of date
number values and then multiplied by 65536, which
yields a dimension specifying how far down from the
top of the timeline the entry should be placed.

The actual placement is accomplished with the
`\dlap` macro from the toolbox of TeXMaG Vol. 1
No. 3 [by Barbara Beeton]. By placing the necessary text after a vertical `\kern`, inside a vertical
lap, we are able to print information anywhere on
the timeline without changing our vertical position.
This does have the disadvantage of using a lot of box
memory and may run into problems with very complicated timelines, but it seemed like a good idea at
the time.

The final interesting facet of the macros is the
(simple) way that two entries that are close together
are resolved. After an entry is printed, the vertical dimension specifying its placement is stored in
the dimen register `\itwashere`. When the next entry is to be printed, the current vertical placement
is compared to `\itwashere`; if the difference is less
than 12pt, and the entry would normally be placed
on the left, then the entry is printed on the right.

This is a timeline of the history of the first year of
TeXMaG.

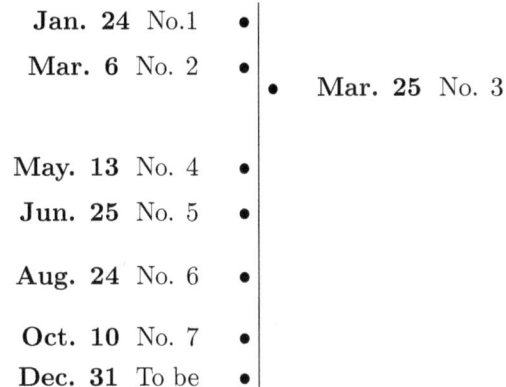

If text immediately follows the end of the timeline
then a comment is required otherwise there is an
extraneous space at the start of the text. A blank
line following the end behaves normally, whether or
not there has been a comment.

Figure 16.1: First timeline

Otherwise it is printed on the left. This algorithm
works well for two closely placed entries but fails for
three closely placed entries (the two on the left will
likely overlap).

The macros presented work for simple timelines,
but probably will be deficient for more complex timelines. Hopefully, this explanation of the macros will
help in customizing them for your own purpose, or
in writing timeline macros of your own.

```
%%% File: timeline.sty
%%% Works with either LaTeX or plain TeX
%%%
%%% In LaTeX:
%%% \begin{timeline}{length}(start,stop)
%%%    . . .
%%% \end{timeline}
%%%
%%% in plain TeX
%%% \timeline{length}(start,stop)
%%%    . . .
%%% \endtimeline
%%% in between the two, we may have:
%%% \item{date}{description}
%%% \item[sortkey]{date}{description}
%%% \optrule
%%%
%%% the options to timeline are:
%%%     length\Dash The amount of vertical
%%%        space that the timeline should use.
%%%     (start,stop)\Dash indicate the range of
```

```
%%%        the timeline. All dates or sortkeys
%%%        should lie in the range [start,stop]
%%%
%%% \item without the sort key expects date to
%%%        be a number (such as a year).
%%% \item with the sort key expects the sort
%%%        key to be a number; date can be
%%%        anything. This can be used for log
%%%        scale timelines or dates that
%%%        include months or days.
%%% putting \optrule inside of the timeline
%%%        environment will cause a vertical
%%%        rule to be drawn down the center
%%%        of the timeline.

\catcode'\@=11     % Pretend @ is a letter
\newcount\startat     \newcount\tllength
\newdimen\putithere   \newdimen\itwasthere
\newcount\scr@tchi    \newdimen\scr@tchii


% A vertically centered lap
\long\def\ylap#1{\vbox to \z@{\vss#1\vss}}


% Vertical 'laps'; cf. \llap and \rlap
\long\def\ulap#1{\vbox to \z@{\vss#1}}
\long\def\dlap#1{\vbox to \z@{#1\vss}}


\def\timeline#1(#2,#3){%
  \ifvmode\else\par\fi$$\vbox to#1\bgroup
          % The \vbox command is
          % surrounded by $$..$$ to make it
          % fit in well with paragraphs.
  \offinterlineskip
  \startat=#2\tllength=#3
    \advance\tllength by-\startat
% \tllength should be the total length of
%  the timeline.
  \def\item{\@ifnextchar[\@item\@itemnosrtkey}
  \def\@item[##1]##2##3{\scr@tchi=##1
    \advance\scr@tchi by-\startat
    \putithere=#1
    \divide\putithere by 65536 % avoid overflow
% only remain accurate to 1pt in the
% next set of calculations
    \multiply\putithere by \scr@tchi
    \divide\putithere by\tllength
    \multiply\putithere by 65536
% Now \putithere has how far
% down we should go for this item.
    \scr@tchii=\putithere
    \advance\scr@tchii by -\itwasthere
    \ifdim\scr@tchii<12pt
      \ifx\lrswitch L
        \@putright{\putithere}{##2}{##3}
      \else
        \@putleft{\putithere}{##2}{##3}
      \fi
    \else
      \@putleft{\putithere}{##2}{##3}
```

```
    \fi
    \itwasthere=\putithere}
  \def\@itemnosrtkey##1##2{%
    \@item[##1]{##1}{##2}}
  \def\@putright##1##2##3{\dlap
    {\kern##1\centerline
      {\rlap
        {\ $\bullet$\hskip1.5em{\bfseries ##2}
        \ ##3}}}}
  \let\lrswitch=R}
  \def\@putleft##1##2##3{\dlap
    {\kern##1\centerline
      {\llap
        {{\bfseries ##2} \ ##3\hskip1.5em%
        $\bullet$
        \ }}}
  \let\lrswitch=L}
  \def\optrule{\dlap
    {\centerline
% This calculation is kept local
      {\dimen0=#1 \advance\dimen0 by 6pt
        \vrule depth \dimen0 height-6pt}}}}
% Put the extra \vskip in a \vbox to hide
% it from the math gods.
\def\endtimeline{%
  \vfill\egroup\vbox{\vskip\baselineskip}$$}
\ifx\@latexerr\undefined
  \def\@ifnextchar#1#2#3{%
    \let\@tempe #1
    \def\@tempa{#2}\def\@tempb{#3}
    \futurelet\@tempc\@ifnch}
  \def\@ifnch{%
    \ifx \@tempc \@sptoken
      \let\@tempd\@xifnch
    \else
      \ifx \@tempc \@tempe
        \let\@tempd\@tempa
      \else
        \let\@tempd\@tempb
      \fi
    \fi \@tempd}
% NOTE: the following hacking must precede
%       the definition of \: as math medium
%       space.
% make \@sptoken a space token
  \def\:{\let\@sptoken= } \:
  \def\:{\@xifnch}
  \expandafter\def\: {\futurelet\@tempc\@ifnch}
\catcode'\@=12 % Stop pretending @ is a letter
\fi
\endinput
```

Using the above code, the result of the initial example is in Figure 16.1 and the second is in Figure 16.2.

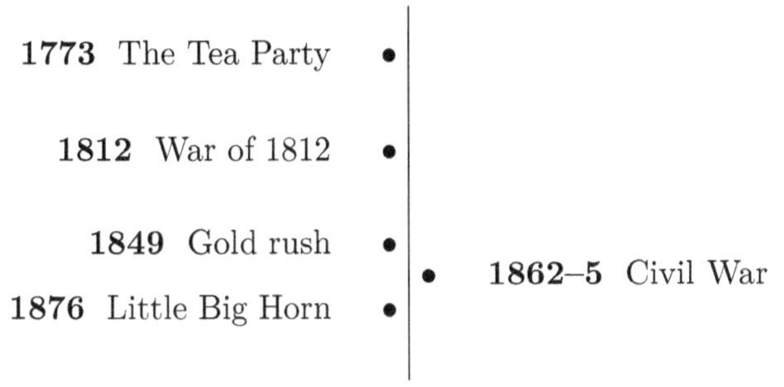

1773	The Tea Party	●		
1812	War of 1812	●		
1849	Gold rush	●	●	**1862–5** Civil War
1876	Little Big Horn	●		

Figure 16.2: Second timeline

16.2 Parsing a filename

> Gaul as a whole is divided into three parts.
>
> *De Bello Gallico*, JULIUS CAESAR

This is a (slightly edited) article by John McClain from a later issue of TEXMAG [86].

Sometimes it is nice to be able to use the pieces of a file name as information in a particular document. For example, suppose I wanted to typeset TEXMAG on real paper, and be able to have the volume and issue numbers read from the title of the file that TEX was processing, and subsequently assigned to tokens for use in the document, perhaps in a header. Say my file was named TEXMAG-5-1.TEX. The following would isolate the 5 and the 1 for use within the TEX document:

```
% This particular idea was developed by our
% chief consultant Dr John McClain

\newtoks \volumenumber
\newtoks \issuenumber

\def\parse#1-#2-#3-{\global\volumenumber={#2}
                    \global\issuenumber={#3}}

\expandafter\parse\jobname-

%%% for a TeX headline
\headline={Volume \the\volumenumber,
           Number \the\issuenumber
\hfil page \folio}
% end of macro
```

Notice the \jobname contains the name of the file (without any extension, see *The TEXbook*, p. 213). The \expandafter allows you to piece apart this token into its volume and number. We also had to chose a special delimiter which would conform to standards of a filename and be a legal parameter delimiter in TEX. A space would not have worked as a legal file name. A hyphen was our best choice. When you test this, remember that the filename must conform to the parameter specs of \parse (in this case, two minus signs, i.e., XXXX-N-N.TEX).

The essence of the code in the TEXMAG article is the \parse macro. The \jobname of the document you are now reading is 'glisterb', which does not match the requirements of \parse. The following code demonstrates that macros based on \parse can work with names other than \jobname provided that they expand into the expected format.

For instance:

```
\newcommand*{\jname}{glisten-n16-v3.tex}
\newtoks \pwfirstsub
\newtoks \pwsecondsub
\def\parse#1-#2-#3.#4-{%
    \global\pwfirstsub={#2}
    \global\pwsecondsub={#3}}
\newcommand*{\parsit}[1]{\expandafter\parse#1-}

\verb?\parsit{\jname}? \parsit{\jname}
  File \jname\ with: \\
Number \the\pwfirstsub,
and Version \the\pwsecondsub
```

And the result of the above code is:

\parsit{\jname}   File glisten-n16-v3.tex with: Number n16, and Version v3

The basic idea of \parse can be applied to any multipart string that has a well-defined delimiter between the parts.

Catching fire, taking hold
All that glisters leaves you cold
No-one is near, no-one will hear
Your changeling song take shape
In Shadowtime.

Shadowtime, SIOUXSIE AND THE
BANSHEES

17.1 Cutout windows

Twixt the optimist and pessimist
The difference is droll:
The optimist sees the doughnut
But the pessimist sees the hole.

Optimist and Pessimist,
McLANDBURGH WILSON

While winnowing my shelves and piles of books, journals, magazines, paper, etc., in anticipation of a move from the US to the UK I came across a *TUGboat* article by Alan Hoenig [63] in which he provides TeX code for creating an open window in the middle of a paragraph. An example of a paragraph with a cutout is in Figure 17.1. This was produced by:

```
\input{cutsty.tex}
\window{2}{0.4\textwidth}{0.25\textwidth}{5}
   This paragraph is set within the ...
...in a minipage in a \TUB\ \texttt{figure*}).
\endwindow
```

I tried out the code as given but found that it needed a tweak here and there to improve the spacing. Here is my version of Alan's code for rectangular cutouts, which can be used in both TeXed and

LaTeXed documents.[1] Most of my changes to the code are changes of name and argument specification to make it acceptable to both TeX and LaTeX.

```
% cutsty.tex  Based on Alan Hoenig,
%  'TeX Does Windows\Dash The Conclusion',
%  TUGboat 8:2, pp.211-215, 1987
```

First some counts, lengths, and boxes are needed (I have used `cut` as the start of each of these names to try and avoid clashes with other code):

```
\newcount\cutlines \newcount\cuttoplines
\newdimen\cutlftside \newdimen\cutrtside
\newtoks\cuta
\newcount\cutn
\newbox\cutrawtext \newbox\cutholder
\newbox\cutwindow \newbox\cutfinaltext
\newbox\cutaslice \newbox\cutbslice
\newdimen\cuttopheight
\newdimen\cutilgvs % glue or shift
```

The main user commands are `\window` and the accompanying `\endwindow`. The first of these takes four arguments as:
`\window{`⟨*top-lines*⟩`}{`⟨*left*⟩`}{`⟨*right*⟩`}{`⟨*cut-lines*⟩`}`
where ⟨*top-lines*⟩ is the number of lines before the window cutout, ⟨*left*⟩ is the width of the text at the left of the window and ⟨*right*⟩ the width of the text at the right, and ⟨*cut-lines*⟩ is the number of lines used for the window (i.e., the height of the window). The macro gets a `\parshape` for the forthcoming

---

[1] Alan also gave code for creating arbitrary shaped holes.

This paragraph is set within the `window` environment. There are limitations on the `window` arguments and text. There must be at least one line of text above the window and if the number of lines spec- ified for the opening exceeds the available lines then the text after the `window` environment will be moved down by an amount corre- sponding to the excess. A window will not extend into a second paragraph. The environ- ment is effectively a box and will not break across a page boundary. There should be enough space at the left and right of the window for a few words on each side (don't try to make either of these zero in an attempt to have a window opening to the margin). There is usually not enough width to put a significant window into a column on a two-column page (this has been set in a minipage in a *TUGboat* `figure*`).

Figure 17.1: A generated window

text, gets and applies any vertical shift, opens a box for the text and then applies the \parshape.

```
\def\window#1#2#3#4{%
  \cuttoplines=#1\relax
  \cutlines=#4\relax
  \cutlftside=#2\relax
  \cutrtside=#3\relax
  \cuta={}%
  % calculate the \parshape spec
  \parshapespec
  % reset these arguments
  \cuttoplines=#1\relax
  \cutlines=#4\relax
  % calculate and apply any vertical shift
  \cutshift \vskip-\cutilgvs
  % start a box for collecting the text
  \setbox\cutrawtext=\vbox\bgroup
  \parshape=\cutn \the\cuta}
```

The text, in the form of a single paragraph with a constant \baselineskip is put between the two \...window commands; in the case of LaTeX you can, but don't need to, use a window environment instead.

The general scheme is to use a specially shaped paragraph which effectively splits the text into three sets of lines; those before the cutout; those that will form the cutout; and the rest. The lines forming the cutout are short while the others are full length. An example is shown in Figure 17.2. The final output is assembled from the top set of lines, the cutout lines combined in pairs, and the remainder. The final form of a paragraph with a cutout is shown in Figure 17.3.

```
\def\endwindow{%
  \egroup       % end \box\cutrawtex
  \parshape=0 % reset parshape
  \computeilg % find ILG using current font
  \setbox\cutfinaltext=
    \vsplit\cutrawtext
      to\cuttoplines\baselineskip
  \cuttopheight=\cutlines\baselineskip
  \cuttopheight=2\cuttopheight
  \setbox\cutholder=
    \vsplit\cutrawtext
      to\cuttopheight
  % \cutholder contains the narrowed text
  %  for window sides. Slice up \cutholder
  %  into \cutwindow
  \decompose{\cutholder}{\cutwindow}
  \setbox\cutfinaltext=\vbox{%
    \unvbox\cutfinaltext\vskip\cutilgvs
      \unvbox\cutwindow%
      \vskip-\cutilgvs\unvbox\cutrawtext}%
  \box\cutfinaltext}
```

If you have to have a cutout in a narrow column keep the words short. Use one or two or maybe one or more
extra letters so that
they may fit into the
available area with-
out too much odd
spacing. If the words
are hyphenatable this will help a lot as then a long one may be cut into two short bits.

Figure 17.2: Split window lines

If you have to have a cutout in a narrow column keep the words short. Use one or two or maybe one or more   extra letters so that
they may fit into the   available area with-
out too much odd   spacing. If the words
are hyphenatable this will help a lot as then a long one may be cut into two short bits.

Figure 17.3: Assembled window lines

The \parshape primitive is used to specify quite general paragraph shapes [71, Ch. 14] or [38, Ch. 18]. Its $2n + 1$ parameters specify the indentation and length of the first n lines in the following paragraph which must start immediately (no empty line after the parameters). The first parameter is n followed by n pairs of indentation and line length values. In general:

\parshape n i_1 l_1 i_2 l_2 ... i_n l_n

If there are more than n lines then the specification for the last line (i_n l_n) is used for the rest of the lines in the paragraph.

\parshapespec calculates the \parshape parameters to generate a paragraph with ⟨top-lines⟩ full lines followed by ⟨cut-lines⟩ of length ⟨left⟩ alternating with ⟨cut-lines⟩ of length ⟨right⟩.

```
\def\parshapespec{%
  \cutn=\cutlines \multiply \cutn by 2
    \advance\cutn by \cuttoplines
    \advance\cutn by 1\relax
  \loop
    \cuta=\expandafter{\the\cuta 0pt \hsize}
    \advance\cuttoplines -1\relax
    \ifnum\cuttoplines>0\repeat
  \loop
    \cuta=\expandafter{\the\cuta
          0pt \cutlftside 0pt \cutrtside}%
    \advance\cutlines -1\relax
  \ifnum\cutlines>0\repeat
  \cuta=\expandafter{\the\cuta 0pt \hsize}}
```

An example paragraph at this stage of the process is in Figure 17.2.

The `\decompose{⟨narrow⟩}{⟨split⟩}` command takes a box ⟨narrow⟩ and for each pair of lines puts the first at the left and the second at the right of the box {⟨split⟩}. That is, it converts pairs of lines into single lines with text at the left and the right with a space between.

```
\def\decompose#1#2{%
  % loop over the windowed lines
  \loop\advance\cutlines -1
   % get a pair of lines
  \setbox\cutaslice=\vsplit#1 to\baselineskip
  \setbox\cutbslice=\vsplit#1 to\baselineskip
  % split into the two sides
  \prune{\cutaslice}{\cutlftside}%
  \prune{\cutbslice}{\cutrtside}%
  % assemble into one line
  \setbox#2=\vbox{\unvbox#2\hbox
  to\hsize{\box\cutaslice\hfil\box\cutbslice}}%
  \ifnum\cutlines>0\repeat}
```

For the example in Figure 17.2 the `\decompose` macro converts the 6 narrow lines into the 3 cutout lines shown in Figure 17.3.

`\prune{⟨vbox⟩}{⟨width⟩}` is used to prune the glue that TeX puts at the end of a short `\parshape` line. It takes a `\vbox` containing a single `\hbox`, `\unvboxes` it, cancels the `\lastskip` and puts it in a box of ⟨width⟩ wide; a `\strut` is needed to keep the spacing consistent.

```
\def\prune#1#2{%
  \unvbox#1\relax
  \setbox#1=\lastbox % \box#1 is now an \hbox
  \setbox#1=\hbox to#2{\strut\unhbox#1\unskip}}
```

`\cutshift` calculates the amount that the windowed paragraph must be raised, which is half a `\baselineskip` for each windowed line. (This is my addition).

```
\def\cutshift{%
  \cutilgvs=\cutlines\baselineskip
  \cutilgvs=0.5\cutilgvs}
```

`\computeilg` computes the interline glue in the windowed paragraph. This is the last macro so finish the file with an `\endinput`.

```
\def\computeilg{%
  \cutilgvs=\baselineskip
  \setbox0=\hbox{()
    \advance\cutilgvs-\ht0
    \advance\cutilgvs-\dp0}
\endinput
```

Artwork or text may be placed in the cutout. How to do that is a very different problem and one that I am not intending to address here, but zero-sized pictures and headers or footers come to mind [152]. Perhaps solutions will have been published by the time this article appears.

Since the preceding was first written, the cutwin package [153] has appeared which lets you create variously shaped cutouts and place things in the resulting window.

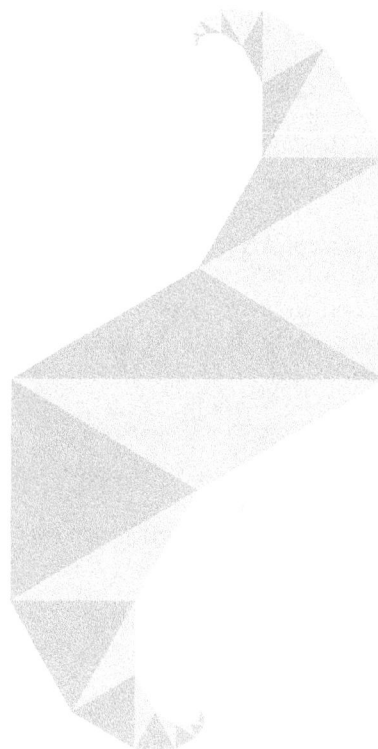

Snail, snail, glister me forward,
Bird, soft-sigh me home.
Worm, be with me.
This is my hard time.

———

The Lost Son, THEODORE ROETHKE

18.1 Repetition

We'll meet again,
Don't know where, don't know when,
But I know we'll meet again
Some sunny day.

———

We'll Meet Again, ROSS PARKER &
HUGHIE CHARLES

In September 2009 JT posed the following to the `comp.text.tex` newsgroup (ctt).

I have numbered propositions of the form:

(P1) Some proposition.

(P2) Another proposition.

(P3) Yet another proposition.

which are in a custom list environment and I can refer to the labels (P1, P2, etc.) later in the document. However I sometimes want to also repeat the corresponding proposition like this:

> *Recall P2 from Chapter 1:*
>
> *(P2) Another proposition.*

Is there any way to output the entire list item without having to retype it?

Lars Madsen [82] responded with the following example code.

```
\documentclass[a4paper]{memoir}
\makeatletter
\newcommand{\Reuse}[1]{\@nameuse{forlater@#1}}
\newcommand{\ForLater}[2]{%
  \item[(#1)]\def\@currentlabel{#1}\label{#1}%
  \global\long\@namedef{forlater@#1}{#2}%
  \Reuse{#1}}
\makeatother
\begin{document}
\begin{itemize}
\ForLater{P1}{Some long text}
\ForLater{P2}{More longer text.\par
        In paragraphs.}
```

```
\end{itemize}

Recall \ref{P2}:
\begin{itemize}
\item[(\ref{P2})] \Reuse{P2}
\end{itemize}
\end{document}
```

As a demonstration that Lars' `\ForLater` and `\Reuse` macros work, I used them in the description above of JT's request.

In an earlier column (Chapter 10; [150]) I had tackled the question of repeating work in a somewhat different, and a not quite so elegant, manner.

18.2 Verbatims

verbatim et litteratim — word for word and letter for letter.

———

Chambers Dictionary

18.2.1 \verb with an argument

Luca Merciadri asked on ctt if there was a way of defining a `\verb` macro that took the verbatim material as an argument enclosed in braces.

Ulrich Diez [32] responded with three solutions, the last two of which avoided any assignments. The first, shown below, looked much simpler to me.

```
\edef\verba#1#{\noexpand\verb#1\string}%
    \let\noexpand\next=}
```

```
\edef\verba#1#{%
  \noexpand\verb#1\string}%
  \noexpand\expandafter
  \noexpand\fi
  \noexpand\if{\noexpand\iffalse}\noexpand\fi}
```

```
\edef\verba#1#{%
  \noexpand\verb#1\string}%
  \noexpand\expandafter\expandafter
  \noexpand\csname @gobble\endcsname
  \noexpand\string}
```

You can use `\verba` like this:

```
'You can use either \verba{the \verba macro} or
\verba*{the \verba* macro}, whichever suits
your purpose best.'
```

which will produce:

'You can use either `the \verba` macro or `the␣\verba*␣macro`, whichever suits your purpose best.'

However, just like `\verb`, `\verba` with its argument cannot be used in an argument to another macro, not even in the argument to `\verba`.

18.2.2 Automatic line breaking

Hans Balsam asked on `ctt`:

I'm looking for a way to combine the features of the verbatim environment and LaTeX's automatic line breaking.

'Zappathustra' (Paul) responded with [66]:

```
\makeatletter
\def\@xobeysp{ }
\makeatother
```

This redefines `\@xobeysp`, *to which the space character is* `\let` *in verbatim text, to a normal space instead of an unbreakable space. Then you can use the usual 'verbatim' environment.*

This proposal works, albeit with at least one surprise — a space following a comma gets swallowed so a double space should be used instead of a single space. The other potential surprise is that hyphenation is disabled and multiline verbatim text is set raggedright.

18.3 Small pages

> If any man will draw up his case, and put his name at the foot of the first page, I will give him an immediate reply. Where he compels me to turn over the sheet, he must wait my leisure.
>
> *Memoirs*, LORD SANDWICH

Harald Hanche-Olsen asked this [slightly edited] on `ctt`:

I'd like to make some PDF files specially for reading on screen, more specifically on the iPhone. For much of this, a fixed page length seems like a straitjacket. I want to divide the material into pages so that one topic will fit on one page. Some pages will be very short while others will be very long. I don't want oceans of white space at the bottom of the pages.

I imagine doing this with LaTeX . . . [but] the output routine gives me goose bumps. . . I don't plan on using marginal notes and if I must do without floats and footnotes, that is fine too. I could of course do it in plain TeX, but would like to have the added power of LaTeX available.

Will Robertson [114] responded with a potential solution based on the preview package [70]. His code follows, and I have taken the liberty of extending it very slightly to enable it to work with a variety of classes, and also extending the example document..

```
%\documentclass[article]{memoir}
\documentclass{article}
\usepackage{charter}% more readable on a screen
\usepackage{lipsum}
\makeatletter
%% PW's extension here
\@ifclassloaded{memoir}{%
    \let\section\chapter
    \let\raggedy\raggedyright
}{\usepackage{ragged2e}
    \let\raggedy\RaggedRight}
\makeatother

\usepackage[active,tightpage]{preview}
\usepackage{hyperref}
\newenvironment{page}{%
    \begin{preview}
    \begin{minipage}{5cm}
    \medskip \centering
    \begin{minipage}{4.5cm}
    \footnotesize\raggedy
    \parindent=2em
}{%
    \end{minipage}
    \medskip
    \end{minipage}\end{preview}}

\begin{document}

\begin{page}\tableofcontents\end{page}
\begin{page}
\section{Foo}
\lipsum[1]
\end{page}
\begin{page}
\section{Bar}\lipsum[2-5]\end{page}
\begin{page}
\section{Fuz}
Some text here. I wonder if one can have a
marginal note. %\marginpar{At the side}
It doesn't work!
\section{Fuzzy}
What if we have two 'sections' on the
same page?
\end{page}
\begin{page}
\section{Fie}
Some text here. I wonder if one can have a
footnote.\footnote{At the end like this}
It works!\par
\lipsum[2-5]
```

```
\end{page}
\end{document}
```

It is not possible to demonstrate Will's `page` environment here, but it does seem to meet Harald's request as far as I understand it. Floats do not work, nor are page numbers printed, but `\tableofcontents` and the hyperref package [110] work (at least as used in the test code above), if needed.

18.4 Prefixing section heads

> He fixed thee 'mid this dance
> Of plastic circumstance.
>
> *Rabbi Ben Ezra*, ROBERT BROWNING

'Ghoetker' wrote to ctt along the following lines:
I have changed the formatting of subsections in my document to start with the term 'Activity' (trust me, it made sense). So, the subsection heading is 'Activity A.1. Test'. When I cross-reference, however, this isn't what I want — I just want the 'A.1' part....

As is so often the case, Donald Arseneau came up with an elegant solution [14] shown below. But first, to set the context:

The LaTeX kernel `\@seccntformat` macro typesets the number of a (sub-)section head, and takes one argument which is the name of the section head. Its default definition is:

```
\newcommand*{\@seccntformat}[1]{%
  \csname the#1\endcsname\quad}
```

and in, for example, a `\subsubsection` it would be called as:
```
... \@seccntformat{subsubsection}...
```
resulting in the code:
```
... \thesubsubsection\quad...
```

Donald proposed:

```
\makeatletter
\renewcommand*{\@seccntformat}[1]{%
  \@ifundefined{#1prefix}{}%
    {\csname #1prefix\endcsname\ }%
  \csname the#1\endcsname. \quad}
\makeatother
\renewcommand*{\thesubsection}{%
  \Alph{section}.\arabic{subsection}}
\newcommand*{\subsectionprefix}{Activity}
```

As well as putting 'Activity' before subsection head numbers it also has the effect of putting a '.' at the end of every sectional number. Using the above will result in

- `\section` heads like **2. Title**,
- `\subsection` heads like **Activity A.2. Title**,
- `\subsubsection` heads like **A.2.3. Title**.

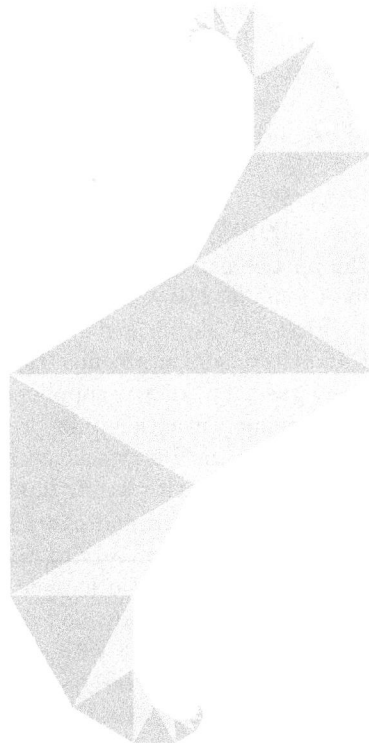

If the '.' after every sectional number is not required this can be dealt with by extending Donald's code to cater for putting something specific after the heading number, which can then be different for each section level:

```
\makeatletter
\renewcommand*{\@seccntformat}[1]{%
  \@ifundefined{#1prefix}{}%
    {\csname #1prefix\endcsname\ }%
  \csname the#1\endcsname
  \@ifundefined{#1postfix}{}%
    {\csname #1postfix\endcsname}\quad}
\makeatother
\renewcommand*{\thesubsection}{%
  \Alph{section}.\arabic{subsection}}
\newcommand*{\subsectionprefix}{Activity}
\newcommand*{\subsectionpostfix}{.}
```

Using the above will result in

- `\section` heads like **2 Title**,
- `\subsection` heads like **Activity A.2. Title**,
- `\subsubsection` heads like **A.2.3 Title**.

This simple bug is tied from black Glister which is a synthetic material with iridescence and peacock like colouration.

Black Glister Bug, HARTLEY FLY FISHING

19.1 Fonts

Slow, slow, fresh fount, keep time with my salt tears.

Cynthia's Revels, BEN JONSON

19.1.1 A font of fleurons

In an earlier column (Chapter 14), I showed how printers' ornaments and flowers could be combined to make interesting patterns. Subsequently, I obtained John Ryder's book on flowers, flourishes, and fleurons [121] in which he discussed a rather fine set of fleurons that are thought to have been cut by Robert Granjon around 1565. These are known collectively as *Granjon's Arabesque* or *Granjon's Fleurons*. I found a commercial font of these, the Lanston Type Company's *LTC Fleurons Granjon* (https://fonts.com/browse/designers/lanston-type-company), for Mac or Windows. I purchased the Windows version which came as both TrueType and Type 1 fonts. The Type 1 files were `LTCFleurGranj.afm` and `LTCFleurGranj.pfb`. The question then was: How do I use these in LaTeX?

I read Philipp Lehman's wonderful guide to installing Type 1 fonts for LaTeX and it seemed pretty simple [72]. First, decide on a name for the font using the Karl Berry naming scheme. But Lanston Type Company was not a 'known' supplier and other aspects of the naming convention didn't really seem to apply, so I ignored the Berry scheme and made up a name; the `zlgf` font with family name `lgf`.

Next, copy the original `afm` and `pfb` font files to our newly named font (thus preserving the original files in case of disaster, which did happen — several times). So, we now have `zlgf.afm` and `zlgf.pfb`.

I then blindly used `fontinst` with the 'default' `latinfamily` which produced various files which I then installed in their proper locations, and ran a test file meant to show all the glyphs. It didn't.

After much huffing and puffing, trying to read encrypted binary files, looking at the font in George Williams' amazing `FontForge` [137], and other possibly useful things I eventually managed to install the font on, I think, the 5th attempt (I had paid money for the font and I wasn't going to give up).

`FontForge` revealed that the actual font name was `LTCFleuronsGranjon` and the font's family name was `LTC Fleurons Granjon`. It also turned out from using `FontForge` to check the font that some of the glyphs were in LaTeX's normal range of 0–255 while others were above that, and LaTeX couldn't deal with the higher level numbered ones. I read the *Font Installation Guide* several more times and with its help eventually came up with the following:

- Opened `zlgf.pfb` in `FontForge` and reencoded it into *Glyph Order* which just numbered the glyphs continuously in the order they appeared in the file, then used *Generate Fonts* to keep the new encoding and regenerate `zlgf.afm` to match.

- Followed Lehman's example of installing symbol fonts. That is, I created two files, the first based on [72, p. 46] I named `makelgf.tex`:

```
% makelgf.tex fontinst file
%            for Granjon's Fleurons
\input fontinst.sty
\recordtransforms{lgf-rec.tex}
\installfonts
\installfamily{U}{lgf}{}
\installrawfont{zlgf}{zlgf}%
  {txtfdmns,zlgf mtxasetx}{U}{lgf}{m}{n}{}
\endinstallfonts
\endrecordtransforms
\bye
```

And the second, based on [72, p. 17], I named `maplgf.tex`:

```
% maplgf.tex fontinst file to
%            generate map for lgf font
\input finstmsc.sty
\resetstr{PSfontsuffix}{.pfb}
\adddriver{dvips}{lgf.map}
\input lgf-rec.tex
\donedrivers
\bye
```

Then I ran TeX on them, in that order. The result was two files: the file `ulgf.fd`:

	0		1		2		3		4		5		6		7
	8		9		10		11		12		13		14		15
	16		17		18		19		20		21		22		23
	24		25		26		27		28		29		30		31
	32		33		34		35		36		37		38		39
	40		41		42		43		44		45		46		47
	48		49		50		51		52		53		54		55
	56		57		58		59		60		61		62		63
	64		65		66		67		68		69		70		71
	72		73		74		75		76		77		78		79
	80		81		82		83		84		85		86		87
	88		89		90		91		92		93		94		95
	96		97		98		99		100		101		102		103
	104		105		106		107		108		109		110		111

Figure 19.1: The Granjon Fleurons glyphs

```
%Filename: ulgf.fd
% other comments
\ProvidesFile{ulgf.fd}
  [2009/10/10 Fontinst v1.929
  font definitions for U/lgf.]
\DeclareFontFamily{U}{lgf}{}
\DeclareFontShape{U}{lgf}{m}{n}{<-> zlgf}{}
\endinput
```

and the file `lgf.map` (one line):

```
zlgf  LTCFleuronsGranjon <zlgf.pfb
```

Then I ran the program `afm2tfm` on `zlgf.afm` to create `zlgf.tfm`.

- Moved the various files to their proper places in the TDS tree. I made a `lanston` directory in each place to hold the files in case I ever wanted to install another of the Lanston Type Company fonts. The several files ended up in the `texmf-local` tree as:

```
.../fonts/map/dvips/lanston/lgf.map
.../fonts/afm/lanston/zlgf.afm
.../fonts/tfm/lanston/zlgf.tfm
.../fonts/type1/lanston/zlgf.pfb
.../tex/latex/lanston/ulgf.fd
```

and then *refreshed the database*, in my case by running `texhash`.

- Ensured the new `.map` file can be found by running `updmap[-sys]`. (Make sure that you either always run `updmap` and never `updmap-sys`, or you always run `updmap-sys` and never run `updmap`.[1] If you should ever alternate these then access to your fonts is likely to be all messed up.) In my case, as administrator/root I ran:

```
updmap-sys --enable Map=lgf.map
```

The fonts should now be available for use. I wrote a little test file to see if all the glyphs were available by generating a font table, using the fonttable package [149], and a macro to print a glyph by giving its number in the font table:

```
% testlgf.tex Test the lgf font family
\documentclass{article}
\usepackage[T1]{fontenc}
\usepackage{fonttable}
% typeset a character by number
\newcommand*{\F}[1]{{%
    \usefont{U}{lgf}{m}{n}\char#1}}
% zero extra line spacing
\newcommand*{\zeroxls}{%
    \lineskip=0pt\lineskiplimit=0pt}

\begin{table*}
\centering
```

---

[1] Update for 2020: `updmap` is now a no-op, and `updmap-user` serves its purpose. The advice here still holds, *mutatis mutandis*.

```
\caption{The Granjon Fleurons glyphs}
    \label{tab:lgf}
\nohexoct
\fontsize{12}{12}
\xfonttable{U}{lgf}{m}{n}
\end{table*}
```

```
    And here are some examples of
how they can be used.
```

```
\begin{center}\zeroxls
\fontsize{24}{24}\F{11}\F{12}\\
                \F{13}\F{14}
\end{center}
```

```
\begin{center}\zeroxls
\fontsize{24}{24}\F{14}\F{13}\\
                \F{12}\F{11}
\end{center}
```

```
\begin{center}\zeroxls
\fontsize{24}{24}%
  \F{26}\F{47}\F{75}\F{54}\\
  \F{27}\F{46}\F{74}\F{55}
\end{center}
\end{document}
```

The results from the test file are in Table 19.1 and the three arabesques below.

And many other arabesques may be created, like those below and the 'moustachios' used earlier as anonymous divisions setting off the T_EXM_AG articles.

All was well with using my fleurons font until I

came to install the next version of TeX Live, when the fleurons suddenly became unfindable. Apparently new fonts installed as I had done had to be reinstalled whenever TeX Live was (re)installed. Norbert Preining advised me on how to go about avoiding this problem.

[Update: as of 2017, the best advice is different now, so I won't include the obsolete information. Please see the web page https://tug.org/texlive/scripts-sys-user.html.]

19.1.2   Fonts, GNU/Linux and X_ETeX

Having gone to the trouble to get LaTeX to use my new fleurons font I thought that it might have been easier to use X_ETeX as I understood that it could handle any system font without the contortions involved in setting one up for LaTeX. It seems that if you are on a Mac or Windows machine installing a new system font is trivial. However, I work on a GNU/Linux box and my first difficulty was in finding out how to install a new system font. All articles on the subject that I googled had different ideas on the subject, some very complicated. I eventually, with much trepidation, tried what appeared to be the simplest method which was to:

- Copy the font and files into a directory under /usr/share/fonts, which I created and called Lanston.[2]

- As root, run fc-cache -f -v so that it will cache the new font for use.

- Run fc-list, which returns a list of the system fonts, to check that the new font is now among them.

Now for the test. A simple X_ELaTeX file:

```
\documentclass{article}
\usepackage{fontspec}
\fontspec{LTCFleuronsGranjon}
\begin{document}
ABCDEFGHI
\end{document}
```

which produced:
ABCDEFGHI
an abject failure! It should have typeset the corresponding fleurons.

I had come across a method for displaying a table of all the glyphs in a font by Guido Herzog in a posting to the X_ETeX mailing list [61]. I used X_ETeX on this for my fleurons font:

---

[2]I tend to uppercase the first letter of directory names, but not necessarily consistently.

```
%!TEX TS-program = xetex
%!TEX encoding = UTF-8 Unicode
% glyphs.tex -- find glyphs and their index
\parindent 0pt
%% the font to test
\font\test="LTC Fleurons Granjon" at 14pt
% this next one also works
%\font\test="LTCFleuronsGranjon" at 14pt

\newcount\charcountA \charcountA 0
\newcount\charcountB
  \charcountB \XeTeXcountglyphs\test
  \advance\charcountB -1\relax
\newcount\charcountC \charcountC 0

\def\ystrut{%
  \vrule height 15pt depth 5.5pt width 0pt}
\advance\vsize 4\baselineskip

\loop
  \advance\charcountC 1\relax
  \leavevmode
  \hbox{\hbox to 10mm{%
    \hss\number\charcountA\quad}%
  \hbox to 10mm{%
    \test\XeTeXglyph\charcountA\ystrut\hss}}%
  \ifnum\charcountC = 8
      \endgraf \charcountC 0\fi
  \ifnum\charcountA < \charcountB
      \advance\charcountA 1\relax
\repeat

\bye
```

The result was a table similar to Table 19.1, displaying all the fleuron glyphs. This meant that X꜀TEX found my new font but for some reason my use of the fontspec package [115] might have been at fault. I eventually found that I should have done:

```
\documentclass{article}
\usepackage{fontspec}
\begin{document}
\fontspec{LTCFleuronsGranjon}
ABCDEFGHI
\end{document}
```

which made the fleurons the current font, or

```
\documentclass{article}
\usepackage{fontspec}
\setmainfont{LTCFleuronsGranjon}
\begin{document}
ABCDEFGHI
\end{document}
```

which made the fleurons the main (default) font.

Now, it seems simple to typeset with new fonts on a GNU/Linux box also.

Mixing traditional and system fonts

A little while ago I was extending an older document where I had been using several fonts set up for the traditional LATEX methods — Type 1 fonts with tfm and map files. For swapping from one font to another I used

```
\newcommand*{\FSfont}[1]{%
  \fontfamily{#1}\selectfont}
```

where the argument is the font's family name. This worked well.

I then wanted to use a new font, IM_FELL_Double_ Pica_PRO_Roman, that didn't come with the LATEX support files so I added it to the system fonts directory, added it to the document with \FSfont, and used xelatex, together with fontspec, instead of pdflatex for processing. The new font displayed well but all the others reverted to the default Latin Modern fonts.

I eventually had to ask on ctt and Ulrike Fischer responded [45] that with xetex/fontspec the default encoding is set to EU1 but with pdflatex it is set to T1. Therefore I had to take account of encodings when moving from pdflatex to xelatex.

In my case I was only using the normal alphanumeric and punctuation characters which are in the same slots in the EU1 and T1 encodings. Changing my \FSfont macro to:

```
\newcommand*{\FSfont}[1]{%
  \fontencoding{T1}\fontfamily{#1}\selectfont}
```

fixed the problem for me.

Ek gret effect men write in place lite;
Th' entente is al, and nat the lettres space.

Troilus and Criseyde, GEOFFREY
CHAUCER

20.1 Asterism

There is a symbol that is called *asterism* which is a
simple kind of ornament consisting of three asterisks
and is supplied in some fonts. It is typically used as
an anonymous division looking like this.

*
**

Recently Stephen Moye [90] posted a macro to
make one if it was not available otherwise. This was
based on some earlier code from Peter Flynn [48].
The code below is my version.

```
\newcommand*{\asterism}{%
  \raisebox{-.3em}[1em][0em]{%  OK for 10-12pt
    \setlength{\tabcolsep}{0.05em}%
    \begin{tabular}{@{}cc@{}}%
      \multicolumn{2}{c}*\\[-.75em]%
      *&*%
    \end{tabular}%
}}
```

The asterism above was printed by:

```
\par{\centering \asterism\par}
```

20.2 Raising a character

'Maximus_Rumpas' wrote to `ctt` along the following lines:
I am writing some Latin text within a document:
GALL : REG : IACO : MAG : BRITA : REG
I need to raise the colon between the abbreviated
text to the centre of the text line rather than, as
normal, aligned at the bottom of the text. I use
\textperiodcentered for a single period but I can't
find anything similar for colons.
Heiko Oberdiek [98] responded with:
The following solution centers the colon using an
uppercase letter for comparison. Also it makes the
colon active inside an environment for easier writing.

```
\documentclass{article}
\begingroup
  \lccode`\~=`\:%
  \lowercase{\endgroup
  \newenvironment{vccolon}{%
    \catcode`\:=\active
    \let~\textcoloncentered
    \ignorespaces
}{\ifhmode\unskip\fi}}
\newcommand{\textcoloncentered}{}
\DeclareRobustCommand*{\textcoloncentered}{%
  \begingroup
    \sbox0{T}%
    \sbox2{:}%
    \dimen0=\ht0 %
    \advance\dimen0 by -\ht2 %
    \dimen0=.5\dimen0 %
    \raisebox{\dimen0}{:}%
  \endgroup}

\begin{document}
\begin{vccolon}
GALL : REG : IACO : MAG : BRITA : REG
\end{vccolon}
\end{document}
```

Following on from this Dan Luecking suggested
using a \valign:

```
% works for 2018 and earlier LaTeX
\def\textcoloncentered{%
  \valign{&##\cr\vphantom{T}
  \cr\vfil\hbox{:}\vfil\cr}}
% works for 2019 LaTeX
\def\textcoloncentered{%
  \valign{&##\cr\hbox{\vphantom{T}}
  \cr\vfil\hbox{:}\vfil\cr}}
```

also remarking that perhaps a simple box raised by
some multiple of ex would do as well.

I tried all three suggestions and decided that

```
\DeclareRobustCommand*{\textcoloncentered}{%
  \raisebox{.2ex}{:}}
```

gave a satisfying result, also enabling the height to
be adjusted to optically center the colon if necessary.

Heiko's result:

GALL : REG : IACO : MAG : BRITA : REG

Dan's current result:

GALL : REG : IACO : MAG : BRITA : REG

Karl Berry[1] sent me the revised version of Dan's code that works in this document as

```
% works for 2019 LaTeX
\def\textcoloncentered{%
  \valign{&##\cr\hbox{\vphantom{T}}%
  \cr\vfil\hbox{:}%
  \vfil\cr}}
```

His explanation was:

A change in the LaTeX December 2018 release was to force horizontal mode for commands that are 'only' intended for horizontal mode, such as \thinspace ... but also including \smash and \phantom. See section 'Start L-R mode for \thinspace and friends' in LaTeX News 29, page 2, https://tug.org/TUGboat/tb40-1/tb124ltnews29.pdf.

Without the explicit \hbox, Dan's code is in \vmode when it did the \phantom, hence the phantom now started horizontal mode, hence it was a whole line of paragraph on its own, hence each word in the vccolon environment was on its own line.

Sometimes you have to be careful when moving to an updated version of LaTeX!

And after all this, my result:

GALL : REG : IACO : MAG : BRITA : REG

20.3 Boxing a glyph

Paul Kaletta wanted to be able to draw a box around a glyph similar to the example in chapter 11 of *The TeXbook*. Herbert Voß responded with [135] [slightly edited]:

```
\documentclass{article}
\usepackage[T1]{fontenc}
\usepackage{lmodern}
\newsavebox\CBox
\makeatletter
```

---

[1] Private email 9 July 2019.

```
\def\Gbox#1{\begingroup
  \unitlength=1pt
  \fboxsep=0pt\sbox\CBox{#1}%
  \leavevmode
  \put(0,0){\line(1,0){\strip@pt\wd\CBox}}%
  \fbox{#1}%
  \put(-\strip@pt\wd\CBox,0){\circle*{4}}
  \endgroup}
\makeatother
\begin{document}
\begingroup
\fontsize{2cm}{2.2cm}\selectfont
\Gbox{g}\Gbox{r}\Gbox{f}%
\Gbox{'}\Gbox{,}\Gbox{T}
\endgroup
\end{document}
```

In this article Herbert's demonstration code results in:

20.4 Glyph widths

'PmI' wrote to ctt:

I'm trying to put some text in a box, so that I can calculate the box dimensions, but [neither] hbox nor mbox seem to want to perform linebreaks, and parbox needs a width argument, which is actually what I want to compute so it's useless ...

```
\filltestbox{I need \\ the width \\
          of this text}
\begin{minipage}{\testboxwidth}
```

Several respondents mentioned that the varwidth package [16] does this, but two other solutions were provided for when the text was simple [46].

Ulrike Fischer proposed using a tabular and measuring its width.

```
\newsavebox\testbox
\newcommand{\filltestbox}[1]{%
  \savebox\testbox{%
    \begin{tabular}{@{}l@{}}#1\end{tabular}}}
\newcommand*{\testboxwidth}{\the\wd\testbox}
```

On the other hand, as an exercise Donald Arseneau, the author of the varwidth package, proposed this:

```
\newcommand{\filltestbox}[1]{%
  \setbox\testbox\vbox{%
  \def\\{\unskip\egroup\hbox\bgroup%
        \ignorespaces}%
  \hbox\bgroup\ignorespaces #1\unskip\egroup}}
```

which makes a vbox (called `\testbox`) containing a list of hboxes whose contents are the pieces of text between \\.

In my limited testing, the two approaches yield the same final result. For instance:

```
\filltestbox{Some \\
             text which I want to know \\
             the width. \\
             There can be \\
             only one paragraph.}
\fbox{%
\begin{minipage}{\testboxwidth}
\usebox\testbox
\end{minipage}}
```

results in:

```
Some
text which I want to know
the width.
There can be
only one paragraph.
```

20.5   Font size

Gonzalo Medina Arellano asked on `ctt`:

Let's say I use 12pt as class option. How can I find the exact values of the size obtained with the standard commands `\tiny`*,* `\scriptsize`*, ...* `\huge`*, and* `\Huge`*?*

Several respondents, Bob Tennent [126] among them, suggested looking at the appropriate `.clo` file, such as `size12.clo` for the article or report classes 12pt option or `bk12.clo` for the book class, which lists the font and baseline sizes for the several size commands.

Dan Luecking [77] added to this saying [slightly edited]:

You can determine the current font size within a document without knowing what size command was last issued. The macro `\f@size` *holds the font size and is updated with each size change. You can print it with a macro like*

```
\makeatletter
  \newcommand*{\currentfontsize}{\f@size}
\makeatother
```

Then `\currentfontsize` *would print it and* `\typeout{\currentfontsize}` *would display it on the terminal screen and in the log file.*

In this document the normal fontsize is 10.

20.6   Long labels

Ernest posted to `comp.text.tex` saying [41]:

I'm trying to change the description environment, so that when labels exceed a certain length, the text following the label starts in the next line instead of starting in the same line. The LATEX Companion book explains how to do this, however when I've tried I've found that the lines that contain a long label are typeset a little bit too close to the previous line, not the usual baselineskip...

The standard `description` environment uses the command `\descriptionlabel` for setting the contents of the `\item` macro. The *Companion* [88, §3.3] describes various methods of modifying the standard layout by using a different definition for `\descriptionlabel` and/or creating a new kind of `description` list. Ernest's requirement can be met just by a modified version of `\descriptionlabel`, the default definition of which is:

```
\newcommand*{\descriptionlabel}[1]{%
  \hspace{\labelsep}%
  \normalfont\bfseries #1}
```

The following is an example of the default appearance of a `description` list:

Short A short label.

Longer label A longer label.

A very long label that exceeds the available width A long label with the text also longer than a single line.

Medium label The more typical length of a label and some text.

As you can easily see it does not handle long `\item` labels in a graceful manner.

This version of the `\descriptionlabel`, namely `\widedesclabel`, meets Ernest's requirements:

```
\usepackage{calc} % or xparse package
\newlength{\dlabwidth}
\newcommand*{\widedesclabel}[1]{%
  \settowidth{\dlabwidth}{\textbf{#1}}%
  \hspace{\labelsep}%
  \ifdim\dlabwidth>\columnwidth
    \parbox{\columnwidth-\labelsep}%
      {\textbf{#1}\strut}%
  \else
    \textbf{#1}%
  \fi}
\let\descriptionlabel\widedesclabel
```

which, when applied to the previous example results in:

Short A short label.

Longer label A longer label.

A very long label that exceeds the available width
    A long label with the text also longer than a single line.

Medium label The more typical length of a label and some text.

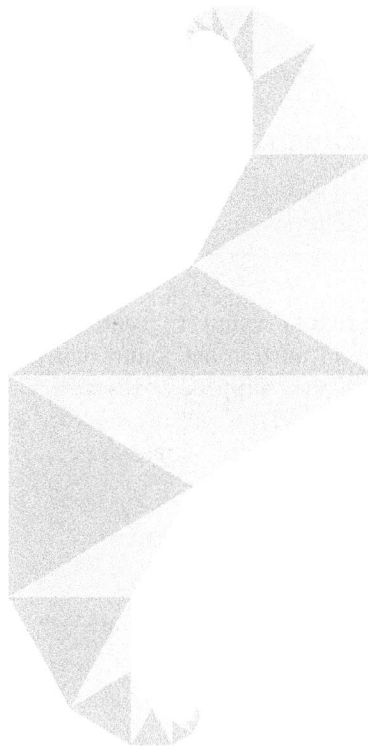

If our understanding have a film of
ignorance over it, or be blear with gazing or
other false glisterings, what is that to truth?

Of Reformation in England, JOHN MILTON

21.1 Ruling off

The lines are fallen unto me in pleasant
places; yea, I have a goodly heritage.

The Bible, Psalm 16, v. 6

Pujo wrote that he wanted to create a box with a line
at the top and bottom but found that the fancybox
package [131] only supplied boxes with all four sides
enclosed. Peter Flynn [49] responded with the following ruledbox, based on fancybox:

```
\documentclass{article}
\usepackage{fancybox,lipsum}
\newenvironment{ruledbox}{%
  \begin{Sbox}
    \begin{minipage}{\columnwidth}}{%
  \end{minipage}\end{Sbox}%
  \centering\medskip
  \vbox{\hrule height1pt
    \par\medskip
    \TheSbox
    \medskip\hrule height1pt}\par\medskip}
\begin{document}
\lipsum[1]

\begin{ruledbox}
\lipsum[2]
\end{ruledbox}
\lipsum[1]
\end{document}
```

Some text, but not as long as lipsum[2].

More text shorter than lipsum[1].

Sometime later I wondered if a box was really
needed, wouldn't just drawing a couple of rules do as
well? I came up with the ruled environment which
let you change the width of the ruled contents.

```
\newdimen\narrowsize
\newenvironment{ruled}[1][0pt]{%
  \par
```

```
  \narrowsize\hsize
  \advance\leftskip#1\advance\rightskip#1
  \advance\narrowsize-2\leftskip
  \noindent%
  \rule{\narrowsize}{3pt}\par
}{%
  \par\noindent
  \rule{\narrowsize}{1pt}
  \par}
```

The optional length argument to the environment
is the distance the left and right margins should be
increased, thus temporarily reducing the apparent
width of the textblock. The next paragraph is set
within \begin{ruled}[1pc] ... \end{ruled}.

The ruled environment produces a result
that might be a little too fancy for your taste,
in which case change the thickness of the rules.

On the other hand, a box will not break across a
page boundary which may be an advantage, but on
the whole I think not.

21.2 Marginal rules

We started off trying to set up a small
anarchist community, but people wouldn't
obey the rules.

Getting On, ALAN BENNET

David Arnold posed the following problem on ctt.

*I'd like to adjust my example environment in the
code below so that each example is bracketed between
two horizontal rules. The first rule should be placed
above the example, align with the inner edge of the
text and flow to the outer edge of the text, add a
couple of spaces in the outer margin, typeset 'You
Try It!', then continue to flow to within 1cm of the
page edge.*

*Similarly, for the rule at the bottom of the exam-
ple, I'd like to start it at the inner edge of the text,
flow into the outer margin, then typeset the square
that is flush right within 1cm of the paper edge.*

I'm not showing David's code here. Instead,
the below is effectively the code that I responded
with [151]. Drawing the rules across the textblock is

no problem. Also typesetting in the margins can be catered for by using the `\rlap` and `\llap` macros, in order to avoid LaTeX getting huffy about overlong lines. The only tedious part of the code is calculating the length of the two rules in the margin area. Hopefully the comments in the code explain sufficiently what is done in this regard.

```
\documentclass[twoside]{report}
\usepackage{lipsum}
\usepackage{amssymb}

\newcounter{example}[section]
\renewcommand{\theexample}{\arabic{example}}

%% insert lengths
\newdimen\uwidth
\newcommand*{\Utryit}{%
  \space\space You Try It!\space}
\settowidth{\uwidth}{\Utryit}
\newdimen\sqwidth
\newcommand*{\Usq}{{\Large$\square$}}
\settowidth{\sqwidth}{\Usq}

%% rule length in the oddpage margins =
%% paperwidth - textwidth - 1cm - 1in
%% - oddmargin - insert
% odd page rule lengths
\newdimen\uxtra  % Utryit
\newdimen\sqxtra % Square
\uxtra=\paperwidth
\advance\uxtra-\textwidth
\advance\uxtra-1cm
\advance\uxtra-1in
\advance\uxtra-\oddsidemargin
\sqxtra=\uxtra
\advance\uxtra-\uwidth
\advance\sqxtra\sqwidth

%% rule length in the evenpage margins =
%% 1in + evenmargin - 1cm - insert
\newdimen\uxtrav  % Utryit
\newdimen\sqxtrav % Square
\uxtrav=\evensidemargin
\advance\uxtrav 1in
\advance\uxtrav-1cm
\sqxtrav=\uxtrav
\advance\uxtrav-\uwidth
\advance\sqxtrav-\sqwidth

\makeatletter
\newenvironment{example}{%
\medskip\refstepcounter{example}%
\ifodd\c@page%     odd page
  \noindent\rule{\hsize}{3pt}%
    \rlap{\Utryit\rule{\uxtra}{3pt}}
\else
  \noindent\llap{\rule{\uxtrav}{3pt}\Utryit}%
    \rule{\hsize}{3pt}
```

```
\fi
\par\noindent\textbf{Example \theexample.}}%
{%
\ifodd\c@page
  \par\noindent\rule{\hsize}{1pt}%
  \rlap{\rule{\sqxtra}{1pt}
  \Usq}
\else
  \par\noindent\llap{\Usq\rule{\sqxtrav}{1pt}}%
    \rule{\hsize}{1pt}
\fi
  \par\medskip}
\makeatother

\begin{document}
\lipsum[1]
\begin{example}
\marginpar{Simplify: $33+28$}
\lipsum[2]
\end{example}
\lipsum[1]
\end{document}
```

The code just shown is intended for use in single column documents, and as *TUGboat* uses two columns it will not work here (account must be taken of which column the example is in). Extending it to cater for two columns is left as an exercise.

21.3 Preventing an awkward page break

Szabolcs Horvát requested help on `ctt`:
I would like to have an environment that starts and ends with a horizontal line (`\hrule`), with text in smaller type in between. The text may run several pages long. How can it be prevented that the page be broken right after the first `\hrule` or right before the last one?

As so often happens Donald Arseneau came up with an answer [15].
The answer to the question is easy: insert `\par` and `\nobreak` and `\@nobreaktrue`.

The tricky problem is getting the spacing right! `\hrule` causes normal `\baselineskip` to be omitted, but `\rule` takes a full baseline which leaves too much whitespace. Try this:

```
\makeatletter
\newenvironment{aside}{%
  \list{}{\leftmargin 5ex
          \rightmargin\leftmargin}
  \vtop{\hrule width\columnwidth}%
  \nobreak\@nobreaktrue
  \vspace{0.5ex}%
  \item\relax\small
}{%
```

```
\par\nobreak\@nobreaktrue
\advance\baselineskip -0.7ex
\vtop{\hrule width\columnwidth}%
\endlist}
\makeatother
```

I tried the `aside` environment and it worked even better than requested as it kept a rule and at least two lines of text together.

I haven't tried to combine the `aside` and `ruled` environments which I leave as an interesting exercise.

From a slightly different viewpoint, Nick Urbanik posted to `ctt` that he wanted to keep a list of items always on a single page [129]. In particular, to keep a question and its suggested answers together, where there was a list of questions each with its list of answers. There were some six respondents to Nick's request for help but the discussion for some reason veered from the `enumitem` package to the `titlesec` package that had no relevance to the initial posting. Donald Arseneau again provided a simple solution to the original problem [20], resulting in questions and answers for a possible accountant's interview being coded like:

```
\textbf{Accountancy test}
\begin{questions}
\Qitem What is $2+2$?
  \begin{enumerate}
  \item 3
  \item 4
  \item Whatever you want it to be.
  \end{enumerate}
\Qitem What is the essence of double-entry
      bookkeeping?
  \begin{enumerate}
  \item Each transaction recorded twice,
      in the credit and debit ledgers.
  \item Two sets of books, the real ones and
      the ones for the tax inspectors.
  \item Don't know.
  \end{enumerate}
\Qitem What ...
\end{questions}
```

When processed this will result in a question and all its potential answers being kept together on a page and, depending on their length, there may be several sets of questions and answers on a page.

Accountancy test

1. What is $2 + 2$?

    a) 3

    b) 4

    c) Whatever you want it to be.

2. What is the essence of double-entry bookkeeping?

    a) Each transaction recorded twice, in both the credit and debit ledgers.

    b) Two sets of books, the real ones and the ones for the tax inspectors.

    c) Don't know.

3. What ...

Donald's method to make this happen is:

```
\newcommand*{\Qitem}{\pagebreak[0]\item}
\newenvironment{questions}%
  {\enumerate\samepage}%
  {\endenumerate}
```

which says that the `questions` environment should be all on one page except that a page break is allowed just before a question's `\Qitem`.

21.4   Not at a page break

Sometimes it may be desirable to have a divisional marker of some kind disappear at a page break. I have forgotten the details but someone once had a supplement (with a title such as 'Notes') at the end of each chapter in the document and wanted to have a rule before the supplement unless the supplement started a new page.

A TeX *leader* is not a permissible breakpoint and may vanish at a page break and so provides a potential means of meeting such a requirement. Just before this paragraph I specified:

```
\newskip\rulebreakskip
  \rulebreakskip=\baselineskip
\newcommand*{\filler}{\hbox to \hsize{%
  \hss \rule{0.7\hsize}{1pt} \hss}\vskip 1pt}
\newcommand*{\rulebreak}{%
  \vskip\rulebreakskip
  \cleaders\filler
  \vskip\rulebreakskip}
\rulebreak
```

which resulted in either a centered rule or, if at the bottom of the column, nothing.

* * *

Just before this paragraph I specified:

```
\renewcommand*{\filler}{%
  \hbox to \hsize{\hss * * * \hss}}
\rulebreak
```

which resulted in either three centered asterisks or, if at the bottom of the column, nothing.

You can put different elements in the \filler box, such as an \asterism or a moustachio but you might have to adjust the value of \rulebreakskip for the best optical effect.

21.5 Line backing

'talazem' presented ctt with a problem that has never been completely solved in LATEX — namely typesetting to a grid. TEX was not designed with this in mind. Slightly edited, his presentation was:

I am typesetting a book in Memoir and want to ensure that the lines register well to avoid shine through. The book is mainly in English with a font size 10/12.5. However there are some paragraphs that are causing alignment problems.

There are some paragraphs that have to be set to a 0.8 ratio of the primary face with a 0.5 ratio of line spacing. There are others in a non-English typeface where the font is about 1.4 times bigger than the Roman font for the English text.

Paragraphs of this kind throw off the alignment of text lines on adjacent pages, and causing shine through on the recto and verso sides of a page.

The basic requirement here is that these irregular paragraphs should take up a space that is an integral number of the normal **\baselineskip**.

The one potential solution provided came from an exchange of views between Donald Arseneau and Dan Luecking [21], as follows, where the environment will occupy an integral number of the normal lines.

```
\makeatletter
\@ifundefined{@tempdimc}{\newdimen\@tempdimc}{}
\newenvironment{gridblock}{\par
  \setbox\@tempboxa\vtop\bgroup
}{\par\egroup
% measurement of top
  \@tempdima=\ht\@tempboxa
  \@tempdimc=\dp\@tempboxa
  \ifdim\@tempdima>\ht\strutbox
    \advance\@tempdimc\@tempdima
    \@tempdima=\ht\strutbox
% \@tempdima is the top height.
    \advance\@tempdimc-\@tempdima
  \fi
% measurement of bottom
  \setbox\@tempboxa\vbox{\unvbox\@tempboxa}%
  \ifdim\dp\@tempboxa>\dp\strutbox
```

```
    \@tempdimb=\dp\strutbox
  \else
    \@tempdimb=\dp\@tempboxa
  \fi
% \@tempdimb is the bottom depth.
  \advance\@tempdimc-\@tempdimb
% \@tempdimc is distance between the top
% and bottom baselines.
% The excess, \@tempcnta, is the number
% of baselines.
  \@tempcnta=\@tempdimc
  \divide\@tempcnta\baselineskip
  \advance\@tempdimc -\@tempcnta\baselineskip
  \ifdim\@tempdimc >2\vfuzz
    \advance\@tempdimc-\baselineskip \fi
  \divide\@tempdimc\tw@
  \vbox to\@tempdima{}%
  \nobreak \nointerlineskip
    \kern-\@tempdima \kern-\@tempdimc \nobreak
  \box\@tempboxa
  \nobreak \nointerlineskip
    \kern-\@tempdimb \kern-\@tempdimc \nobreak
  \hbox{\vrule
    height \z@ width \z@ depth \@tempdimb}}
\makeatother
```

The **gridblock** environment doesn't cater for footnotes, floats, or really anything other than plain text. It certainly does *not* handle page breaks.

This is \tiny text in the gridblock environment. I'm not sure how well the effect will be demonstrated as the adjacent column may, or may not, be evenly spaced vertically.

Did that work out? Are the lines in this paragraph aligned with those on the adjacent columns, or pages? If not it may be because the adjacent columns are not set on a grid. Incidentally, the relatively recent package **grid** may be of interest, though it is not a complete solution either.

21.6 Linespacing

Pander wrote [105]:

I have some questions on line spacing (leading) that should respect font size. It mainly concerns non-uniform line spacing that doesn't reserve space for ascenders and descenders and line spacing that is too big or too small for small and large font sizes.

Please see the following TeX [code] for the exact questions. I know this is tricky in TeX, but have to ask anyway.

```
\noindent
{\tiny aeou\\aeou\\}%too much leading
{\normalsize aeou\\aeou\\}
{\Huge aeou\\aeou\\}%not enough leading
{\tiny gpqy\\gpqy\\}%too much leading
{\normalsize gpqy\\gpqy\\}
```

aeou

aeou

aeou

aeou

aeou

aeou

gpqy

gpqy

gpqy

gpqy

gpqy

gpqy

bdfhkl

bdfhkl

bdfhkl

bdfhkl

bdfhkl

bdfhkl

gpqybdfhkl

gpqybdfhkl

gpqybdfhkl

gpqybdfhkl

gpqybdfhkl

gpqybdfhkl

Figure 21.1: Different font sizes in a paragraph: (left) Pander's problem; (right) following Donald Arseneau

```
{\Huge gpqy\\gpqy\\}%no space for descenders
{\tiny bdfhkl\\bdfhkl\\}%too much leading
{\normalsize bdfhkl\\bdfhkl\\}
{\Huge bdfhkl\\bdfhkl\\}%no space for ascenders
{\tiny gpqybdfhkl\\gpqybdfhkl\\}%too much leading
{\normalsize gpqybdfhkl\\gpqybdfhkl\\}
{\Huge gpqybdfhkl\\gpqybdfhkl\\}
```

The result of processing this is shown in the left side of Figure 21.1. Pander also noted a similar problem when using different fonts in a `tabular`.

There were several respondents all of whom noted that Pander's example consisted of a single paragraph within which the several font size changes were closed within groups. Further, that TeX takes the font size in effect at the end of a paragraph as applying throughout the paragraph, and hence that the leading is constant.

Donald Arseneau [19] replied with:
Set `\baselineskip=0pt` *or some small value*
Set `\lineskip=\lineskiplimit=` *desired space*

```
\baselineskip=8pt
\lineskip=4pt
\lineskiplimit=\lineskip
```

Then be aware that font-change commands reset `\baselineskip`, *so that font changes that span the end of a paragraph will go back to some larger* `\baselineskip`.

In `tabular` *put* `\strut` *in with all your variant fonts.*

Roughly speaking, the normal spacing between the baselines of text is `\baselineskip` but if the 'top' of a line is closer than `\lineskiplimit` to the bottom of the previous line then the spacing will be increased so that the top to bottom space is `\lineskip` [71, Ch. 12]. The results of applying Donald's settings are shown at the right of Figure 21.1.

Blasing markes are most shot at,
glistering faces chiefly marked

School of Abuse, STEPHEN GOSSON

22.1 Here or there

In a civil war, a general must know — and
I'm afraid it's a thing rather of instinct
than of practice — he must know exactly
when to move over to the other side.

*Not a Drum was Heard: The War
Memoirs of General Gland*, (unpublished
radio play, 1959) HENRY REED

Paul Kaletta asked on `ctt` [slightly edited]:

*I am writing a twoside document which means that
even and odd pages have different margins. Unfortunately all images I include are aligned with the left
side of the text on every page. Some of them are
broader than the line width and protrude into the
right margin, which is nice for odd pages, but looks
weird for even ones.*

*I would love to align the images to the inner mar-
gin, so that they always protrude to the outer one.
Is this possible?*

Heiko Oberdiek gave a solution so that an image would not exceed the width of the text plus the
marginpar area [102].

This has been a problem that has cropped up from
time to time on `ctt`. More generally the problem is
how to decide into which margin something should
be put, and then put it there. The code below for
the first problem is based on code that I wrote for my
memoir class. This version requires the `changepage`
package [147] for correctly deciding whether an odd
or even page is being typeset.[1]

The `\pikmargin` workhorse macro, used for specifying a margin, takes one argument which must be
one of: `left`, `right`, `outer`, or `inner`. The result
is `\pkmarg` which is in the range 0–3 for the allowed
arguments, otherwise it is −1. The code is rather
tedious.

```
\usepackage{changepage}
\newcommand*{\pikmargin}[1]{\bgroup
```

---

[1]Because of the asynchronous nature of TeX's page
breaking algorithm, simply checking the page number does
not always lead to the correct result. The `changepage`
macros are an integral part of `memoir`.

```
\def\targ{#1}\def\parg{left}%
\ifx\targ\parg
  \gdef\pkmarg{0}%
\else
  \def\parg{right}%
  \ifx\targ\parg
    \gdef\pkmarg{1}%
  \else
    \def\parg{outer}%
    \ifx\targ\parg
      \gdef\pkmarg{2}%
    \else
      \def\parg{inner}%
      \ifx\targ\parg
        \gdef\pkmarg{3}%
      \else
        \gdef\pkmarg{-1}%
      \fi
    \fi
  \fi
\fi
\egroup}
```

The `\settheside` workhorse macro takes one argument, the value of `\pkmarg` from `\pikmargin`,
and sets `\ifputatright` TRUE or FALSE according
to whether material should be put into the right or
left margin. The basic algorithm is:

1. A negative argument is converted to 2 (outer).

2. For two columns always the nearest margin.

3. For one sided documents:

   0 (left) FALSE

   not 0 (all else) TRUE

4. For two sided documents:

   0 (left) FALSE

   1 (right) TRUE

   2 (outer) TRUE on an odd page and FALSE on
   an even page

   3 (inner) FALSE on an odd page and TRUE on
   an even page

The code is tedious, even more so than for the previous macro.

```
\newif\ifputatright
\makeatletter
\newcommand*{\settheside}[1]{%
  \def\m@rgcode{#1}%
  \ifnum #1<0\relax
    %% error! write message and set to 'outer'
  \typeout{Error! arg is '#1'. Set to 'outer'}%
    \def\m@rgcode{2}%
  \fi
  \if@twocolumn
    \if@firstcolumn
      \putatrightfalse
    \else
      \putatrighttrue
    \fi
  \else
    \checkoddpage%  from the changepage package
    \if@twoside
      \ifcase\m@rgcode\relax
        \putatrightfalse
      \or%    1 = left
        \putatrighttrue
      \or%    2 = outer
        \ifoddpage
          \putatrighttrue
        \else
          \putatrightfalse
        \fi
      \or%    3 = inner
        \ifoddpage
          \putatrightfalse
        \else
          \putatrighttrue
        \fi
      \fi
    \else%   1-sided
      \ifnum\m@rgcode=0\relax
        \putatrightfalse
      \else
        \putatrighttrue
      \fi
    \fi
  \fi}
\makeatother
```

You can use the \pikmargin and \settheside macros directly but in case there might be more than one kind of material to be put into the margins it is better to be conservative and use them indirectly.

With the two workhorse macros in hand, here is code for letting overwide images extend a particular distance, \ximwidth, into the margin.

\pikimagemargin is for selecting the margin for a wide image. The margin code is stored as \pkimg.

```
% \usepackage{graphicx} need this package
\newcommand*{\pikimagemargin}[1]{%
  \pikmargin{#1}%
  \ifnum \pkmarg<0\relax
```

```
    %% error! write message and set to 'outer'
    %% or perhaps to something more appropriate
  \typeout{Error! arg is '#1'. Set to 'outer'}%
    \def\pkimg{2}%
  \else
    \let\pkimg\pkmarg
  \fi}
```

The next bit of code sets the maximum width for an image.

```
\newdimen\ximwidth% extra width
\newdimen\maximwidth% max total width
\makeatletter
\newcommand*{\maxiw}{%   MAX Image Width
  \ifdim\Gin@nat@width>\maximwidth
    \maximwidth
  \else
    \Gin@nat@width
  \fi}
\makeatother
```

An external image is included by calling \MaxImage which is a wrapper around the regular graphicx package's \includegraphics macro and takes the same arguments, except for the optional width argument which is supplied internally.

```
\newcommand*{\MaxImage}[2][]{%
  \par\noindent
  \settheside{\pkimg}%
  \ifputatright
  \else
    \hspace{0pt minus \ximwidth}% move left
  \fi
  \includegraphics[{#1,width=\maxiw}]{#2}%
  \ifputatright
    \hspace{0pt minus \ximwidth}%
  \fi
  \par}
```

The general user scheme is:

```
%% set the dimensions
\setlength{\maximwidth}{\textwidth}
\setlength{\ximwidth}{\marginparwidth}
\addtolength{\maximwidth}{\ximwidth}
%% specify the margin (say the outer)
\pikimagemargin{outer}
...
%% image may be in a figure, but need not be
\begin{figure}
\centering
\MaxImage[height=\textheight,
          keepaspectratio]{myimage}
\caption{...}
\end{figure}
```

22.2 Parallel texts

22.2.1 Opposites

> To do just the opposite is also a form of imitation.
>
> *Aphorismen*, GEORG CHRISTOPH LICHTENBERG

On occasion somebody wants to set two documents in parallel on facing pages. This is typically in the form of an original in one language on even numbered pages and a translation in another language on the facing odd numbered pages. The ledpar package [144] is designed for this purpose, enabling individual line numbering and multiple footnotes on the parallel pages.[2] But sometimes this may be overkill. Stephen Hicks [62] presented a method in response to a query on texhax, where it didn't matter if one of the texts was much longer than the other (if necessary the shorter text being 'completed' with blank pages). He explained his basic algorithm as:

1. *Load both documents into separate boxes (i.e., galleys)*
   ```
   \setbox\left@box\vbox\bgroup
       \input left\egroup
   \setbox\right@box\vbox\bgroup
       \input right\egroup
   ```
   This might lead to difficulties if anything in the documents have, say, \eject or anything else weird re: page handling, or it might just work if the whatsits behave well inside boxes.

2. *Alternately* \vsplit *off* \textheight *from each box and* \unvbox *it into the current page, followed by a* \clearpage.

Stephen's code for implementing this was as follows, except that I have made a minor change described later, and exercised some editorial privilege.

```
\documentclass{report}% or other class
...
\makeatletter
\newbox\left@box \newbox\right@box
\newenvironment{leftpage}{%
  \global\setbox\left@box\vbox\bgroup}%
  {\egroup}
\newenvironment{rightpage}{%
  \global\setbox\right@box\vbox\bgroup}%
  {\egroup}
\def\alternate{%\cleardoublepage
  \cleartostart
```

```
  \let\@next\@alternate
  \ifdim\ht\left@box=\z@\ifdim\ht\right@box=\z@
    \let\@next\relax\fi\fi
  \@next}
\def\@unvsplit#1{\ifdim\ht#1=\z@\vbox{}\else
  \setbox\z@\vsplit#1 to\textheight\unvbox\z@
  \fi}
\def\@alternate{\@unvsplit\left@box\eject
  \@unvsplit\right@box\eject\alternate}
\makeatother
...
\begin{document} ...
\begin{leftpage}
\input{lefttext}
\end{leftpage}
\begin{rightpage}
\input{righttext}
\end{rightpage}
\alternate
... \end{document}
```

As Stephen said, there are limits to what can be successfully included in the parallel texts. For example, footnotes may throw things out of kilter and page headings can get out of sync if they are changed inside either of the texts by, say, including some \sections.

The technical change I made was replacing the macro \cleardoublepage with the new one named \cleartostart. This is called just before the left–right printing starts. With \cleardoublepage the left text starts on an odd page and continues on odd pages while the right text then starts on the following even page. It seems more logical to me that the left text should start on an even numbered page, this being the left of a two-page spread. The standard \clearpage moves to the next page, which may be odd or even, while the \cleardoublepage moves to the next odd page. The \cleartostart macro, which is based on \cleartoevenpage from the memoir class [142], moves to the next even page.

```
\newcommand*{\cleartostart}{\clearpage
  \ifodd\c@page\hbox{}\newpage\fi}
```

22.2.2 Equals

> The true virtue of human beings is fitness to live together as equals.
>
> *The Subjection of Women*, JOHN STUART MILL

Thomas Thurman, who described himself as a poet and programmer, posted to ctt saying [128]:

> *I have a particular typesetting task, described below. Can you tell me whether it's possible in TeX without major upheaval? (Pointers as to how it's*

---

[2]Since the original column was published the ledpar package has been transmuted into the reledmac package [120] by Maïeul Rouquette.

possible are welcomed, but at the moment I want to check that it's possible at all.)

I have two source documents P and Q. P consists (as you might expect) of a series of words separated by spaces and punctuation. Q consists of exactly the same number of entirely different words, but separated by the same punctuation. The words may not necessarily be the same length, but there will be the same number of them.

So P might run "I am (of course) shocked! and appalled!" and Q might run "We drink (in summer) lemonade! and Pimms!"

What I want to do is to turn P and Q into a TeX document that either:

- consists of two columns per page, the left from P and the right from Q, but on each line the number of words in each column is the same. (So if there are five words from the P column on the first line, there are five words from the Q column on the first line.)
or

- consists of pages alternately from P and Q, but for each line the number of words on that line is equal to the number of words on the same line on the facing page.

Either is a good solution. (Both would be wonderful.)

Of course if P has a run of long words then the matching Q line will contain a lot of whitespace. This is quite all right.

This resulted in a conversation between Bruno Le Floch and Jean-François Burnol ending with essentially the following code from Jean-François [25] (I have edited it slightly to better fit the two-column format). I can't explain how it works any better than what you see.

```
\makeatletter
% ======== Some helper macros
\let\xpf\expandafter
\def\addtobuff#1#2{\xpf\def\xpf#1%
               \xpf{#1 #2}}
\long\def\ifneitherempty#1#2{%
  \xpf\ifx\xpf a\detokenize{#1}a%
    \xpf\@gobble
  \else
    \xpf\ifx\xpf a\detokenize{#2}a%
      \xpf\xpf\xpf\@gobble
    \else
      \xpf\xpf\xpf\@firstofone
    \fi
  \fi}
```

```
% ======== Splitting into paragraphs

\long\def\longsbs #1#2{%
  \longsbs@aux #1\par\Q #2\par\Q}
```

```
\long\def%
\longsbs@aux #1\par#2\Q #3\par#4\Q{%
  \sidebyside{#1}{#3}% do one paragraph
  \bigskip % space between paragraphs
  % If either is empty, we're done
  % else do "\sidebyside"
  \ifneitherempty{#2}{#4}%
  {\longsbs@aux #2\Q #4\Q
  }}
```

```
% ======== Splitting at each space

\def\sbs@parse #1 #2 \Q #3 #4 \Q{%
  \sbs@step{#1}{#3}%
  % if either text is empty,
  % we are (almost) done
  % else continue
  \ifneitherempty{#2}{#4}%
  {\sbs@parse #2 \Q #4 \Q}}
```

```
% ======= Checking the size of each line
% ======= and printing it when it's ready

\newif\ifsbs@break
\def\sbs@step#1#2{%
    \setbox1=\hbox{\sbs@buffi{} #1}%
    \setbox2=\hbox{\sbs@buffii{} #2}%
    \ifdim\wd1>.4\hsize\sbs@breaktrue\else
    \ifdim\wd2>.4\hsize\sbs@breaktrue\else
    \sbs@breakfalse\fi\fi
    \ifsbs@break\sbs@writeline%
      \def\sbs@buffi{#1}%
      \def\sbs@buffii{#2}%
    \else
      \addtobuff\sbs@buffi{#1}%
      \addtobuff\sbs@buffii{#2}%
    \fi}
```

```
\def\sbs@writeline{%
    \hbox to \hsize{\hss%
        \hbox to .4\hsize{\pr@buffi}%
        \hskip.1\hsize%
        \hbox to .4\hsize{\pr@buffii}%
    \hss}}
```

```
% ========= Master function

\def\sidebyside#1#2{%
    \def\sbs@buffi{\noindent}%
    \def\sbs@buffii{\noindent}%
    \sbs@parse #1 \Q #2 \Q
    \sbs@writeline% flush the last line
}
```

I have added the following code so that the user can specify if the left and right texts are to be set flush left ([l]), centered (the default) or flush right ([r]).

```
\newcommand*{\setsbsleft}[1][c]{%
  \def\pr@buffi{\hfill\sbs@buffi\hfill}%
```

```
\def\@tempa{#1}\def\@tempb{l}
  \ifx\@tempb\@tempa
    \def\pr@buffi{\sbs@buffi\hfill}%
  \else
    \def\@tempb{r}%
    \ifx\@tempb\@tempa
      \def\pr@buffi{\hfill\sbs@buffi}%
    \fi
  \fi}
\newcommand*{\setsbsright}[1][c]{%
  \def\pr@buffii{\hfill\sbs@buffii\hfill}%
\def\@tempa{#1}\def\@tempb{l}
  \ifx\@tempb\@tempa
    \def\pr@buffii{\sbs@buffii\hfill}%
  \else
    \def\@tempb{r}%
    \ifx\@tempb\@tempa
      \def\pr@buffii{\hfill\sbs@buffii}%
    \fi
  \fi}

%% center the texts
\setsbsleft
\setsbsright
\makeatother
```

The following is a short example of using the \longsbs macro which, unfortunately, may have difficulties if either of its arguments includes any macros. In this case the texts are set flush right and flush left.

```
\setsbsleft[r]
\setsbsright[l]
\longsbs {%
    I am (of course) ...

    Can you tell ...
}{%
    We drink (in summer) ...

    P consists ...
}
```

I am (of course) shocked! and appalled! I have a particular typesetting task, described herein.	We drink (in summer) lemonade! and Pimms! I have two source documents P and Q.
Can you tell me whether it's possible in TeX ... at all.	P consists (as you might expect) of a series ... same punctuation.

22.3 Abort the compilation

> Eternity's a terrible thought. I mean, where's it all going to end?
>
> *Rosencrantz and Guildenstern are Dead,*
> Tom Stoppard

Rasmus Villemoes wrote to ctt [133]:

I have a document which is only meant to be typeset using pdflatex. It is rather large, and the first pdf-only stuff doesn't occur until quite late. So if one accidentally compiles with latex *it takes a couple of minutes before the error is discovered. I would therefore like to insert some code shortly after* \documentclass *which aborts the compilation with an error message unless running under pdflatex.*

Both Lars Madsen and Heiko Oberdiek replied and the following code is a merge and extension of their responses. The definition of \abort is from Heiko and following a comment by Lars I included using the ifxetex package [113][3] in addition to the originally suggested ifpdf package [96] as both pdflatex and xelatex generate pdf output.

```
\documentclass[...]{...}
\usepackage{ifpdf}
\usepackage{ifxetex}
\newcommand*{\abort}{}
\ifpdf\else
  \ifxetex\else
    \typeout{You must be in PDF mode.
      Use pdflatex (or xelatex) instead.}
    \def\abort{\csname @@end\endcsname}
%   or \def\abort{\stop}
  \fi
\fi
\abort
...
\begin{document}
...
```

If desired, it would be simple to recast this as a package (a .sty file), which is what Lars exemplified in his response.

---

[3] As of 2019, the iftex package subsumes ifxetex and several other similar packages, providing many kinds of engine conditionals.

Plain as the glistering planets shine
When winds have cleaned the skies,
Her love appeared, appealed for mine,
And wantoned in her eyes.

Songs of Travel, ROBERT LOUIS STEVENSON

23.1 Longest string

The chief defect of Henry King
Was chewing little bits of string.

Cautionary Tales, HILLAIRE BELLOC

Romildo wrote to `comp.text.tex` saying that he tried to implement a macro for determining the longest string in a list but was having problems with the code [118]. Romildo's user view of the macro (\Widest) was like this:

```
\newdimen\mydimen
\def\Format#1{{\itshape\tiny #1}}
\Widest{\mydimen}{\Format}{Good,morning,world}
\the\mydimen
```

There were several responses, including ones from GL [54] and Heiko Oberdiek [101] who got into a bit of a discussion about their suggested solutions, partly because GL preferred the strings to look like multiple arguments (e.g., {a}{bbb}{cc}) and Heiko appeared to lean more towards a single argument with the strings being separated by commas (e.g., (a,bbb,cc)).

GL suggested (I have used \Widestg for GL's macro and \Widesth for Heiko's to distinguish between them):

```
\makeatletter
\newskip\result
\def\Widestg#1#2#3\Widestg{% #1 = Format
  \setbox\z@\hbox{#1{#2}}%
  \ifdim\wd\z@>\result
    \result\wd\z@
    \edef\longest{#2}% % added by PW
    \def\flong{{#1{\longest}}}% % added by PW
  \fi
  \ifx\relax#2\else
    \Widestg{#1}#3\Widestg
  \fi}
\makeatother
...
\result=0pt
```

```
\Widestg{\textbf}{one}{two}{three}\relax\Widestg
\the\result \\
\longest\ \the\result\\      % added by PW
\flong\ \the\result          % added by PW
```

I added the code for \longest which contains the longest string and \flong to typeset it using the specified format. This code, applying the macro to the list {one}{two}{three}, results in:

26.13898pt
three 26.13898pt
three 26.13898pt

Heiko's version uses the kvsetkeys package [99] for parsing a comma-separated list where spaces at the beginning and end of an entry are ignored.

```
\usepackage{kvsetkeys}
\newcommand*{\Format}[1]{\textit{\tiny #1}}
\newlength\WidestResult
\makeatletter
\@ifdefinable{\Widesth}{%
  \def\Widesth#1#2(#3){%
    #1=\z@ % 0 pt
    \comma@parse{#3}{%
      \settowidth\dimen@{#2{\comma@entry}}%
      \ifdim#1<\dimen@
        #1=\dimen@
        \edef\longest{\comma@entry}% PW added
        \def\flong{#2{\longest}}%   PW added
      \fi
      \@gobble % ignore list entry argument
    }%
  }%
}
\makeatother
...
\Widesth{\WidestResult}{\Format}(Good,morning,
                                  world)
\the\WidestResult \\
\longest\ \the\WidestResult\\    % added by PW
\flong\ \the\WidestResult        % added by PW
```

Just as with \Widestg I added the \longest and \flong code. Note that the comma-separated list of strings is enclosed in parentheses and not braces. The result from Heiko's example is:

25.97304pt

morning 25.97304pt

morning 25.97304pt

Applying GL's macro to Romildo's example as:

```
\result=0pt
\Widestg{\tiny\textit}{Good}{morning}
               {world}\relax\Widestg
\longest\ \the\result \\
\flong\ \the\result
```

results in:

morning 25.97304pt

morning 25.97304pt

which is the same as that from `\Widesth`.

Although both macros give the same result I prefer Heiko's user interface to GL's, but then you may think it should be the other way round.

23.2 Marching along

> Tear along the dotted line.
>
> *Instruction*, ANONYMOUS

23.2.1 Oddment

On `ctt` Roger said that he was
... planning to take a string of the form mm.nn.pp where mm, nn, and pp are all integers, and test if pp is odd. So I'd like to write a macro that does that and use that as the parameter to `\ifodd`.

Joseph Wright responded [155] that it sounded as though he wanted something like:

```
\makeatletter
\newcommand*{\MyFunction}[1]{%
  \My@function#1..\@nil\@stop}
\def\My@function#1.#2.#3#4\@stop{%
  \def\My@mm{#1}%
  \def\My@nn{#2}%
  \def\My@pp{}%
  \ifx#3\@nil\else
    \My@function@#3#4
  \fi
% 0 below makes the test work when
% \My@pp is empty
  \ifodd0\My@pp\relax
    Odd
  \else
    Even
  \fi}
\def\My@function@#1..\@nil{\def\My@pp{#1}}
\makeatother
...
\MyFunction{11.22.33}
```

```
\MyFunction{11.22.44}
\MyFunction{11.22.}
\MyFunction{11}
```

With Joseph's code, running his suggested test examples results in:

Odd   Even   Even   Even

Quite frankly, I do not understand just how his code works. In order to get a better feel for it I decided to write my own macros for dot-separated lists of one, two, and three numbers and then try to extend them to deal with a list of arbitrary extent. Here are my efforts for the one, two, and three length lists. I included some diagnostic output to help when my code didn't work as I thought that it should.

Firstly, here are the code shorthands that I have used for the diagnostics — the `\cs` macro is defined in the ltugboat class, as shown.

```
%\DeclareRobustCommand\cs[1]{%
%   \texttt{\char`\\#1}}
\newcommand*{\sarg}[1]{\texttt{\{#1\}}}
\newcommand*{\csparg}[2]{\cs{#1}\sarg{#2}}
\newcommand*{\LRA}{%
  \ensuremath{\Longrightarrow} }
```

For a single number the command is:
`\MyFunctionI{⟨N⟩}`

```
\newcommand*{\MyFunctionI}[1]{%
  \csparg{MyFunctionI}{#1} \LRA
  \ifodd0#1\relax
    #1 Odd
  \else
    #1 Even
  \fi}
```

Some example results are:

MyFunctionI (11) $\Longrightarrow$ 11 Odd
MyFunctionI (22) $\Longrightarrow$ 22 Even
MyFunctionI () $\Longrightarrow$ Even

For a list of two numbers the command is:
`\MyFunctionII{⟨N.N⟩}`

```
\makeatletter
\newcommand*{\MyFunctionII}[1]{%
  \csparg{MyFunctionII}{#1} \LRA
  \My@FunctionII#1\@nil
  \ifodd0\My@last\relax
    \My@last\ Odd
  \else
    \My@last\ Even
  \fi}
```

```
\def\My@FunctionII#1.#2\@nil{%
  \def\My@last{#2}}
\makeatother
```

Example results are:

MyFunctionII (11.22) $\implies$ 22 Even
MyFunctionII (11.33) $\implies$ 33 Odd
MyFunctionII (11.) $\implies$ Even

For a list of three numbers the command is:
`\MyFunctionIII{`$\langle N.N.N\rangle$`}`

```
\makeatletter
\newcommand*{\MyFunctionIII}[1]{%
  \csparg{MyFunctionIII}{#1} \LRA
  \My@FunctionIII#1\@nil
  \ifodd0\My@last\relax
    \My@last\ Odd
  \else
    \My@last\ Even
  \fi}
\def\My@FunctionIII#1.#2.#3\@nil{%
  \def\My@last{#3}}
\makeatother
```

Some results are:

MyFunctionIII (11.22.33) $\implies$ 33 Odd
MyFunctionIII (11.22.44) $\implies$ 44 Even
MyFunctionIII (11.33.) $\implies$ Even

Based on the underlying idea—delimited arguments [2, 38, 71, 148]—of the above macros I then tried to develop one that would take a dot-separated list of any length and return whether the last number was odd or even.

I failed.

Eventually I remembered that the LaTeX kernel includes an `\@for` macro for marching along a comma-separated list of elements and decided to try and create a version that would handle dot-separated lists. It is effectively a copy of the `\@for` code replacing every ',' with a '.'. I can't pretend to understand how it works. I have named it `\@ford` as shorthand for `'\@fordot-separated-list'`.

```
\makeatletter
% \@ford NAME := LIST \do {BODY}
\long\def\@ford#1:=#2\do#3{%
  \expandafter\def\expandafter\@fortmp
  \expandafter{#2}%
  \ifx\@fortmp\@empty \else
    \expandafter
    \@forloopd#2.\@nil.\@nil\@@#1{#3}
  \fi}
```

```
\long\def\@forloopd#1.#2.#3\@@#4#5{%
  \def#4{#1}\ifx #4\@nnil \else
    #5\def#4{#2}\ifx #4\@nnil
      \else #5\@iforloopd #3\@@#4{#5}\fi\fi}
```

```
\long\def\@iforloopd#1.#2\@@#3#4{%
  \def#3{#1}\ifx #3\@nnil
    \expandafter \@fornoop \else
    #4\relax
    \expandafter\@iforloopd\fi#2\@@#3{#4}}
\makeatother
```

I did use this for a macro to handle unlimited length lists of the kind that Roger was interested in. Then there was a further posting from him [116] in response to Joseph (which I have abbreviated):

Thank you. That works (and was quite educational). However, I failed to completely specify my problem ...

Here's what I have:
`{a.b.c, x.y.z}` *or*
`{x.y.z}` *or*
`{, x.y.z}`
where `a,b,c`, `x,y,z` *are integers.*

What I would like to do is to be able to set a switch in the file that if set then the ... would be included only if `z` *is odd, but if the switch is not set then all ... will be included.*

This requirement seemed to me to be a candidate for a combination of `\@for` to handle the comma-separated parts and `\@ford` for the portions that are dot-separated.

Below is what I ended up with to handle an unlimited comma-separated list of unlimited dot-separated lists determining whether the last entry of all is odd or even.

First the `\DotFunction` for a dot-separated list of numbers. I have added some diagnostic print out just in case together with a means (`\ifop`) for enabling it. The macro is called like:
`\DotFunction{`$\langle N.N.N...N\rangle$`}`
and sets `\gotoddtrue` if the last number in the list is odd.

```
\newif\ifgotodd
\newif\ifop
\optrue
```

```
\makeatletter
\def\DotFunction#1{%
  \ifop \csparg{DotFunction}{#1} \LRA \fi
  \def\My@last{0}% in case arg is empty
  \@ford\scratch:=#1\do{%
    \edef\My@last{\scratch}}%
  \ifodd0\My@last\relax
    \gotoddtrue
    \ifop \My@last\ Odd \fi
```

```
\else
  \gotoddfalse
  \ifop \My@last\ Even \fi
\fi}
\makeatother
```

Some example results are:

```
DotFunction () ⟹ 0 Even
DotFunction (11) ⟹  11 Odd
DotFunction (11.22) ⟹  22 Even
DotFunction (11.22.33) ⟹  33 Odd
DotFunction (11.22.33.44) ⟹  44 Even
DotFunction (11.nowt.33.44.55) ⟹  55 Odd
DotFunction (11..33.44.55) ⟹  55 Odd
\newcommand*{\numM}{11.22.33.44.55.66.77}
\DotFunction{\numM} ⟹
DotFunction (11.22.33.44.55.66.77) ⟹  77 Odd
```

Note that for \DotFunction, only the last element in the list must be an integer (or blank), earlier elements can be, for example, text. Further, unlike all the previous \MyFunction... macros, the argument may be a macro.

Finally, here is the end of the exercise — a generalised solution to Roger's requests, called as \HisFunction{⟨N.N...N, N...N, ..., N...N⟩}.

```
\makeatletter
\def\DotCommaFunction#1{%
\csparg{DotCommaFunction}{#1} \LRA
\opfalse % stop \DotFunction printing
  \@for\first:=#1\do{%
    \DotFunction{\first}}%
  \ifgotodd
\My@last\ Odd
  \else
\My@last\ Even
  \fi}
\makeatother
```

Some results of using \DotCommaFunction:

```
DotCommaFunction (1.2.3, 4.5.7) ⟹  7 Odd
DotCommaFunction (, 4.5.7) ⟹  7 Odd
DotCommaFunction (4.5.7) ⟹  7 Odd
DotCommaFunction (1, 2.3, , 4.5, 7.8) ⟹  8 Even
DotCommaFunction (1,2.3, ,4.5,7.8) ⟹  8 Even
```

All that remains is for the user to make appropriate changes to the actions of the odd/even result and to eliminate, or change, the diagnostic outputs to suit the application at hand.

23.2.2 Indexing into a list

Alastair asked [5]:

I've got a question about comma separated lists. Is there any way that you can index elements in a list. Lists can be iterated over in the PGF/TikZ package's \foreach *loop. How can you access an element whilst not in a loop?*

Often responses to questions on ctt provide the bare bones of a solution, leaving the questioner to adapt or extend it to his own situation. There were several responses and the one I found that would best suit me was from Ulrike Fischer [44]. The following is essentially Ulrike's code, edited to better fit the column:

```
\usepackage{tikz}
\def\values{i5, i4, i3, i2, i1}
\newcounter{loc}
\newcommand{\getitem}[1]{%
  \setcounter{loc}{0}
  \foreach \x in \values{%
    \stepcounter{loc}%
    \expandafter\xdef\csname
      alsval\the\value{loc}\endcsname{\x}}%
  \csname alsval#1\endcsname}
```

Ulrike's \getitem{⟨N⟩} macro returns the item that is in the ⟨N⟩th location in \values as \alsvalN. With:

```
\getitem{1}, \getitem{4}, \getitem{8}.
```

the result is:

i5, i2, .

I wondered if there was a solution that did not involve calling the tikz package and came up with the following which does not require any packages, being based on the LaTeX kernel's \@for construct.

```
\let\xpf\expandafter % just to save some space
\makeatletter
\newcount\vindex
\newcommand*{\getit}[2]{%
  \xpf\xpf\xpf\@getit\xpf{#2}{#1}%
  \theans}

\newcommand*{\@getit}[2]{%
  \vindex=0
  \def\theans{[index #2 out of range]}%
  \xdef\alist{#1}%
  \@for\tmp := #1 \do{%
    \advance\vindex 1\relax
    \ifnum\vindex=#2\relax
      \xdef\theans{\tmp}%
    \fi}}
\makeatother
```

The macro `\getit{`⟨*N*⟩`}{`⟨*list*⟩`}` returns `\theans` as the value of the ⟨*N*⟩th item in the ⟨*list*⟩ where ⟨*list*⟩ may be either a comma-separated list or a macro defined as one. I have included a check on whether ⟨*N*⟩ is valid for the given list (this would be better in the form of an error report in the `log` file external to the document instead of being typeset).

With these inputs (and the previous definition of `\values`)

```
\getit{1}{\values},
\getit{4}{\values},
\getit{8}{\values},
\getit{9}{\values}.

\getit{1}{i5, i4, i3, i2, i1},
\getit{4}{i5, i4, i3, i2, i1},
\getit{8}{i5, i4, i3, i2, i1}.

\getit{1}{i5,i4,i3,i2,i1},
\getit{4}{i5,i4,i3,i2,i1},
\getit{9}{i5,i4,i3,i2,i1}.
```

the results are:

> i5, i2, [index 8 out of range], [index 9 out of range].
> i5, i2, [index 8 out of range].
> i5, i2, [index 9 out of range].

The key problem that I had to solve in my method is that the 'list' that `\@for` operates on must be an actual sequence of comma-separated items and not a macro defined as such a list. That is why I have separated the code into two macros. The first to grab the list, be it actual or as a macro, and then to hand that over to `\@getit` as an actual list by utilising a series of `\expandafter`s within `\getit`.[1]

It is important to note that the internal `\@for` takes account of any spaces in the list. Above I have provided examples of comma separated lists with and without spaces so that you can see the difference; specifically, the `\getit{4}` in the second line of output has a preceding space because that is present in the list of input values, which is not the case for the last line of output. Adding `\ignorespaces` before `\tmp` in the definition of `\theans` would remove such leading spaces, if desired.

---

[1] `\expandafter` and when it should be used is to me among the more difficult aspects of TeX code. I usually come to a solution by either following what others have done in similar circumstances or by much experimentation — otherwise known as errors and trials.

23.3 A blank argument

> The tumult and the shouting dies,
> The captains and the kings depart,
> And we are left with large supplies
> Of cold blancmange and rhubarb tart.
>
> *After the Party*, RONALD KNOX

The title of a posting by Matthew to `texhax` was *Finding blank argument to a macro*. There is a long history behind this kind of macro, initially posed as a challenge in Michael Downes' *Around the Bend* [37] series in the early 90s, and without looking any further I assumed that the solution would be the `ifmtarg` [22] package which provides a test as to whether a macro argument consists of zero or more blank spaces.

However, I was mistaken, as Matthew's posting continued [84]:

I am trying to solve a problem in LaTeX that I thought would be relatively straightforward. I would like to make a macro that will evaluate its argument and tell me whether the result is blank or not ... I managed to come up with a TeX macro that handles different types of 'blank' pretty well. It properly recognizes an empty argument, empty braces, spaces, etc. It even works on another macro that evaluates to a blank, so I thought I was home free. However, as soon as I fed it a macro that takes an argument, bad things happen. I've attached a simple document below that shows the problem.

The 'simple document' contains many lines of code implementing his `\blankArgTest{`⟨*arg*⟩`}`, together with examples of when it worked and when it didn't give the required result. With the macros:

```
\usepackage{ifthen}
\newcommand{\testA}{%
  \ifnum10=10 \empty\else A\fi}
\newcommand{\testB}{%
  \ifthenelse{10=10}{\empty}{B}}
\newcommand{\testC}[1]{%
  \ifnum#1=10 \empty\else C\fi}
```

`\blankArgTest` worked when ⟨*arg*⟩ was `\testA` but failed for `\testB` and `\testC`.

Michael Barr [23] came up with a remarkably simple solution which I am presenting as:

```
\newcommand{\IfBlank}[1]{%
  \setbox0\hbox{$#1$}%
  \ifdim\wd0=0pt
    Blank
  \else
    Not blank
  \fi}
```

The basic idea is to put the argument into math material inside an `\hbox` and check if the box's width is zero. Math mode causes the spaces to be ignored.[2] (For full generality `\mathsurround` must also be set to zero, but we won't worry about that here.) This assumes that a 'blank' argument is one that results in no typeset material (or rather, anything typeset ends with zero width). With the following definitions:

```
\newcommand{\blank}{ }
\newcommand{\tout}{\typeout{Typeout}}
```

example uses of the `\IfBlank` macro are:

```
\IfBlank{} Blank
\IfBlank{   } Blank
\IfBlank{Text} Not blank
\IfBlank{\blank} Blank
\IfBlank{\tout} Blank
\IfBlank{{ }} Blank
\testA Blank
\testB Blank
\testC{10} Blank
```

A somewhat different need for an empty/blank argument was expressed by Timothy Murphy who wrote [93]:

I have a macro `\cmd#1#2` *. Both arguments are given in the form* {...}*. I'd like an empty second argument* {} *to be added if none is given, i.e., if the next character after* `\cmd{...}` *is not* { *.*

What is the simplest way to do this?

There were three interesting proposed solutions which I have given below.[3]

Heiko Oberdiek's was the first positive response and was essentially as follows [100] defining `\CmdH`:

```
\newcommand*{\CmdH}[1]{%
  \begingroup
  % remember parameter
  \toks0={#1}%
  % look forward
  \futurelet\NextToken\CmdI}
\newcommand*{\CmdI}{%
  \ifx\NextToken\bgroup
    \edef\next{\endgroup
      \noexpand\CmdImpl{\the\toks0}}%
```

```
\else
  \edef\next{\endgroup
    \noexpand\CmdImpl{\the\toks0}{}}%
\fi
\next}
\newcommand{\CmdImpl}[2]{%
  \textbf{Heiko:}
  this is (#1) and here's (#2).}
\CmdH{abc}{def} \\
\CmdH{ghi}\relax \\
\CmdH{jkl} %
```

which results in:

Heiko: this is (abc) and here's (def).
Heiko: this is (ghi) and here's ().
Heiko: this is (jkl) and here's ().

Dan Luecking [76], noting *that there were probably better ways (see Heiko's reply)*, responded with `\CmdD`:

```
\makeatletter
\newcommand*{\CmdD}[1]{%
  \@ifnextchar\bgroup
    {\Cmd@i{#1}}{\Cmd@i{#1}{}}}
\newcommand*{\Cmd@i}[2]{%
  \textbf{Dan:}
  this is (#1) and here's (#2).}
\makeatother
\CmdD{abc}{def} \\
\CmdD{ghi}\relax \\
\CmdD{jkl} %
```

which results in:

Dan: this is (abc) and here's (def).
Dan: this is (ghi) and here's ().
Dan: this is (jkl) and here's ().

Dan pointed out that his code does not examine the actual *next* character, but rather the next *nonspace* character. He also commented that Heiko's solution emulates a portion of `\@ifnextchar` without the skipping of spaces.

Joseph Wright [154] proposed a solution (`\CmdJ`) based on the xparse package [127] developed as part of the LaTeX3 project. From the user's viewpoint it appears to be the simplest of the three proposed solutions.

```
\usepackage{xparse}
\NewDocumentCommand\CmdJ{mG{}}{%
  \textbf{Joseph:}
  this is (#1) and here's (#2).}
```

---

[2]Another approach to ignoring spaces would be to set the catcode of space to 9 (ignored) and `\endlinechar=-1`. Yet another approach would be to set `\fontdimen2` and `\fontdimen7` to zero. All of these have their own advantages and drawbacks.

[3]I have slightly edited the code, principally by using distinguished macro names instead of the somewhat generic `\cmd`, and using a common set of tests.

```
\CmdJ{abc}{def} \\
\CmdJ{ghi}\relax \\
\CmdJ{jkl} %
```

which results in:

Joseph: this is (abc) and here's (def).
Joseph: this is (ghi) and here's ().
Joseph: this is (jkl) and here's ().

The three very different implementations each handled all the test cases correctly.

23.4   A centered table of contents

> America is a land whose center is nowhere;
> England one whose center is everywhere.
>
> *Pick Up Pieces*, John Updike

Bogdan Butnaru[4] uses the memoir class and asked me how to have a centered table of contents (ToC). I came up with one solution and passed Bogdan's request on to Lars Madsen, who is now memoir's maintainer, and he came up with a better solution; both of these were based on memoir's tools for manipulating the ToC. I then came up with a more basic solution which is also applicable to the standard book and report classes.

In these classes a chapter entry is set by the `\l@chapter` macro, a section entry by `\l@section`, and so on. These may be redefined to produce centered entries. These macros have the general calling form of:
`\l@chapter{`⟨*number-and-title*⟩`}{`⟨*page*⟩`}`
where ⟨*number-and-title*⟩ has the form:
`{{\numberline}{num} title}`
where `\numberline` typesets the chapter number. The `\l@...` macros also take into account whether or not the entry should be printed and the surrounding vertical spacing. The *LATEX Companion* [88, §2.3] provides further information about ToCs and related packages.

The following redefinition of `\l@chapter` will center the chapter entries, with the chapter number above the title, and a middle-dot between the title and page number.

```
\makeatletter
\renewcommand*{\l@chapter}[2]{%
  \ifnum\c@tocdepth>\m@ne % print chapter entry
  \addpenalty{-\@highpenalty}%
  \vskip 1em plus 0pt
  \begingroup
```

---

[4]Private email, 2010/07/21

```
  \def\numberline##1{##1\\\nobreak}% number
    {\centering\bfseries
      #1~\textperiodcentered~#2\par}%
  \endgroup
  \fi}
\makeatother
```

The `\tableofcontents` macro uses `\chapter*` to set the title ragged right. A hack to that can be used to center the title is to make `\raggedright` into `\centering`.

```
\let\saverr\raggedright
\newcommand*{\rrtocenter}{%
  \let\raggedright\centering}
\newcommand*{\restorerr}{%
  \let\raggedright\saverr}
\let\oldtoc\tableofcontents
\renewcommand*{\tableofcontents}{%
  {\rrtocenter\oldtoc}}
```

To typeset the ToC with the heading and chapter entries centered is now as easy as:
`\tableofcontents`

If you wanted the section entries to be centered then `\l@section` can be redefined in a similar, but not identical, manner to `\l@chapter`. However, centered section entries following a centered chapter entry in my view looks rather confusing.

If you want chapter headings to be centered, you can do:

```
{\rrtocenter
    \chapter[...]{...}
}
```

or

```
\rrtocenter
    \chapter[...]{...}
\restorerr
```

In each case the effect of `\rrtocenter` is limited to `\chapter`; if it were not then surprises could be in store later on.

A stately rocke beset with Diamonds faire,
And pouldred round about with Rubies red,
Where Emeralds greene doo glister in the air,
With Mantill blew of Saphyres ouer spread.

The Ship of Safegarde, BARNABE GOOGE

24.1 Assemblies

Eric, or, Little by Little

Book title, FREDERICK W. FARRAR

24.1.1 Adding to a macro

On occasions it is useful to be able to extend a pre-existing macro. For instance, to assemble a list of the names of the members of some organization, or the reviewers of some article, and then print them. In simple cases the LaTeX kernel
\g@addto@macro{⟨*macro*⟩}{⟨*addition*⟩}
can be used for this.

```
\makeatletter
\newcommand*{\member}[1]{%
  \@ifundefined{@members}{%
% a new list of members
% define it as the argument (member name)
    \newcommand{\@members}{#1}}{%
% a list exists, add the argument to it
    \g@addto@macro{\@members}{, #1}}}
\newcommand*{\showmembers}{%
  \ignorespaces\@members}
\newcommand*{\themembers}{\showmembers
  \let\@members\relax}
\makeatother
```

The macro \member{⟨*name*⟩} can be used several times to add ⟨*name*⟩ to the \@members macro. The macro \themembers can then be called to print the contents of \@members and clear \@members so a new list may be started. If you want to print the list more than once then use \showmembers which prints, but does not clear, the list.

```
\member{Fred} \member{Joe}
\member{Susan} \member{Faye}
```

\themembers ⟹ Fred, Joe, Susan, Faye

For more complex additions, for instance when the macro to be extended takes arguments, then the patchcmd package [34] could be the answer.

Once having created a list of members it might have to be changed because one or more members have left. This is more complicated and I present it only as an example of what could be done.

The \deletemember{⟨*name*⟩} will go over the list of members, creating a new temporary working list with the exception of the ⟨*name*⟩ member, then replace the original list with the working one.

```
\makeatletter
\let\xpf\expandafter%  just a shorthand
\newcommand*{\deletemember}[1]{%
  \let\@tempmembers\relax
  \def\@dm@num{1}%
  \@for\member@:=\@members\do{%
    \ifnum\@dm@num<2\relax
      \def\t@mp@b{#1}%              initial entry
      \ifx\member@\t@mp@b%
        \def\@dm@num{0}%
      \else
        \def\t@mp@b{\space #1}% later entries
        \ifx\member@\t@mp@b%
          \def\@dm@num{0}%
        \fi
      \fi
    \fi
    \ifnum\@dm@num=0\relax
      \def\@dm@num{2}%
    \else
      \xpf\xpf\xpf\transfer\xpf{\member@}%
    \fi}%
  \let\@members\@tempmembers}
\makeatother
```

The coding of \deletemember is not straightforward. The LaTeX kernel's \@for construct is used to loop over the comma-separated entries in \@members, putting, in turn, each entry into the \member@ macro. Due to the way that \@members is constructed, the name of the initial entry is recovered as **name**, while a later entry is recovered as ␣**name**; hence the two tests for the argument ⟨*name*⟩ against the recovered \member@ name.

The \@dm@num macro is used to track the state of the process. At the start it is set to 1. If it is less than 2, attempts are made to match the argument with the current list name and if a match is found then \@dm@num is set to 0. After the argument check, if the argument is matched (\@dm@num = 0) then \@dm@num is reset to 2, otherwise the current member name is added to the working list. This all means that once the list name matches the argument then no further attempts at matching are needed or done, and the remaining original members are simply added to the working list. At the end the original list is set to the temporary working list.

The tricky part is that the current contents of \member@, not the macro itself, should be added to the working list.[1] The bunch of \expandafters around the call to \transfer expands \member@ to its definition before it gets handed over as the argument to \transfer.

The macro \transfer{⟨name⟩} adds ⟨name⟩ to the macro \@tempmembers containing a list of comma separated names. It has the same general form as the earlier \member macro.

```
\makeatletter
\newcommand*{\transfer}[1]{%
  \@ifundefined{@tempmembers}{%
    \newcommand*{\@tempmembers}{#1}%
  }{%
    \g@addto@macro{\@tempmembers}{,#1}%
  }}
\makeatother
```

Here are some examples of adding and deleting members to and from the original member list above.

```
\member{Alice} \member{Bob} \member{Claire}
\member{David} \member{Erica}
```

\showmembers ⟹ Fred, Joe, Susan, Faye, Alice, Bob, Claire, David, Erica
\deletemember{David}\showmembers ⟹ Fred, Joe, Susan, Faye, Alice, Bob, Claire, Erica
\deletemember{Fred}\showmembers ⟹ Joe, Susan, Faye, Alice, Bob, Claire, Erica

```
\member{Xerxes} \member{Zeno}
```

\showmembers ⟹ Joe, Susan, Faye, Alice, Bob, Claire, Erica, Xerxes, Zeno
\deletemember{Miriam}\showmembers ⟹ Joe, Susan, Faye, Alice, Bob, Claire, Erica, Xerxes, Zeno

24.1.2   Piecing a paragraph

Ron Aaron wanted a different kind of assembly. He wrote [1]:

---

[1] If the macro is added then the list will consist of nothing but a series of \member@, thus all expanding to the identical name (the current definition of \member@ when the list is printed).

What I wish to do is accumulate text into a paragraph 'as I go'. My simple approach is to allocate a box, and then unbox and add the text. But this doesn't work as I intend:

```
\newbox\textbox
\def\addbox#1{%
  \setbox\textbox\vbox{%
    \unvbox\textbox#1}}
\addbox{Hello}
\addbox{there!}
\box\textbox
```

What I get is each appended bit of text in a separate line. I've tried to '\unskip' and '\unkern' etc. after the \unvbox but whatever I do I get a list of lines.

Trying out Ron's example the result is:

Hello,
there!

The squashed vertical spacing between the lines is real, not an artifact of this article.

In responding, Philip Taylor [125], having said that using a \vbox would be difficult, gave two suggestions; either use an \hbox directly or a token-list register. His \hbox solution (and my example) is:

```
\newbox\textbox
\def\addbox #1{%
  \setbox \textbox = \hbox
  \bgroup
    \unhbox \textbox #1%
  \egroup}
\addbox{Hello}
\addbox{ World!}
\addbox{ Now isn't that a rather
        common saying?}
\unhbox\textbox
```

with the result:

Hello World! Now isn't that a rather common saying?

At various points after this I have used code like
\addbox{ (n) text}
as an example of assembling a paragraph piece by piece and at the end showing the result via:
\unhbox\textbox.

```
\addbox{(1) Start of a paragraph.}
```

Philip's second solution uses a token register:

```
\newtoks\texttoks
\def\addtoks #1{%
  \texttoks =
  \expandafter {\the \texttoks #1}}
\addtoks {Goodbye}
\addtoks { \emph{vain} world. Ah, the
            weariness in that statement
            does one no good.}
\the \texttoks
```

and the example produces:

Goodbye *vain* world. Ah, the weariness in that statement does one no good.

```
\addbox{ (2) After an interruption
         add more.}
```

Note that with both of Philip's solutions you have to explicitly incorporate spaces where you want them to occur in the assembled paragraph. It seemed, though, that Ron really wanted to use a \vbox but I have neither seen nor been able to come up with satisfactory code.

```
\addbox{ (3) This is the end
         of the piecewise
         paragraph.}
\unhbox\textbox
```

Now print the piecewise paragraph giving:

(1) Start of a paragraph. (2) After an interruption add more. (3) This is the end of the piecewise paragraph.

24.2 Table talk

> Beneath those rugged elms, that
> yew-tree's shade,
> Where heaves the turf in many a
> mouldering heap,
> Each in his narrow cell for ever laid,
> The rude forefathers of the hamlet sleep.
>
> *Elegy Written in a Country Churchyard,*
> THOMAS GRAY

Arbo [8] wanted a tabular layout like the one shown in Figure 24.1 and tried using code like this to produce it.

```
\begin{tabular}{r|c|l}
\hline
First & Second & Third \\
Text &
  \multicolumn{1}{c|c|c|c|}%
```

First	Second				Third
Text	C 1	C 2	C 3	C 4	More text
Words	C 5		C 6		C 7	text
Title	C 8			C 9		Some text

Figure 24.1: Desired tabular layout

```
               {C 1 & C 2 & C 3 & C 4}
    & More text \\
Words &
  \multicolumn{1}{c|c|c}%
               {C 5 & C 6 & C 7}
    & Text \\
Title &
  \multicolumn{1}{c|c}%
             {C 8 & C 9}
    & Some text \\
\hline
\end{tabular}
```

If you try it you will find, like Arbo, that it doesn't work, resulting in a string of error messages beginning with:

```
! Missing } inserted.
<inserted text>
                 }
1.6945  {C 1 & C 2 & C 3 & C 4}
```

The problem is that \multicolumn merges multiple columns into one whereas the requirement here was to split one column into several.

Donald Arseneau [18] responded that *'They don't look aligned at all, so don't call them columns'*, and provided code for an \addcell macro. Arbo modified it very slightly to center the \vlines, with the final version as follows:

```
\newcommand{\addcell}{\unskip\hfill
  \hspace\tabcolsep\vline\hspace\tabcolsep
  \hfill % added by Arbo
  \ignorespaces}
```

Using this, the tabular in Figure 24.1 is created by:

```
\begin{tabular}{|r|c|l|}\hline
First & Second & Third \\
Text & C 1
       \addcell C 2 \addcell C 3 \addcell C 4
    & More text \\
Words & C 5
       \addcell C 6 \addcell C 7
    & text \\
Title & C 8 \addcell  C 9 & Some text \\
\hline
\end{tabular}
```

Yet Tarquyne pluckt his glistering grape,
And Shake-speare, paints poor Lucrece
rape.

————————————————

Willobie His Avisa, HENRY WILLOBIE?

25.1 Index headers

*La dernière chose qu'on trouve faisant un
ouvrage, est de savoir celle qu'il faut
mettre la première.*
The last thing one knows in constructing
a work is what to put first.

————————————————

Pensées, BLAISE PASCAL

In the manual for the memoir class the headers for
the index included the first and last main index entries on the page in question. The technique I used
was fairly simple and can be applied to any document whose index is generated via the MakeIndex
program. It consists of defining a macro in the
document's preamble (or a package) and a simple
MakeIndex style file [30, 88, 142].

Below is an example document, where the new
macro is \idxmark and the fancyhdr package [130] is
used for specifying the page headers and footers.

\idxmark{⟨entry⟩} prints ⟨entry⟩ and also sets
both the marks to ⟨entry⟩, where \leftmark resolves
to the first mark on the page and \rightmark to the
last mark on the page.

```
\documentclass[...twoside]{...}
\usepackage{makeidx,fancyhdr}
\newcommand*{\idxmark}[1]{#1\markboth{#1}{#1}}
\pagestyle{fancy}
%% set up general fancy headers/footers
\makeindex
\begin{document}
... % many \index{...} ...
\clearpage
%% fancy headers/footers for index pages
\fancyhead{}
\fancyhead[LE,RO]{%
  \rightmark\space---\space\leftmark}
\fancyfoot{}
\fancyfoot[C]{\thepage}
\printindex
\end{document}
```

The index is typically set in two columns and
LaTeX's marking system did not always function well

in this case; in the past, including the fixltx2e package was needed to fix that, but nowadays it is included by default.

In the example the general header/footer styles
are set in the preamble using the fancyhdr package facilities. The (special) headers and footers for
the index are set just before the index commences.
When looking for something in a book I flick it half
closed only seeing the outer portion of each page.
Consequently, in this case I have put the first and
last index entries on the page at the outer of the
headers where they are easy to see and the page
number, which is not particularly important when
looking through the index, centered at the foot of
the page.

Here are the essentials of the MakeIndex style file
flindex.ist for the application. For each main
entry, ⟨entry⟩ in the input .idx file it outputs
\idxmark{⟨entry⟩} in the .ind file which is used by
pdflatex to print the index.

```
% MakeIndex style file flindex.ist
% output main entry as <entry> as:
%     \item \idxmark{<entry>}
item_0 "\n\\item \\idxmark{"
delim_0 "}, "
% not forgetting subitem
\item_X1 "} \n \\subitem "
```

The memoir manual, has an index that is over
40 pages long with each alphabetic section headed
by the letter (A, B, C, etc.). The hyperref package
is used to enable PDF bookmarks and Lars Madsen developed code so that the index letter subheads would appear in the bookmark listing. Here
is the skeleton of how this was done, where the
\doidxbookmark{⟨head⟩} macro does the work. The
⟨head⟩ argument is an index subhead and the macro
adds it to the list of bookmarks at one level below the Index entry. The default MakeIndex generated subhead for entries that do not commence with
an alphanumeric is 'Symbols', but I felt that 'Anal-
phabetics' was a better subhead. \doidxbookmark
prints the appropriate subhead centered in a bold
font and adds it to the bookmark list.

```
...
\usepackage{ifpdf}
\ifpdf
  \usepackage[pdftex,
```

```
            plainpages=false,
            pdfpagelabels,
            bookmarksnumbered,
            colorlinks,
            ocgcolorlinks,
          ]{hyperref}
\else
  \usepackage[plainpages=false,
            pdfpagelabels,
            bookmarksnumbered,
            colorlinks,
          ]{hyperref}
\fi
\makeatletter
\newcommand*{\doidxbookmark}[1]{{%
  \def\@tempa{Symbols}\def\@tempb{#1}%
  \centering\bfseries \ifx\@tempa\@tempb
    Analphabetics
    \phantomsection%
    \belowpdfbookmark{Analphabetics}%
                  {Analphabetics-idx}%
  \else
    #1%
    \phantomsection%
    \belowpdfbookmark{#1}{#1-idx}%
  \fi
  \vskip\baselineskip\par}}
\makeatother
...
\begin{document}
...
\clearpage
\pdfbookmark{Index}{Index}
\phantomsection
\printindex
\end{document}
```

The MakeIndex style file must be written so that it wraps the \doidxbookmark around the subheads, like this:

```
% MakeIndex style file flindex.ist
% output main entry ...
% Wrap and uppercase head letters
headings_flag 1
heading_prefix "\\doidxbookmark{"
heading_suffix "}"
```

And here is the sequence of commands to generate the indexed **file.tex** document:

```
> pdflatex file
> makeindex -s flindex.ist file
> pdflatex file
```

25.2 Numerations

As yet a child, nor yet a fool to fame,
I lisped in numbers, for the numbers came.

An Epistle to Dr Arbuthnot, ALEXANDER
POPE

25.2.1 Sorted lists

Reza wrote to ctt [111] saying that he had developed code that would sort the items in a description environment and asked if there was a way to enumerate the entries.

I had no idea that you could sort items within LATEX but it appears that Nicola Talbot's incredible datatool package [124] enables you to do that, and much more.

Here is Reza's original code, to which I have added some comments to try and indicate what is happening and changed the environment name to distinguish it from other later code:

```
%%%% Reza's code
\usepackage{datatool}
\newcommand{\sortitem}[2]{%
    % start a new row in the db
  \DTLnewrow{list}%
    % add key/value to row
  \DTLnewdbentry{list}{label}{#1}%
    % add another key/value to the row
  \DTLnewdbentry{list}{description}{#2}%
}
\newenvironment{sorteddesc}{%
  % use or create a db called 'list'
  \DTLifdbexists{list}
    {\DTLcleardb{list}}{\DTLnewdb{list}}%
}{%
  % at the end of the environment sort the
  % db in ascending order of the label
  \DTLsort{label}{list}%
  % start a description environment
  \begin{description}%
    % iterate through the db,
    % picking out the keys/values
    \DTLforeach*{list}%
      {\theLabel=label,\theDesc=description}{%
        \item[\theLabel]\theDesc
      }%
  \end{description}%
}
```

As an example,

```
\begin{sorteddesc}
\sortitem{zz}{description of zz}
\sortitem{mm}{description of mm}
\sortitem{aa}{description of aa}
\end{sorteddesc}
```

results in:

aa description of aa

mm description of mm

zz description of zz

Reza wanted to know if there was a way to enumerate the entries. That is, so the output would look like:

```
1. aa description of aa
2. mm description of mm
3. zz description of zz
```

Christian Anderson [7] responded with the following based on using the **enumerate** environment (I have changed the name of the sorting environment to distinguish it from the other proposals):

```
\newenvironment{sortedenum}{%
  \DTLifdbexists{list}%
    {\DTLcleardb{list}}{\DTLnewdb{list}}%
}{%
  \DTLsort{label}{list}%
  \begin{enumerate}%
    \DTLforeach*{list}%
      {\theLabel=label,\theDesc=description}{%
      \item \theLabel\ \theDesc% original
      % bolds the descriptive label
%      \item \textbf{\theLabel}\ \theDesc
      }%
  \end{enumerate}%
}
```

As an example of Christian's proposal

```
\begin{sortedenum}
\sortitem{zz}{description of zz}
\sortitem{mm}{description of mm}
\sortitem{aa}{description of aa}
\end{sortedenum}
```

results in:

```
1. aa description of aa

2. mm description of mm

3. zz description of zz
```

It was unclear as to how Reza wanted the combination of number and label to be typeset. Christian indicated how the label could be typeset in a bold font, but the number would still be set in the normal font.

Alan Munn [91] also responded as follows, taking advantage of the `\DTLcurrentindex` macro from **datatool** (again I have changed the name of the sorting environment).

```
\newenvironment{sorteditemdesc}{%
  \DTLifdbexists{list}%
    {\DTLcleardb{list}}{\DTLnewdb{list}}%
}{%
  \DTLsort{label}{list}%
  \begin{description}%
    \DTLforeach*{list}%
      {\theLabel=label,\theDesc=description}{%
      \item[{\normalfont
            \DTLcurrentindex.\ }
            \theLabel]\theDesc}%
  \end{description}%
}
```

As an example of Alan's proposal

```
\begin{sorteditemdesc}
\sortitem{zz}{description of zz}
\sortitem{mm}{description of mm}
\sortitem{aa}{description of aa}
\end{sorteditemdesc}
```

results in:

```
1.  aa description of aa

2.  mm description of mm

3.  zz description of zz
```

Alan also indicated how the number could be set in bold to match the label. By suitable application of `\normalfont` both could instead be set in the normal font. In this sense Alan's solution is slightly more general than Christian's.

25.2.2 Autotab

Jeremy wrote to ctt [68]:
I want to create a table and I want the first column of the table to have incrementing numbers ... I would like to avoid having to manually enter the numbers in the first column. Is there a way to do this automatically?

Alan Munn responded with [92] `\newcolumntype` and `\resetrownum`:

```
%\usepackage{booktabs}
%\usepackage{array}
\newcounter{rownum}
\newcolumntype{N}{%
  >{\stepcounter{rownum}\therownum.\ }l}
\newcommand*{\resetrownum}{%
  \setcounter{rownum}{0}}
\begin{tabular}{Nll} \toprule
\multicolumn{1}{>{\resetrownum}l}{I}
& A & B \\ \midrule
& blah & blah \\
& foo & foo \\ \bottomrule
\end{tabular}
```

I	A	B
1.	blah	blah
2.	foo	foo

In the same thread Heiko Oberdiek noted that the \resetrownum could be taken out of the tabular:

```
\resetrownum
\begin{tabular}{Nll} \toprule
\multicolumn{1}{l}{I}& A & B \\ \midrule
& blah & blah \\
& foo & foo \\ \bottomrule
\end{tabular}
```

In a later thread on a similar but extended topic Romildo posed [119],

I want to typeset an enumeration list in a tabular format, building a table with automatic numbered items and sub-items in different rows. [An example layout followed.]

Jean-François Burnol [26] responded with:

```
\newcounter{bitmi}
  \renewcommand{\thebitmi}{%
    \arabic{bitmi}}
\newcounter{bitmii}[bitmi]
  \renewcommand{\thebitmii}{%
    \thebitmi.\arabic{bitmii}}
\newcounter{bitmiii}[bitmii]
  \renewcommand{\thebitmiii}{%
    \thebitmii.\arabic{bitmiii}}
\newcommand{\bitm}{\stepcounter{bitmi}
  \hbox to 1.5em{\thebitmi.\hfil}}
\newcommand{\bsubitm}{\stepcounter{bitmii}
  \hbox to 1.5em{}
  \hbox to 2.5em{\thebitmii\hfil}}
\newcommand{\bsubsubitm}{%
  \stepcounter{bitmiii}
  \hbox to 4em{}
  \hbox to 3.5em{\thebitmiii\hfil}}
```

```
\begin{tabular}{llll}
Subject           & Class & Total & Notes \\
\bitm First topic  & 2     & 2 & a, b      \\
\bitm Second topic & 12    & 14 &          \\
  \bsubitm Aaaa    &       & & b, c, d \\
    \bsubsubitm M1 &       & & a        \\
    \bsubsubitm M2 &       & & b, e, f \\
  \bsubitm Bbbb    &       & & a, b     \\
\bitm Third topic  & \ldots & &         \\
\end{tabular}
```

Subject		Class	Total	Notes
1.	First topic	2	2	a, b
2.	Second topic	12	14	
	2.1 Aaaa			b, c, d
	2.1.1 M1			a
	2.1.2 M2			b, e, f
	2.2 Bbbb			a, b
3.	Third topic	...		

Just a little later Peter Flynn proposed [51]:

```
\usepackage{array}
\newcounter{topic}
  \renewcommand{\thetopic}{\arabic{topic}}
\newcounter{topici}[topic]
  \renewcommand{\thetopici}{%
    \thetopic.\arabic{topici}}
\newcounter{topicii}[topici]
  \renewcommand{\thetopicii}{%
    \thetopici.\arabic{topicii}}
\newcommand{\topic}[1]{%
  \stepcounter{topic}%
  \vrule height1.2em width0pt\thotopic. &
  \multicolumn{3}{l}{#1}}
\newcommand{\subtopic}[1]{%
  \stepcounter{topici}%
  \vrule height1em width0pt & \thetopici &
  \multicolumn{2}{l}{#1}}
\newcommand{\subsubtopic}[1]{%
  \stepcounter{topicii} & &
  \thetopicii&#1}

\begin{tabular}{rrrlr<{\quad}r<{\enspace}l}
  \multicolumn{4}{l}{\textbf{Subject}} &
    \multicolumn{1}{r}{\textbf{Class}} &
    \multicolumn{1}{r}{\textbf{Total}} &
    \textbf{Notes}\\[2pt]
\topic{First topic}  & 2 & 2 & a, b    \\
\topic{Second topic} & 12 & 14 &       \\
  \subtopic{Aaaa}    & & & b, c, d \\
    \subsubtopic{M1} & & & a        \\
    \subsubtopic{M2} & & & b, e, f \\
  \subtopic{Bbbb}    & & & a, b     \\
\topic{Third topic}  & \ldots & & &   \\
\end{tabular}
```

Subject		Class	Total	Notes
1.	First topic	2	2	a, b
2.	Second topic	12	14	
	2.1 Aaaa			b, c, d
	2.1.1 M1			a
	2.1.2 M2			b, e, f
	2.2 Bbbb			a, b
3.	Third topic	...		

Jean-François's approach to me is the simpler and easier of the two as he designed it so that all the main entries go into the first column and internally uses empty \hboxes to indent the several (sub) item levels. Peter's approach is more complex in that it involves several \multicolumns to control the (sub) topic indentations; he also uses zero-width vertical rules to enable different vertical spacing between the topic levels. My feeling is that the combination of Jean-François's horizontal positioning and Peter's vertical adjustments might be closest to an optimum solution to Romildo's needs.

25.3   Real number comparison

Tenants of life's middle state,
Securely placed between the small and great.

Tirocinium, WILLIAM COWPER

On `ctt` Pluto noted that \ifnum could be used to compare integer values and wondered if there was a similar method for comparing real numbers [109]. This led to a spirited discussion involving several people and over 50 postings at my last count. The two that struck me the most were from Donald Arseneau and 'GL'.

For demonstration purposes assume that the following are defined:

```
\def\fourfive{4.5}
\def\fivefive{5.5}
\def\sixseven{6.7}
\def\threetwo{3.2}
```

Donald gave concise and elegant code,[1] shown later, that could be used like this:
`\ifrnum <condition> \then...\else...\fi`
as in:

```
\ifrnum 4.5 > 5.5
  \then 4.5 is larger than 5.5
```

---

[1] Which I cannot interpret for you, beyond saying that the basic idea is to convert the numbers to dimensions and use \ifdim for the comparison.

```
  \else 4.5 is not larger than 5.5\fi. \\
\ifrnum \sixseven > \threetwo
  \then \sixseven\ is larger than \threetwo
  \else \sixseven\ is not larger than
      \threetwo \fi.
```

4.5 is not larger than 5.5.
6.7 is larger than 3.2.

Here is Donald Arseneau's code [17]:

```
\let\then\iffalse
\def\gobblejunk#1\delimeter{}
\def\ifrnum#1\then{\ifdim
  \ptlt\ptgt\pteq #1pt\gobblejunk<=>\delimeter}
\def\ptlt#1<{#1pt<}
\def\ptgt#1>{#1pt>}
\def\pteq#1={#1pt=}
```

GL also provided code, shown later, that could be used like this:

```
\unless\Realnums\ifnum <condition>
    \Then ... \else ... \fi
```

as in:

```
\unless\ifnum\Realnums\fourfive>\fivefive
  \Then \fourfive\ is not larger than \fivefive
  \else \fourfive\ is larger than
      \fivefive\fi. \\
\unless\ifnum\Realnums 6.7 > 3.2
  \Then 6.7 is not larger than 3.2
  \else 6.7 is  larger than 3.2\fi.
```

4.5 is not larger than 5.5.
6.7 is larger than 3.2.

In GL's original posting [53], which was in response to Donald, he reused, modified, and extended Donald's code. I have renamed some of the macros in GL's code so that the two sets are distinct, which means that both styles can be used in the same document, as I have done here.

```
\def\gobblejunk#1\delimeter{}
\def\Realnums#1\Then{\dimexpr
  \Ptlt\Ptgt\Pteq #1pt\gobblejunk<=>\delimeter}
\def\Ptlt#1<{#1pt<\dimexpr}
\def\Ptgt#1>{#1pt>\dimexpr}
\def\Pteq#1={#1pt=\dimexpr}
```

The \unless macro is defined in ε-TeX, which all recent LaTeX systems automatically utilise. Personally I find the \unless construct hard to get my mind around; it's the reverse of the traditional \if....

So, with his daughters three, th'
unsceptered Lear
Heaved the loud sigh, and pour'd the
glistering tear.

The Loves of the Triangles:
A mathematical and philosophical
poem, JOHN HOOKHAM FRERE

26.1 Hanging

We must indeed all hang together, or most
assuredly, we shall all hang separately.

Spoken at the signing of the Declaration of
Independence, BENJAMIN FRANKLIN

26.1.1 Overhangs

Rui Maciel asked about a notation for the closure of
a set, saying that [81]:

When I need to refer to the closure of a set I tend
to use the \bar{} *command. So, considering the set*
Ω *then the closure of that set would be:*
$\bar{\Omega}$ -> $\bar{\Omega}$
However, I've noticed that when the symbol used to
reference a given set also has a superscript then $\bar{\Omega}^s$

doesn't look very good. I've also tried \overline{}
instead but it appears even worse
$\overline{\Omega^{s}}$ -> $\overline{\Omega^s}$.

Enrico Gregorio recommended [56] \closureG:

```
% \closureG{right shift}{symbol}
\newcommand*{\closureG}[2][3]{%
  {}\mkern#1mu\overline{\mkern-#1mu#2}}
```

while Bill Hammond said [59] that he found the following \closureH to work better, also noting that
he used amsmath:

```
% \closureH{right shift}{symbol}
\newcommand*{\closureH}[2][3]{%
  \overline{{}\mkern#1mu#2\mkern-#1mu}}
```

In each case the optional argument is the value of
an \mkern (in mu) applied to the overline to move
it sideways; the default is 3.

Dan Luecking felt [79] that there should be two
controls over the overline — one to shift the line
(which is provided by the previous macros) and a
second to adjust the length of the line — and suggested the \closureL macro.

'closure'	Ω	Ω^*	Ω_s	B	B^*	B_s
\overline{...}	$\overline{\Omega}$	$\overline{\Omega^*}$	$\overline{\Omega_s}$	$\overline{B}$	$\overline{B^*}$	$\overline{B_s}$
\closureG[-3]{...}	$\overline{\Omega}$	$\overline{\Omega^*}$	$\overline{\Omega_s}$	$\overline{B}$	$\overline{B^*}$	$\overline{B_s}$
\closureG[0]{...}	$\overline{\Omega}$	$\overline{\Omega^*}$	$\overline{\Omega_s}$	$\overline{B}$	$\overline{B^*}$	$\overline{B_s}$
\closureG[3]{...}	$\overline{\Omega}$	$\overline{\Omega^*}$	$\overline{\Omega_s}$	$\overline{B}$	$\overline{B^*}$	$\overline{B_s}$
\closureH[-3]{...}	$\overline{\Omega}$	$\overline{\Omega^*}$	$\overline{\Omega_s}$	$\overline{B}$	$\overline{B^*}$	$\overline{B_s}$
\closureH[0]{...}	$\overline{\Omega}$	$\overline{\Omega^*}$	$\overline{\Omega_s}$	$\overline{B}$	$\overline{B^*}$	$\overline{B_s}$
\closureH[3]{...}	$\overline{\Omega}$	$\overline{\Omega^*}$	$\overline{\Omega_s}$	$\overline{B}$	$\overline{B^*}$	$\overline{B_s}$
\closureL{-3}{-3}{...}	$\overline{\Omega}$	$\overline{\Omega^*}$	$\overline{\Omega_s}$	$\overline{B}$	$\overline{B^*}$	$\overline{B_s}$
\closureL{-3}{0}{...}	$\overline{\Omega}$	$\overline{\Omega^*}$	$\overline{\Omega_s}$	$\overline{B}$	$\overline{B^*}$	$\overline{B_s}$
\closureL{-3}{3}{...}	$\overline{\Omega}$	$\overline{\Omega^*}$	$\overline{\Omega_s}$	$\overline{B}$	$\overline{B^*}$	$\overline{B_s}$
\closureL{0}{-3}{...}	$\overline{\Omega}$	$\overline{\Omega^*}$	$\overline{\Omega_s}$	$\overline{B}$	$\overline{B^*}$	$\overline{B_s}$
\closureL{0}{0}{...}	$\overline{\Omega}$	$\overline{\Omega^*}$	$\overline{\Omega_s}$	$\overline{B}$	$\overline{B^*}$	$\overline{B_s}$
\closureL{0}{3}{...}	$\overline{\Omega}$	$\overline{\Omega^*}$	$\overline{\Omega_s}$	$\overline{B}$	$\overline{B^*}$	$\overline{B_s}$
\closureL{3}{-3}{...}	$\overline{\Omega}$	$\overline{\Omega^*}$	$\overline{\Omega_s}$	$\overline{B}$	$\overline{B^*}$	$\overline{B_s}$
\closureL{3}{0}{...}	$\overline{\Omega}$	$\overline{\Omega^*}$	$\overline{\Omega_s}$	$\overline{B}$	$\overline{B^*}$	$\overline{B_s}$
\closureL{3}{3}{...}	$\overline{\Omega}$	$\overline{\Omega^*}$	$\overline{\Omega_s}$	$\overline{B}$	$\overline{B^*}$	$\overline{B_s}$

Figure 26.1: Various closures

```
% \closureL{right shift}{trim}{symbol}
\newcommand*{\closureL}[3]{%
  \mkern#1mu\mkern#2mu
  \overline{\mkern-#1mu \mkern-#2mu #3%
            \mkern-#2mu \mkern#1mu}%
  \mkern#2mu\mkern-#1mu}
```

Table 26.1 shows the results of applying the three closure macros to a variety of variables with a range of kerns, along with the result of a vanilla \overline.

There is no one ideal value for the \mkern; a 'good' value depends on whether the set variable is upright (e.g., Ω) or slanted (e.g., B) and whether or not it has a super- or subscript. Basically it comes down to what you think is most appropriate. In my view I prefer the following:

Upright variable (e.g., Ω) \closureG[0]{}, \closureH[0]{}, \closureL{0}{0}{}, which are all equivalent to \overline{}.

Slanted variable (e.g., B) \closureG[3]{}, \closureH[-3]{}.

I think that \closureL{0}{3}{} and \closureL{3}{0}{} are close but not quite as good. Something like \closureL{1}{2} would seem to give a better result.

As the old saying goes, 'Yer pays yer money and takes yer choice.'

26.1.2   Paragraphs in equations

'Cooch' wrote [31]:

In a number of the chapters for one of my books, I 'define' a series variable, generally embedded in the form

variable = text to define the variable

For example (the page I'm currently staring at)

```
$\phi^{rst}_{i-1,i}$= the probability that
a particle in state \emph{r} at time
\emph{i}-1 and state \emph{s} at time
\emph{i} is in state \emph{t} at time
\emph{i}+1.
```

... I want to force the RHS of the expression to 'wrap' and be indented after the first sentence, to the right of the equal sign. So, that the above looks like:

```
$\phi^{rst}_{i-1,i}$= the probability that
                a particle in state ...
```

In other words, something analogous to a 'hanging indent' after the first line, but where the indentation is relative to where the equal sign falls.

There were several responses to this and for the following, in order to save space and make the examples easier to read, I have defined

```
\newcommand*{\mathdef}{\phi^{rst}_{i-1,i}=}
\newcommand*{\textdef}{the probability that
  a particle in state $r$ at time $i-1$
  and state $s$ at time $i$ is in state
  $t$ at time $i+1$.}
\newcommand*{\smath}{D_{n}=}
\newcommand*{\stext}{the definition of the
  variable as used herein.}
```

All the respondents disagreed with the use of \emph to indicate a math variable. As Enrico Gregorio said [57]:

> Don't use \emph{i} for representing a variable: it's simply i; notice also the difference between $i-1$ ($i-1$) and \emph{i}-1 (i-1); the second one is definitely wrong.

Lars Madsen said [83] that he normally used \equation*[1]

```
\begin{equation*}
\phi^{rst}_{i-1,i}=
\parbox[t]{<length>}{\raggedright the
probability that a particle in state $r$
at time $i-1$ and ...}
\end{equation*}
```

which, with $\langle length \rangle = 0.8$\columnwidth results in

$$\phi^{rst}_{i-1,i} = \text{the probability that a particle in state } r \text{ at time } i-1 \text{ and state } s \text{ at time } i+1.$$

Enrico Gregorio provided [57] the environment qdesc:

```
\newenvironment{qdesc}[1]%
  {\par\addvspace{\medskipamount}
   \sbox{0}{$#1$ }\dimen0=\textwidth
   \advance\dimen0 by -\wd0
   \noindent\usebox{0}
   \begin{minipage}[t]{\dimen0}}%
  {\end{minipage}
   \par\addvspace{\medskipamount}}
```

---

[1] equation* is from the amsmath package.

which applied to the example as

```
\begin{qdesc}{\mathdef}
\textdef
\end{qdesc}
```

and results in:

$\phi^{rst}_{i-1,i} =$ the probability that a particle in state r at time $i - 1$ and state s at time $i + 1$.

Jean-François Burnol presented [27] the `\start` macro:

```
\newcommand{\start}[1]{%
  \setbox0=\hbox{#1}%
  \hangindent\wd0
  \noindent\box0}
```

```
\start{$\phi^{rst}_{i-1,i}$= }\textdef
```

$\phi^{rst}_{i-1,i}=$ the probability that a particle in state r at time $i - 1$ and state s at time $i + 1$.

Jean-François' `\start` macro is a TEX version of the LaTeX kernel's command `\@hangfrom`, which the memoir class provides as a user-level macro `\hangfrom{text}` by copying the original definition:

```
\newcommand{\hangfrom}[1]{%
  \setbox\@tempboxa\hbox{{#1}}%
  \hangindent \wd\@tempboxa%
          \noindent\box\@tempboxa}
```

`\hangfrom{⟨text⟩}` puts text in a box and makes a hanging paragraph of the following material (somewhat like a description item). Applying this:

```
\hangfrom{$\mathdef$ }\textdef \par
\hangfrom{$\smath$ }\stext
```

$\phi^{rst}_{i-1,i} =$ the probability that a particle in state r at time $i - 1$ and state s at time $i + 1$.
$D_n =$ the definition of the variable as used herein.

As the last example shows, each 'definition' is treated individually. If it is required that, say, several definition texts should be aligned in a set of definitions then using one of the `tabular` environments could be an advantage. For example:

```
Using \texttt{tabular}: \\
\begin{tabular}{lp{0.7\columnwidth}}
$\mathdef$ & \textdef \\
$\smath$ & \stext \\
\end{tabular}
```

```
\noindent Using \texttt{tabularx}: \\
\begin{tabularx}{\linewidth}{lX}
$\mathdef$ & \textdef \\
$\smath$ & \stext \\
\end{tabularx}
```

Using **tabular**:

$\phi^{rst}_{i-1,i} =$ the probability that a particle in state r at time $i - 1$ and state s at time $i + 1$.
$D_n =$ the definition of the variable as used herein.

Using **tabularx**

$\phi^{rst}_{i-1,i} =$ the probability that a particle in state r at time $i-1$ and state s at time $i+1$.
$D_n =$ the definition of the variable as used herein.

Some of the suggestions require a length to be specified for the definition text while others automatically use all the available space. It is just a matter of individual preference which is most suited for a particular desired outcome.

26.2 Safety in numbers

> It was a bright cold day in April, and the clocks were striking thirteen.
>
> *Nineteen Eighty-Four*, GEORGE ORWELL

Gordon Haverland posted [60] to the **texhax** mailing list:

I don't suppose there is some easy way to deal with superstitions in LaTeX? I looked around CTAN a bit and nothing jumped out at me.

I suspect the company I am doing work for is superstitious, or customers are. But I ran across an enumerated list where there is no 13th element. What I've done is:

13. Purposely blank.

But is there something else that is more universal?

Heiko Oberdiek responded [103] with a universal solution by changing the definition of `\@arabic`, which is the underlying LaTeX macro for typesetting the value of a counter in arabic form:

```
\makeatletter
\newcommand*{\safe}{%
\renewcommand*{\@arabic}[1]{%
\ifnum##1=13\relax
  12a%
\else
  \ifnum##1=-13\relax
    -12a%
  \else
\expandafter\@firstofone\expandafter{\number##1}%
  \fi
\fi}}
\makeatother
```

Following the \safe declaration *every* setting '13' will be typeset as '12a'.

To save space in the following examples I have defined \setlistctr:

```
\makeatletter
\newcommand*{\setlistctr}[1]{%
  \setcounter{\@listctr}{#1}%
  \protected@edef\@currentlabel
    {\csname p@\@listctr\endcsname
      \csname the\@listctr\endcsname}}
\makeatother
```

which can be used to reset the enumerate list counter.

Applying Heiko's suggestion to an enumerate list as:

```
Standard enumeration:
\begin{enumerate}
\item One \par
\ldots \setlistctr{11}
\item Twelve
\item Thirteen
\item Fourteen
\end{enumerate}
```

```
'Safe' enumeration:
\begin{enumerate}\safe
\item One \par
\ldots \setlistctr{11}
\item Twelve
\item Thirteen
\item Fourteen
\end{enumerate}
```

the result is:

Standard enumeration:

1. One

   . . .

12. Twelve

13. Thirteen

14. Fourteen

   'Safe' enumeration:

1. One

   . . .

12. Twelve

12a. Thirteen

14. Fourteen

However, Gordon had explicitly asked about the enumerate list and I thought that perhaps something specific for that would suit. To that end I defined the \skipit macro that ensures that the counter in an enumerate skips the value '13', and the macro \fixitem to append it to the end of LATEX's internal \@item macro.

```
\makeatletter
\newcommand*{\skipit}{%
  \if@nmbrlist
    \ifnum12=\csname c@\@listctr\endcsname
      \refstepcounter\@listctr
    \fi
  \fi}
\let\old@item\@item
\newcommand{\fixitem}{%
  \def\@item[##1]{\old@item[##1]\skipit}}
\makeatother
```

An example of this approach is:

```
'skipit' enumeration:
\begin{enumerate}\fixitem
\item One \par
\ldots \setlistctr{11}
\item Twelve
\item Thirteen
\item Fourteen
\end{enumerate}
```

'skipit' enumeration:

1. One

   ...

12. Twelve

14. Thirteen

15. Fourteen

With a second level list, though, you might not get what you expect:

```
Standard enumeration:
\begin{enumerate}
\item Including a 'skipit' enumeration:
\begin{enumerate}\fixitem
\item One \par
\ldots \setlistctr{11}
\item Twelve
\item Thirteen
\item Fourteen
\end{enumerate}
\item Two \par
\ldots \setlistctr{11}
\item Twelve
\item Thirteen
\item Fourteen
\end{enumerate}
```

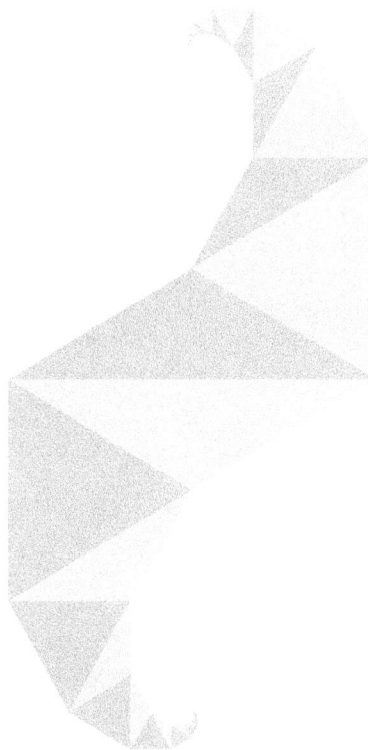

Standard enumeration:

1. Including a 'skipit' enumeration:

   a) One

      ...

   l) Twelve

   n) Thirteen

   o) Fourteen

2. Two

   ...

12. Twelve

13. Thirteen

14. Fourteen

Our stars must glister with new fire, or be
To daie extinct;

The Two Noble Kinsmen,
John Fletcher
(and William Shakespeare?)

27.1 Reading lines

And scribbled lines like fallen hopes
On backs of tattered envelopes.

Instead of a Poet, Francis Hope

The \input macro reads a complete file into TeX as
an atomic action. This was not what Lars Madsen
needed when he posted to ctt wanting to be able to
read a file that consisted of blocks of lines of text,
where a block was ended by a blank line, and then do
something with the last non-blank of the block(s).
The impetus for the following was Dan Luecking's
posting [80], which was one of several responses.

The basis of a solution to Lars' problem is the TeX
construct

```
\read ⟨stream⟩ to \mymacro
```

which reads one line from the file associated with
⟨*stream*⟩ and defines \mymacro to be the contents of
that line.

Let's start with a file of the kind that Lars is
concerned with. Using the filecontents environment, putting the following in the preamble will, if it
does not already exist, create the file glines16.txt
which will start with four TeX comment lines written by filecontents, stating how and when the
file was created; if the filecontents* environment
is used instead then the initial four comment lines
are not output, just the body of the environment as
given [104].

```
\begin{filecontents}{glines16.txt}
This is the file glines16.txt
containing some text lines.

They come in blocks
with blank lines between.


This is the third block
consisting of
three lines.
```

```
\end{filecontents}
```

We need to set up a \read stream and associate it
with a file to be read, making sure that the file does
exist, along the lines of:

```
\newread\instream \openin\instream= qwr!?.tex
\ifeof\instream
  \message{No file 'qwr!?.tex'!^^J}
  \textbf{File 'qwr!?.tex' not found!}
\else
  \message{File 'qwr!?.tex' exists.^^J}
  \textbf{File 'qwr!?.tex' exists.}
  % do something with qwr!?.tex
\fi
\closein\instream
```

which results in:

File 'qwr!?.tex' not found!

Dan's statement was that:
If you
```
    \def\ispar{par}
```
and then
```
    \read <handle> to \myline
```
you will find that
```
    \ifx\myline\ispar
```
will be true for a blank line and also true for a \read
taken after that last line of a file (when \ifeof *is
also true).*

Putting all this together, the next piece of code
produces the result shown afterwards.

```
\newcommand*{\ispar}{\par}
\newcommand*{\processfile}[1]{%
  \openin\instream=#1\relax
  \ifeof\instream
    \message{No file '#1'!^^J}%
    \textbf{File '#1' not found!}%
  \else
    \message{File '#1' exists.^^J}%
    \textbf{File '#1' exists!}%
    \par\noindent
    \loop
      \let\lastline\aline
      \read\instream to \aline
    \ifeof\instream\else
    \ifx\aline\empty (commentline) \\ \else
      \ifx\aline\ispar
```

```
    \ifx\lastline\ispar
      (blankline) \\
    \else
      (lastline) \lastline (followed by)\\
      (blankline) \\
    \fi
  \else
    (aline) \aline\\
  \fi
 \fi
 \repeat
\fi
\closein\instream}
\processfile{glines16.txt}
```

File 'glines16.txt' exists.
(commentline)
(commentline)
(commentline)
(commentline)
(aline) This is the file glines16.txt
(aline) containing some text lines.
(lastline) containing some text lines. (followed by)
(blankline)
(aline) They come in blocks
(aline) with blank lines between.
(lastline) with blank lines between. (followed by)
(blankline)
(blankline)
(aline) This is the third block
(aline) consisting of
(aline) three lines.
(lastline) three lines. (followed by)
(blankline)

27.2 Paragraph endings

> When to the sessions of sweet silent thought
> I summon up remembrance of things past,
> I sigh the lack of many a thing I sought,
> And with old woes new wail my dear times' waste.

Sonnet 30, WILLIAM SHAKESPEARE

In earlier columns I described several aspects related to the typesetting of paragraphs [146, 148] (Chapter 7 and Chapter 8) and here are some additions to those.

27.2.1 Singletons

Andrei Alexandrescu wrote to ctt [6] that:
My publisher has the rule that a single word on a line should not end a paragraph, as long as reflowing wouldn't make things really ugly otherwise. So I defined this macro:

```
\newcommand\lastwords[2]{%
  #1\leavevmode\penalty500\ \mbox{#2}}
```

and used it like this:
`Lorem ipsum yadda \lastwords{amet}{dolor}.`

The macro forces the last word never to be hyphenated, and imposes a penalty of 500 for inserting a line break between the first-to-last and the last word. My understanding is that 500 is the same penalty as that of a hyphen (by default).

Things work pretty well, but it turns out quite a lot of paragraphs need `\lastwords` *— a whole 188 for a 500 page book …*

Is there an automated means to enact the rule above?

Suggestions ranged from ignoring the rule, to using existing code to make the last line at least ⟨*some length*⟩ long (see [146], Chapter 7), to code based on a further suggestion by Andrei and using \everypar that, subject to many caveats, implements the requirement.

Peter Flynn [50] suggested the macro \E

```
\def\E #1 #2.{ \mbox{#1}~\mbox{#2}.}
```

which would be used like:
`Lorem ipsum yadda \E amet dolor.`
He observed that it was faster to type and easier to edit in than \lastword but noted that it might not handle arguments with embedded commands, spaces, curly braces, math, etc.

Dan Luecking [78] came up with corrections to Andrei's second suggestion, together with an extension to handle single-word paragraphs.

```
\usepackage{ifthen}
% handle (one word) paragraph, pass others on
\def\controlorphanword #1 #2\par{%
  \ifthenelse{\equal{#2}{}}
    {#1\par}% one word para
    {\controlorphanwordtwo #1 #2\par}}
% to handle multi-word paragraph
\def\controlorphanwordtwo #1 #2 #3\par{%
  \ifthenelse{\equal{#3}{}}
    {#1\leavevmode\penalty500\ \mbox{#2}\par}
    {#1 \controlorphanwordtwo #2 #3\par}}
```

Dan noted that the macros \controlorphanword and \controlorphanwordtwo will not handle words separated by '\space' or '␣', nor will it work with \obeyspaces in effect.[1] He also commented that the process seemed very inefficient.[2] The code should be called by using \everypar like:

---

[1] For instance, using \verb when \controlorphanword is in effect will cause LaTeX to hiccup violently.

[2] The macros would be called for each word in a paragraph.

```
\begin{document}
Normal paragraph. The macro
\cs{cs}\texttt{\{arg\}} will print \cs{arg}.

Another one, and introducing \cs{everypar}.

\everypar{\controlorphanword}
Almost every place I have ever read about
\cs{everypar} (or redefinition of
\cs{par} or changes to paragraph
parameters) there is this or similar caveat:

    (La)TeX may have strange ideas what is
    counted as a paragraph. Use at your
    own risk, or turn it off in complicated
    circumstances.

Turn off orphan word control by putting
\everypar{}
here.

Turn it back on:

\everypar{\controlorphanword}
Sentence.
```

There was a general consensus among the respondents that the publisher's requirement was not particularly sensible, one going so far as to call it 'crazy'.

(Although not a solution to the given problem, too-short last lines can be mostly avoided in an entirely different way: \parfillskip=.75\hsize plus.06\hsize minus.75\hsize, with the numbers tweaked as desired, and with the usual caveats about packages resetting this primitive, etc.)

27.2.2 All is not what it seems

On rare occasions it may be desirable to either fake the end of a paragraph or to insert an invisible end of paragraph.

Faking the end is simple:

```
\newcommand*{\fakepar}{\\[\parskip]%
  \hspace*{\parindent}}
```

and \fakepar can be used as:

```
\ldots\ the end of a sentence.\fakepar
A new sentence looking as though it starts
a new paragraph\ldots
```

which will be typeset as:

... the end of a sentence.
    A new sentence looking as though it starts a new paragraph...

Sometimes it is useful to nudge TeX into breaking a page, which it is inclined to do at the end of a paragraph while keeping the appearance of unbroken text. From *The TeXbook* [71, Ex. 14.15] and [142] the \parnopar macro accomplishes this:

```
\newcommand*{\parnopar}{{%
  \parfillskip=0pt\par\parskip=0pt\noindent}}
```

TeX typesets paragraph by paragraph, initially taking no account of any page break. Only after the text has been set in lines does TeX consider if there should be a page break within the paragraph. If you need something different about the setting on the two pages, then the original paragraph must be split at the page break.

One application is when using the changepage package [147] to temporarily change the width or location of the textblock (e.g., like the quote environment). If you are trying to extend the textwidth into, say, the outer margin, which in two-sided documents is the left margin on even pages and the right margin on odd pages and there is a page break in the shifted text then the results are not what you hoped for. This can be manually fixed using \parnopar, and splitting the adjustment into two.

```
\usepackage{changepage}
...
% move text 4em into outer margin
\begin{adjustwidth*}{0em}{-4em}
... first part of paragraph with the natural
page break at this point\parnopar
\end{adjustwidth*}%
\begin{adjustwidth*}{0em}{-4em}
but the sentence continues on the
following page ...
\end{adjustwidth*}
```

27.2.3 Paraddendum

Selon Stan posted to texhax, asking [122]:
Is there a way to fill the last line of a paragraph with leaders that extend a fixed width beyond the edge of the paragraph, with right-aligned numbers on the right? I am trying ...

Paul Isambert [67] replied with code that I have cast into the following form as \parend:

```
\def\parend#1{%
  \leaders\hbox{\,.\,}\hfill #1\par}
Here's a sentence.\parend{1}
Here's a sentence \\
on two lines.\parend{291}
```

27.3   In conclusion

> The shades of night were falling fast,
> The rain was falling faster
> When through an Alpine village passed
> An Alpine village pastor;
> A youth who bore mid snow and ice
> With nary a sign of fluster
> A banner with a strange device —
> 'Glisterings glister with lustre'.

The Shades of Night, A.E. HOUSMAN &
PETER WILSON

Some years ago, at Barbara Beeton's suggestion, I agreed to take over Jeremy Gibbons' *Hey — It works!* column which was published between 1993 and 2000 in, firstly, *TeX and TUG News*, and then later in *TUGboat*. He provided many useful tips for solving LaTeX typesetting problems. Between 2000 and 2011 I managed to write some 15 columns, titled *Glisterings* as in 'All that glisters is not gold' carrying on Jeremy's work but then found that my circumstances had changed and I could no longer produce a column on a regular basis. Also, the `comp.text.tex` newsgroup from which I got most of my inspiration seemed to be fading away, being replaced by `tex.stackexchange.com` which appealed to the younger generation but not to a GOM[3] like me where many questions were directed towards problems with `tikz` graphics, the `beamer` package and 'How do I produce this'.

I wrote a final 16th column trying to wrap everything up, but the wrapping ended up being so extensive that it would have taken up most of a *TUGboat* issue, so the *TUGboat* production editor decided that it would be best to split it up into several pieces and publish these over the coming years.[4]

---

[3]Grumpy Old Man
[4]I don't think that either of us thought that 'coming' would turn out to be 'next six years'.
[Editor's note: So true.]

27.4   Sixteen

> You load sixteen tons and what do you get?
> Another day older and deeper in debt.
> Say brother, don' you call me 'cause I can't go
> I owe my soul to the company store.

Sixteen Tons, MERLE TRAVIS

For what I thought would be that final 16th *Glisterings* column I wrote the following, which perhaps might still be a suitable closing.

Sixteen is a rather remarkable number in that it can be expressed in many striking ways.

- In binary sixteen is: 10000
- In octal sixteen is: 20
- In decimal sixteen is: 16
- In hexadecimal sixteen is: 10

In decimal notation, which is the one most people are familiar with, there are quite a few ways in which sixteen can be represented. Among the more eye-catching ones are:

Powers
- $4^2 = 16$
- $2^4 = 16$
- $2^{2^2} = 16$

Additions
- sum of the first $\sqrt{16}$ odd numbers:
  $1 + 3 + 5 + 7 = 16$
- sum of adjacent numbers:
  $1 + 2 + 3 + 4 + 3 + 2 + 1 = 16$
  which can also be expressed as:
  $1 + 4 + 6 + 4 + 1 = 16$

Among other properties sixteen is the smallest number with exactly 5 divisors — 1, 2, 4, 8 and 16. It is also the only number that is expressible as both m^n and n^m, with $m \neq n$.

27.5   Twenty-seven

In the end twenty-seven columns were published.

Like sixteen, twenty-seven has some properties although not nearly as many.

Powers
- $3^3 = 27$
- $(2+1)^{(2+1)} = 27$
- $(2+1)^{(2^2-1)} = 27$

Additions
- sum of the first 5 odd prime numbers:
  $1 + 3 + 5 + 7 + 11 = 27$

BIBLIOGRAPHY

[1] Ron Aaron. How to append text to a paragraph (in an existing vbox)? Post to `xetex` mailing list, 16 July 2010.

[2] Paul W. Abrahams, Karl Berry, and Kathryn A. Hargreaves. *TEX for the Impatient.* Addison-Wesley, 1990. https://ctan.org/pkg/impatient.

[3] William Adams. One typeface, many fonts, 1997.

[4] Hendri Adriaens. The xkeyval package, 2005. https://ctan.org/pkg/xkeyval.

[5] Alastair. Indexing individual elements in a comma separated list. Post to `comp.text.tex` newsgroup, 17 October 2010.

[6] Andrei Alexandrescu. Single word on a line at end of paragraph. Post to `comp.text.tex` newsgroup, 26 April 2010.

[7] Christian Andersen. Re: Sorted items in description environment. Post to `comp.text.tex` newsgroup, 10 October 2010.

[8] Arbo. How to produce multiple columns within a multicolumn. Post to `comp.text.tex` newsgroup, 2 November 2010.

[9] Donald Arseneau. `truncate.sty` truncate text to a specific width, 2001. https://ctan.org/pkg/truncate.

[10] Donald Arseneau. shapepar.sty, 2002. https://ctan.org/pkg/shapepar.

[11] Donald Arseneau. The framed package v0.95, 2007. https://ctan.org/pkg/framed.

[12] Donald Arseneau. Re: Text filling the line. Post to `comp.text.tex` newsgroup, 24 March 2007.

[13] Donald Arseneau. Re: How to limit/cut off text after a number of lines. Post to `comp.text.tex` newsgroup, 16 July 2008.

[14] Donald Arseneau. Re: Not using all of the reference. Post to `comp.text.tex` newsgroup, 1 November 2009.

[15] Donald Arseneau. Re: preventing page breaks at certain positions. Post to `comp.text.tex` newsgroup, 17 November 2009.

[16] Donald Arseneau. The varwidth package, March 2009. https://ctan.org/pkg/varwidth.

[17] Donald Arseneau. Re: \ifnum for real numbers. Post to `comp.text.tex` newsgroup, 16 October 2010.

[18] Donald Arseneau. Re: How to produce multiple columns within a multicolumn. Post to `comp.text.tex` newsgroup, 2 November 2010.

[19] Donald Arseneau. Re: Line spacing respecting space for ascenders / descenders and fontsize. Post to `comp.text.tex` newsgroup, 11 April 2011.

[20] Donald Arseneau. Re: List items always on the same page. Post to `comp.text.tex` newsgroup, 15 March 2011.

[21] Donald Arseneau and Dan Luecking. Re: vertical height of boxes by multiple of baselineskip. Posts to `comp.text.tex` newsgroup, 9–10 December 2009.

[22] Donald Arseneau and Peter Wilson. The ifmtarg package, 2009. https://ctan.org/pkg/ifmtarg.

[23] Michael Barr. Re: [texhax] Finding blank argument to a macro. Post to `texhax` mailing list, 27 May 2010.

[24] Anne C. Bromer and Julian I. Edison. *Miniature Books: 4,000 Years of Tiny Treasures.* Abrams in association with the Grolier Club, 2007. ISBN 978-0-8109-9299-3.

[25] Jean-François Burnol. Re: Arranging parallel texts. Post to `comp.text.tex` newsgroup, 24 February 2011.

[26] Jean-François Burnol. Re: Tabular with enumerated items and sub-items in different rows. Post to `comp.text.tex` newsgroup, 27 April 2011.

[27] Jean-François Burnol. Re: Variable definitions / indenting on = sign. Post to `comp.text.tex` newsgroup, 25 March 2011.

[28] David Carlisle. The keyval package, 1999. https://ctan.org/pkg/keyval.

[29] David Carlisle and Peter Schmitt. Russian paragraph shapes. *Baskerville*, 6(1):13–15, February 1996.

[30] Pehong Chen and Michael A. Harrison. Index preparation and processing. *Software Practice and Experience*, 19(8), September 1988. https://ctan.org/pkg/makeindex.

[31] cooch17. Variable definitions / indenting on = sign. Post to `comp.text.tex` newsgroup, 25 March 2011.

[32] Ulrich Diez. Re: a new \verba command. Post to `comp.text.tex` newsgroup, 23 October 2009.

[33] Susan Dittmar. Variant of \cleardoublepage starting on even page numbers. Post to `texhax` mailing list, 18 August 2005.

[34] Michael J. Downes. The patchcmd package, 2000. https://ctan.org/pkg/patchcmd.

[35] Michael J. Downes. Re: catcodes for jobname macro - stupid question. Post to `comp.text.tex` newsgroup, 25 April 2001.

[36] Angus Duggans. PSUtils, 2008. `https://ctan.org/pkg/psutils`.

[37] Michael Downes (ed. Peter Wilson). *Around the Bend*. The Herries Press, July 2008. `https://ctan.org/pkg/around-the-bend`.

[38] Victor Eijkhout. *TEX by Topic, A TEXnician's Reference*. Addison-Wesley, 1991. ISBN 0–201–56882–9. `http://www.eijkhout.net/tbt/`.

[39] Peter Engel. *The Folding Universe*. Vintage, 1989. ISBN 0394757513.

[40] Dániel Erdély. Idea 1979, first presented on the Twelfth International Conference on Crystal Growth in 1998, 2002.

[41] Ernest. Description environment. Post to `comp.text.tex` newsgroup, 2010.

[42] Robin Fairbairns. The UK TEX FAQ. `https://texfaq.org`.

[43] Adam Fenn. Empty arguments. Post to `texhax` mailing list, 17 August 2005.

[44] Ulrike Fischer. Re: Indexing individual elements in a comma separated list. Post to `comp.text.tex` newsgroup, 18 October 2010.

[45] Ulrike Fischer. Re: XeLaTeX, fontspace and fontfamily. Post to `comp.text.tex` newsgroup, 12 July 2010.

[46] Ulrike Fischer and Donald Arseneau. Re: line breaks in boxes (or 'how do i get paragraph parsing in hbox/mbox?'). Posts to `comp.text.tex` newsgroup, 26–27 November 2009.

[47] Peter Flynn. Re: simultaneous justification in latex. Post to `comp.text.tex` newsgroup, 20 September 2006.

[48] Peter Flynn. Re: uncommon typography. Post to `comp.text.tex` newsgroup, 4 June 2007.

[49] Peter Flynn. Re: Fancybox alternatives. Post to `comp.text.tex` newsgroup, 11 September 2009.

[50] Peter Flynn. Re: Single word on a line at end of paragraph. Post to `comp.text.tex` newsgroup, 1 May 2010.

[51] Peter Flynn. Re: Tabular with enumerated items and sub-items in different rows. Post to `comp.text.tex` newsgroup, 27 April 2011.

[52] Jeremy Gibbons. Hey — it works! *TEX and TUG NEWS*, 2(2):7–11, April 1993.

[53] GL. Re: `\ifnum` for real numbers. Post to `comp.text.tex` newsgroup, 16 October 2010.

[54] GL. Re: Finding the widest string. Post to `comp.text.tex` newsgroup, 4 May 2010.

[55] Enrico Gregorio. Re: Text filling the line. Post to `comp.text.tex` newsgroup, 22 March 2007.

[56] Enrico Gregorio. Re: Math notation for the closure of a set? Post to `comp.text.tex` newsgroup, 30 March 2011.

[57] Enrico Gregorio. Re: Variable definitions / indenting on = sign. Post to `comp.text.tex` newsgroup, 25 March 2011.

[58] Branko Grunbaum and G. C. Shephard. *Tilings and Patterns*. W. H. Freeman, 1987.

[59] William Hammond. Re: Math notation for the closure of a set? Post to `comp.text.tex` newsgroup, 16 April 2011.

[60] Gordon Haverland. [texhax] superstitions. Post to `texhax` mailing list, 23 April 2011.

[61] Guido Herzog. Post to `xetex` mailing list, 24 September 2009.

[62] Stephen Hicks. Re: [texhax] multiple documents within a document. Post to `texhax` mailing list, 30 March 2010.

[63] Alan Hoenig. TEX does windows — the conclusion. *TUGboat*, 8(2):211–215, 1987. `https://tug.org/TUGboat/tb08-2/tb18hoenig.pdf`.

[64] Don Hosek. Timelines with plain tex and latex. *TEXMAG*, 1(7), October 1987. `https://ctan.org/tex-archive/info/digests/tex-mag/v1.n7`.

[65] Roberto Ierusalimschy. *Programming in Lua, Second Edition*. Lua.org, Rio de Janeiro, 2006. ISBN 85-903798-2-5.

[66] Paul Isambert. Re: automatic line break within verbatim-environment. Post to `comp.text.tex` newsgroup, 10 April 2009.

[67] Paul Isambert. Re: [texhax] leaders protruding a fixed width from end of paragrah? Post to `texhax` mailing list, 17 March 2011.

[68] Jeremy. Table with auto-incrementing column. Post to `comp.text.tex` newsgroup, 11 April 2011.

[69] David Kastrup. Completely expansible string comparison. Post to `comp.text.tex` newsgroup, 3 September 2002.

[70] Davis Kastrup. The preview package for LaTeX, 2010. `https://ctan.org/pkg/preview`.

[71] Donald E. Knuth. *The TEXbook*. Addison Wesley, 1994.

[72] Philipp Lehman. The font installation guide, December 2004. `https://ctan.org/pkg/fontinstallationguide`.

[73] Maurizio Loreti. webomints, 2002. `https://ctan.org/pkg/webomints`.

[74] Uwe Lück. Re: [texhax] read and process single characters. Post to `texhax` mailing list, 24 June 2005.

[75] Dan Luecking. Re: Text filling the line. Post to `comp.text.tex` newsgroup, 12 March 2007.

[76] Dan Luecking. Re: A small LaTeX macro question. Post to `comp.text.tex` newsgroup, 4 June 2010.

[77] Dan Luecking. Re: How to find the fontsize? Post to `comp.text.tex` newsgroup, 24 August 2010.

[78] Dan Luecking. Re: Single word on a line at end of paragraph. Post to `comp.text.tex` newsgroup, 28 April 2010.

[79] Dan Luecking. Re: Math notation for the closure of a set? Post to `comp.text.tex` newsgroup, 19 April 2011.

[80] Dan Luecking. Re: package for processing text from external files. Post to `comp.text.tex` newsgroup, 23 May 2011.

[81] Rui Maciel. Math notation for the closure of a set? Post to `comp.text.tex` newsgroup, 30 March 2011.

[82] Lars Madsen. Re: Recall a list item and print it later in the document. Post to `comp.text.tex` newsgroup, 14 September 2009.

[83] Lars Madsen. Re: Variable definitions / indenting on = sign. Post to `comp.text.tex` newsgroup, 25 March 2011.

[84] Matthew. [texhax] finding blank argument to a macro. Post to `texhax` mailing list, 2010.

[85] Andreas Matthias. The pdfpages package, 2008. `https://ctan.org/pkg/pdfpages`.

[86] John McClain. The toolbox. T_EXM_AG, 5(1), September 1992. `https://ctan.org/tex-archive/info/digests/tex-mag/v5.n1`.

[87] Ruari McLean. *The Thames and Hudson Manual of Typography*. Thames and Hudson, 1980. ISBN 0-500-68022-1.

[88] Frank Mittelbach and Michel Goossens. *The LATEX Companion*. Addison Wesley, second edition, 2004. ISBN 0-201-36299-6.

[89] Cherryl Moote. *Copied, Bound & Numbered*. At Your Ease Publications, 2003. ISBN 0-9688811-7-3.

[90] Stephen Moye. Re: asterism. Post to `xetex` mailing list, 11 January 2010.

[91] Alan Munn. Re: Sorted items in description environment. Post to `comp.text.tex` newsgroup, 10 October 2010.

[92] Alan Munn. Re: Table with auto-incrementing column. Post to `comp.text.tex` newsgroup, 11 April 2011.

[93] Timothy Murphy. A small LaTeX macro question. Post to `comp.text.tex` newsgroup, 4 June 2010.

[94] Robert Nyqvist. 'example' environment or command. Post to `comp.text.tex` newsgroup, 11 January 2003.

[95] Heiko Oberdiek. The twoopt package: Definitions with two optional arguments, 1999. `https://ctan.org/pkg/oberdiek`.

[96] Heiko Oberdiek. The ifpdf package, July 2001. `https://ctan.org/pkg/oberdiek`.

[97] Heiko Oberdiek. Re: memoir, ps4pdf and `\ifpdf`. Post to `comp.text.tex` newsgroup, 3-September 2004.

[98] Heiko Oberdiek. Re: Raising a colon to center. Post to `comp.text.tex` newsgroup, 23-November 2009.

[99] Heiko Oberdiek. The kvsetkeys package, 2010. `https://ctan.org/pkg/kvsetkeys`.

[100] Heiko Oberdiek. Re: A small LaTeX macro question. Post to `comp.text.tex` newsgroup, 4 June 2010.

[101] Heiko Oberdiek. Re: Finding the widest string. Post to `comp.text.tex` newsgroup, 4 May 2010.

[102] Heiko Oberdiek. Re: How to make all images protrude into the outer border. Post to `comp.text.tex` newsgroup, 3-January 2010.

[103] Heiko Oberdiek. Re: [texhax] superstitions. Post to `texhax` mailing list, 23 April 2011.

[104] Scott Pakin. The filecontents package, 2009. `https://ctan.org/pkg/filecontents`.

[105] Pander. Line spacing respecting space for ascenders / descenders and fontsize. Post to `comp.text.tex` newsgroup, 11 April 2011.

[106] Ivars Peterson. Swirling seas, crystal balls. *Science News*, 170(17):266–268, 2006.

[107] Tom Phelps. Multivalent, 2008. `http://multivalent.sourceforge.net`.

[108] Nikos Platis. Justify at right margin or in next line. Post to `comp.text.tex` newsgroup, 21 August 2006.

[109] Pluto. `\ifnum` for real numbers. Post to `comp.text.tex` newsgroup, 10 October 2010.

[110] Sebastian Rahtz and Heiko Oberdiek. Hypertext marks in LATEX: a manual for hyperref. `https://ctan.org/pkg/hyperref`.

[111] Reza. Sorted items in description environment. Post to `comp.text.tex` newsgroup, 10 October 2010.

[112] Will Robertson. Re: How to limit/cut off text after a number of lines. Post to `comp.text.tex` newsgroup, 16 July 2008.

[113] Will Robertson. The ifxetex package, 2009. `https://ctan.org/pkg/ifxetex`.

[114] Will Robertson. Re: PDFs with a (very) variable page length. Post to `comp.text.tex` newsgroup, 12 October 2009.

[115] Will Robertson and Khaled Hosny. The fontspec package, 2010. `https://ctan.org/pkg/fontspec`.

[116] Roger. Re: ifodd question. Post to `comp.text.tex` newsgroup, 18 May 2010.

[117] David Romano. Setting counters to output of a `\ref` command. Post to `texhax` mailing list, 8 February 2007.

[118] Romildo. Finding the widest string. Post to `comp.text.tex` newsgroup, 3 May 2010.

[119] Romildo. Tabular with enumerated items and sub-items in different rows. Post to `comp.text.tex` newsgroup, 27 April 2011.

[120] Maieul Rouquette. reledmac - typeset scholarly editions, 2019. `https://ctan.org/pkg/reledmac`.

[121] John Ryder. *Flowers & Flourishes including a newly annotated edition of A Suite of Fleurons*. The Bodley Head for Mackays, 1976. ISBN 0370 11308 X.

[122] Selon Stan. [texhax] leaders protruding a fixed width from end of paragraph? Post to `texhax` mailing list, 17 March 2011.

[123] Nicola L. C. Talbot. Creating flow frames for posters, brochures or magazines using flowfram.sty. `https://ctan.org/pkg/flowfram`.

[124] Nicola L. C. Talbot. datatool: Databases and data manipulation. `https://ctan.org/pkg/datatool`.

[125] Philip Taylor. Re: How to append text to a paragraph (in an existing vbox)? Post to `xetex` mailing list, 16 July 2010.

[126] Bob Tennent. Re: How to find the fontsize? Post to `comp.text.tex` newsgroup, 24 August 2010.

[127] The LaTeX3 Project. The xparse package, 2010. `https://ctan.org/pkg/xparse`.

[128] Thomas Thurman. Arranging parallel texts. Post to `comp.text.tex` newsgroup, 22 February 2011.

[129] Nick Urbanik. List items always on the same page. Post to `comp.text.tex` newsgroup, 13 March 2011.

[130] Piet van Oostrum. Page layout in LaTeX, 2004. `https://ctan.org/pkg/fancyhdr`.

[131] Timothy Van Zandt. Documentation for fancybox.sty: Box tips and tricks for LaTeX. `https://ctan.org/pkg/fancybox`.

[132] Boris Veytsman. Printing Envelopes and Labels in LaTeX 2ε: EnvLab Package User Guide, June 1996. `https://ctan.org/pkg/envlab`.

[133] Rasmus Villemoes. Aborting unless running pdflatex. Post to `comp.text.tex` newsgroup, 2 August 2010.

[134] Paul Vojta. Re: New York Times headline style. Post to `comp.text.tex` newsgroup, 2007.

[135] Herbert Voß. Re: How to draw a box around the boundaries of a glyph? Post to `comp.text.tex` newsgroup, 27 March 2009.

[136] Torsten Wagner. Read and process single characters. Post to `texhax` mailing list, 24 June 2005.

[137] George Williams. Fontforge: An outline font editor, 2009. `http://fontforge.sourceforge.net`.

[138] Peter Wilson. Glisterings. *TUGboat*, 22(4):339–341, December 2001. `https://tug.org/TUGboat/tb22-4/tb72wilson.pdf`.

[139] Peter Wilson. LaTeX for ISO Standards, 2002. `https://ctan.org/pkg/iso`.

[140] Peter Wilson. LaTeX Package Files for ISO 10303, 2002. `https://ctan.org/pkg/iso10303`.

[141] Peter Wilson. The hanging package, April 2004. `https://ctan.org/pkg/hanging`.

[142] Peter Wilson. The memoir class for configurable typesetting, 2004. `https://ctan.org/pkg/memoir`.

[143] Peter Wilson. Glisterings. *TUGboat*, 26(3):253–255, 2005. `https://tug.org/TUGboat/tb26-3/tb84glister.pdf`.

[144] Peter Wilson. Parallel typesetting for critical editions: the ledpar package, 2005. `https://ctan.org/pkg/ledmac`.

[145] Peter Wilson. Printing booklets with LaTeX, 2005. `https://ctan.org/pkg/booklet`.

[146] Peter Wilson. Glisterings. *TUGboat*, 28(2):229–232, 2007. `https://tug.org/TUGboat/tb28-2/tb89glister.pdf`.

[147] Peter Wilson. The changepage package, 2008. `https://ctan.org/pkg/changepage`.

[148] Peter Wilson. Glisterings. *TUGboat*, 29(2):324–327, 2008. `https://tug.org/TUGboat/tb29-2/tb92glister.pdf`.

[149] Peter Wilson. The fonttable package, 2009. `https://ctan.org/pkg/fonttable`.

[150] Peter Wilson. Glisterings. *TUGboat*, 30(2):287–289, 2009. `https://tug.org/TUGboat/tb30-2/tb95glister.pdf`.

[151] Peter Wilson. Re: Marginpar in memoir. Post to `comp.text.tex` newsgroup, 27 December 2009.

[152] Peter Wilson. Glisterings. *TUGboat*, 32(2):202–205, 2011. `https://tug.org/TUGboat/tb32-2/tb101glister.pdf`.

[153] Peter Wilson and Alan Hoenig. Making cutouts in paragraphs, 2010. `https://ctan.org/pkg/cutwin`.

[154] Joseph Wright. Re: A small LaTeX macro question. Post to `comp.text.tex` newsgroup, 4 June 2010.

[155] Joseph Wright. Re: ifodd question. Post to `comp.text.tex` newsgroup, 14 May 2010.